NOTHING BUT THE TRUTH

*This book is dedicated to
Mary Turok
and our sons
Fred, Ivan and Neil
whose story this is too.*

NOTHING BUT THE TRUTH

Behind the ANC's Struggle Politics

BEN TUROK

JONATHAN BALL PUBLISHERS
JOHANNESBURG & CAPE TOWN

All rights reserved.
No part of this publication may be reproduced or transmitted,
in any form or by any means, without prior permission from
the publisher or copyright holder.

© Benjamin Turok, 2003

© The copyright holder of the photographs is credited beneath each picture,
with the exception of the pictures supplied by the author from
his personal files.

Published in 2003 by
JONATHAN BALL PUBLISHERS (PTY) LTD
P O Box 33977
Jeppestown
2043

ISBN 1 86842 176 7

Design by Michael Barnett
Reproduction and typesetting of cover and picture section
by Triple M Design & Advertising, Johannesburg
Typesetting and reproduction of text by Alinea Studio, Cape Town
Index by Owen Hendry, Johannesburg
Printed and bound by CTP Book Printers, Duminy Street,
Parow, 7500, Cape Town, South Africa

CONTENTS

	Preface	7
CHAPTER 1	Rebel son	11
CHAPTER 2	Full-time activist	37
CHAPTER 3	On trial for treason	62
CHAPTER 4	Life underground	97
CHAPTER 5	Prison	135
CHAPTER 6	Escape	174
CHAPTER 7	Crisis in the ANC	193
CHAPTER 8	Changing fortunes	220
CHAPTER 9	The 1990 miracle and its aftermath	250
	Annexures	277

PREFACE

After Mandela's autobiography, *Long Walk To Freedom*, there seemed little more to be said about ordeals in prison, underground, in army camps around the world, and the sheer misery of exile. But each of us who were participants in the momentous struggle for the new South Africa have something personal and intimate to add, perhaps giving even greater depth to this most extraordinary experience.

Much of what follows has not been told before. I am the sole survivor of some crucial events in our history. Of the group that assembled underground in Johannesburg following the mass arrests during the state of emergency in 1960, Moses Kotane, Michael Harmel, Yusuf Dadoo, Ruth First, Jack Hodgson and Bram Fischer have all died. This was the first time the movement's leadership went underground, the first time it gave consideration to the resort to violence, and it also saw the emergence of the underground Communist Party. The story needs to be told.

The exile period has also had little coverage. The ANC has by and large been portrayed in heroic terms, and rightly so, but many serious mistakes were made and these should be contextualised in the tough conditions it faced. I want to give an account of the ups and downs of that struggle, and the tenacity and persistence of the movement against all odds, and I shall do so through my eyes, the eyes of a victim of his own mistakes and abrasiveness in dealing with his comrades. This is a painful business and perhaps a mere exercise in self-justification, but it is no ego-trip. I think it is more a case of wanting to get to grips with the unsavoury side of our communist heritage.

What follows is a story. It is not a formal history, and it is both selective and subjective. Much of what I have to say is subject to other interpretations, as memory plays tricks with us. But the book is also more than a story – it is also a distillation of my insights into our struggle and an expansion of my other writings on the subject. It is above all concerned with analysing strategy and tactics in various aspects of struggle – legal, semi-legal, illegal and military – and how and why the movement shifted gears from one to the other. It also discusses changes in posture such as from protest to defiance, from non-violence to violence, and so on.

We deal with strategic considerations of three parallel levels of struggle: normal political campaigning by a liberation movement with no presence in the formal political system; twilight – where legal and illegal methods are combined; and deep cover – in the underground and military aspect. The book also deals extensively with the relationship between the ANC and the Communist Party, one of the most sensitive issues of the movement, usually glossed over in the interests of unity.

The story extends over a historical epoch much different from the present. It was a period of triumphalism, of the victory of socialism across a third of the globe, of the rise of liberation movements in the Third World and the winning of independence and freedom. The youth of the world, including in the heartland of imperialism, was inspired by the audacity of Che Guevara, the solid achievements of Red China, the personality of Kwame Nkrumah and the power of the international working class. In comparison, our present world order provides little to inspire the young, especially as their environment is pervaded by a banal, media-propagated pop culture.

But the very speed of change brought about by those idealistic movements and personalities also brought serious mistakes and even criminal actions. These need to be analysed, and from the perspective of one engaged in struggle, not only by arm's-length historians.

Our story will deal with issues of political process, the problem of democracy within a movement, leadership style, and the relationship between political organisations and society. However, my approach here is not that of political science but rather the examination of concrete events as they played themselves out around me.

I am also driven by the need to understand the nature of our current transition in South Africa. Much has been achieved; all appreciate the political miracle around us. But there is much more to come and the working through of political dynamics will be decisive. These processes formed themselves within the history of the ANC during the years of the struggle and generated the present leadership in its womb.

I hope to show that despite the many setbacks and mistakes, especially from 1960 to 1990, the ANC was fortunate to have some outstanding leaders, notably Oliver Tambo and Nelson Mandela, with long and deep experience of liberation politics. They went through many different phases of struggle with great flexibility, clarity of vision and profound humanity. The survival of the movement in unity throughout these events was largely due to their wisdom, non-sectarianism and a determination to sustain the ANC as a broad movement of many political trends, driven essentially by a vision that was acceptable to all who wanted an end to apartheid. True, that style was eroded and undermined by the imperatives of maintaining security at home, by the frustrations and isolation brought by life in exile and the infiltration by enemy agents within the structures in camps in Africa. My own unhappy experiences in exile were a function of those pressures, and I concede that my understanding of them was one-sided and subjective, plagued by guilt for having left the country and by a related impatience to return to the fray.

Above all, I want to tell my story and analyse these events in order to answer the question: Can the ANC bring about the transition and transformation promised over all those years? I believe much depends on what is does now, but is also governed by what went before. Hence the need to look behind us.

CHAPTER ONE

REBEL SON

It is February 2003. I am 75 years old. I live in a comfortable, white, middle-class suburb. My father was a fairly well-off owner-manager of a fair-sized factory. I am miles apart, in age, in distance, in lifestyle, in culture, in social class and in political experience from so many young people with whom I share the bond of a total commitment to the African National Congress.

I have a tremendous urge to tell my story about experiences in the old ANC and the Communist Party, about how we worked underground, about leaders like Moses Kotane and Chief Luthuli. There was so little time to explain as we struggled with events, with political theory and policy.

Explaining is a difficult thing to do, even painful. There have been many, many moments of inspiration and success, but there has also been a great deal of pain, of humiliation, of just hanging on, of desperate fatigue with it all.

Since I am going to open up on everything, I need to confess that when one becomes an ANC activist, one soon learns to subordinate one's personal life and feelings to the collective. It is essential that career, ambition, personal preferences, family life, even one's sensibilities, become to some degree subject to the objective struggle. And so it becomes difficult to recover one's deepest thoughts and feelings about events long ago. Wordsworth's *Recollections in Tranquillity* are not possible for me. It is more a question of recovering my past in the midst of turbulence.

This is not because I have any regrets. Not at all! I have had the richest of lives, tough as mine was, even though South Africa still has to complete its transition and press on with transformation. The struggle is by no means over. We had no prospect whatsoever of owning a Mercedes Benz, of holding senior public office, of having formal powers. But we are now in a world of great temptation and of new values. That is why I have to tell my story – the story of the struggle, of the real political traditions of the ANC.

I am able to do so because history was kind to me. It allowed me to occupy a central place in the movement at the most crucial time in its development. I worked closely with all the top leaders including Nelson Mandela, Chief Luthuli, Moses Kotane and many others. I am not name-dropping to gain credibility. I am merely saying that I have had the wonderful opportunity of being on the inside track of the ANC and the party at a crucial period in the struggle and I want to pass on that heritage. Since I am the sole survivor of some of the events I shall recount, I have an additional obligation to reveal what really happened. There are no documents and no one else can tell the tale.

But before dealing with the deeper politics of the movement, I feel that I must explore our origins more fully. We continue to affirm that the ANC has a non-racial vision. This is not always believed, largely because Africans are so predominant now. But we fought hard and over many years for the legitimacy of non-racialism as a principle and so I want to reflect further on how people of such differing origins became part of the same movement.

I grew up in Cape Town, mostly in a ghetto of white immigrants from Eastern Europe. For me the closest people of colour with whom I came into contact were Arabia, our domestic worker of Malay origins, and the coloured people who came to the door selling things. Black people were subordinates who were not admitted to our table, could not use our bath or toilet, or even sit down on a white person's chair. When my parents and brothers went out and I was left alone with Arabia, we spent the evening sitting on the floor.

Young blacks for whom whites were entirely alien objects of fear and hatred moved into political life, adjusted to the legitimacy of whites as acceptable comrades, even friends, while whites had to shake off sensations of superiority, even aversion. I was fortunate in a way – being poor and going to a school that was not too scrupulous about judging the whiteness of skin colour – because I often mixed with children who wore no shoes, who were from underclass families, and lived in twilight zones where race separation was not rigidly enforced. Additionally, Cape Town had a majority of coloured people who were subject to less stringent colour bars than black people in the rest of the country.

No doubt my conversion to non-racialism was greatly assisted by the nature of my origins. My parents came from a poor Jewish working-class community. They were born in Byelorussia and my father lost his father when he was a mere 11 years of age. So he went out to work as a shoemaker's apprentice and his education came to an abrupt end, a fact he deplored for the rest of his life since he never properly realised his inner potential. My mother was a sales assistant in a pharmacy and her brothers became skilled engineering factory workers in post-revolution Russia.

Being Jews and growing up in the highly charged political climate of Tsarist Russia, they were influenced by radical Bundist politics and my father became associated with the Jewish Labour Movement, though I cannot say how actively. They both witnessed the 1917 Bolshevik Revolution, though at a distance, since they lived in White Russia where counter-revolutionary forces were dominant. Indeed, they were subjected to the White Terror of the anti-Semitic Cossacks and witnessed Jews being strung up from lampposts.

Conditions deteriorated, so they sold all their goods and acquired passports illegally, which enabled them to flee to neighbouring Latvia where they settled in Libau, the second-largest city, which had a sizable Jewish population. At first things went well and my father was able to set up a leather-goods shop. He had been trained as a clicker in leather, cutting out pieces according to a pattern, but soon the Depression came and with it fascism. Latvia was one of the first countries in Europe to experience the emergence of a fascist movement of the kind that was later to sweep the rest of Europe.

Bankrupt and faced with rising anti-Semitism, my father migrated once more, but this time alone as an advance guard for the family. He left my mother and three small boys, aged seven, ten and thirteen, to survive somehow in the deep recession hanging over Latvia.

He departed for South Africa with high hopes, believing that the streets of Cape Town were literally 'paved with gold', which was how the message about gold-rich South Africa was transmitted across two continents and in several languages. This was a route followed by several of our movement's leaders such as Ray Alexander, Joe Slovo's parents and others.

Instead of gold, my father encountered oranges, which he sold in the streets from a handcart. However, he soon graduated to a fish-and-chips shop which he opened with his savings of two shillings and sixpence. Being diligent and thrifty, he later graduated to a factory job where he used his training to cut leather pieces for goods such as wallets and belts. From his savings he sent a hundred pounds to us in Latvia, enough to rescue us from serious poverty and political harassment.

While my father was hawking in the streets of Cape Town, my mother was hawking household linen in Libau. It was a very tough existence for a young woman alone and with three small boys to look after. She carried two large suitcases of linen goods from door to door, earning just enough to keep us all in a single unheated room in the Jewish ghetto. We bathed once a week in a tub of hot water heated on an open fire. We ate sparely, the treat of the week being the cake crumbs purchased from the local cake shop.

But worst of all was the increasing racial tension throughout Latvia. We lived in a Jewish area and went to a Jewish school where the instruction was in Yiddish. Unfortunately, the school abutted on a square with non-Jewish schools and fights between groups of racially defined boys became commonplace. My older brother, Hillel, was a member of the Red Youth Movement, a type of Boy Scouts, but when marching through the streets on May Day was met with fascist wrath. He was obliged to burn his red tie in a solemn ceremony at home. We yearned to escape from Latvia to join my father.

One incident in particular haunted me for many years. I was about five years old and walking along the mole in the harbour with my two older brothers. We were throwing stones into the sea, relishing the fresh breeze and the spray as the huge rollers crashed onto the boulders. The mole was narrow and there was sea on either side, ideal for fishermen who were unusually absent that day. I felt somewhat insecure so far from the mainland but felt reassured by having my brothers with me.

But then a group of small boys approached from the end of the mole and we could see their hostility as they came nearer. The biggest picked up some stones, threw one at my brother and called out, 'Jude, Jude!' (Jew!). There were six of them and only three of us. We turned and fled with the boys following, jeering at us. Our sense of vulnerability and remoteness became intensified by the rising tide and crashing waves against the mole so we pressed on harder, but I began to lag behind. We finally reached the shore but continued running until we found safety on a park bench beneath a large, overhanging tree, shielded at last from the people around us.

Why this particular incident stays with me even now, I cannot tell. For there were many incidents of this kind, especially in the grass square in front of our school where the non-Jewish boys were often threatening. The ugliness of their racism made a lasting impression.

I wonder whether people realise that in addition to black skins being used to single people out for racist treatment, there are other identifying physical characteristics that can yield very painful results – a particular physical build, an accent, a particular way of using one's hands, and so on. For most of my life I have been aware of the fact that I am easily identified as being of Jewish origin. Afrikaners, especially in rural areas, readily ask: 'Turok? That is a foreign name. You look Jewish.' This, in a joking, semi-accusatory manner. So I often ask myself whether my African comrades appreciate that racism can take many forms in addition to colour doscrimination.

But to return to my story about Latvia, racism was but one aspect of the emerging fascism, with ever-increasing politically inspired incidents becoming a regular phenomenon. The harbour was the scene of one spectacular event when a ship flying a swastika was attacked by a group of Jewish comrades who tore down the flag, smeared the ship with black paint and made off on motorbikes. Such incidents became more frequent but they did not curb the ascendancy of fascism which soon established jackboot rule over the country. What with the daily struggle by my mother to earn a living, we were immensely relieved when my father sent us tickets for our journey to South Africa. But no one informed us that we were migrating from one fascist country to another.

MIGRATION TO SOUTH AFRICA

In 1932 when I was seven years old, we travelled by train to London where we were housed in a kind of hostel for immigrants. Being in central London, surrounded by surging traffic and having no English at all, our forlorn little group dared not leave the block during the three days of our sojourn. And so we learned nothing of this strange English metropolis. Then, aided by some Jewish network, we found our way to Southampton to board ship for Cape Town. My father had endured four hard years of poverty and like any migrant felt lost, ill at ease and unwanted.

When our ship docked we were entranced by the backdrop of Table Mountain. But my father was nowhere to be seen. Imagine our anxiety! But then he arrived, breathless and agitated, to greet his wife and three children after four long years of loneliness. He had simply overslept.

We were taken to a simple boarding house on the outskirts of the city centre where we were to share two rooms. It took some time to get us into school in a district where white and coloured residential areas met. We soon moved into a semi-detached rented house where the three boys shared a small room with a window overlooking the street that was shuttered at night for privacy and security. Sometimes lovers would lean against the shutters in the evening, breathing heavily as they went about their business and we had to suppress our giggles for fear of arousing their wrath.

Some evenings we could hear the scavenging cats of the neighbourhood competing for the meagre offal from the neighbourhood garbage cans. Underfed dogs were there too, fighting for access to the spilled rubbish and rushing off in packs when disturbed. It was ghetto life all right – dirty, noisy and overcrowded – yet with each family trying to maintain a semblance of respectability and identity.

Our school had a strange mixture of teachers, none more extraordinary than the headmaster who was a typical Afrikaner whose spoken English was so strongly accented that it was difficult to understand. He loved teaching history, especially about the Frontier Wars or the Boer War, where he would glorify the heroism of the Afrikaners. But he was a lovable man who could bring his subject alive with wild gesticulations imitating the actions of soldiers at war or Xhosa warriors throwing spears during the Frontier Wars. My recollection is that he was fair in his commentary and we learned a great deal from him about the dynamics of our history.

Even his canings, which were accompanied by a shower of spittle, were carried out with many expressions of regret. There were quite a few Jewish immigrants at the school so we did not feel too isolated. In any case the three of us brothers were a strong enough team to sustain each other against all the anti-Semitic and anti-foreign attacks. Even then, for all the poverty and inner-city deprivation, the school exuded warmth and friendliness, with none of the snobbery that marked many middle-class, pure-white schools.

By this time my father had become active in the Jewish Workers' Movement in Cape Town that came into being to foster fellowship among the immigrants but which soon became an antifascist movement. White workers were easy targets for racism and fascism. They were persuaded that policies like the 'civilised labour policy' which provided jobs for white workers in the public service or in parastatals best served their interests.

The Jewish Workers' Movement, with its experience of fascism in Europe, confronted the fascists wherever possible and my father put aside his dislike of political activity to join in. In one case, several lorry loads of Jews travelled to Paarl, some 30 miles from Cape Town, to demonstrate against the fascists, only to be met by hundreds of thugs who chased the Jewish contingent through the narrow back streets of the town, forcing them to retreat in their lorries.

My parents were gregarious people, and at meetings and socials in our house these clashes were frequently recalled. I was generally allowed to hang about so that I grew up in the midst of a folklore of antiracism and lively debate about current affairs – at least those aspects which touched the lives of South African Jews, especially the more recent immigrants who were yet to be assimilated into the broader society.

Some of the activities at our house were cultural since both my parents were involved in Yiddish theatre, my mother being a star actress while my father busied himself with administration. There were play readings, poetry evenings, political debates and a host of similar events all focusing on the Jewish way of life. It was as though this little community was holding onto its culture as a lifeline to its past and as a key to survival in the face of the current surrounding hostility.

Much of this activity changed character with the advent of the Second World War. When the Soviet Union entered into hostilities, that part of the Jewish community to which we belonged swung enthusiastically behind the Soviet Union, and the Friends of the Soviet Union became very active, even providing support for people in Birobidzhan, the unwanted homeland for Jews in the Soviet Union. Mother collected money, second-hand clothes and shoes, though we later learned that they did not reach their Jewish targets since the authorities argued that it would be unfair to single them out for special treatment – and that it would foster anti-Semitic sentiments in Russia. All this was accepted with reasonably good grace since the Soviets were our heroes who could defeat fascism in Europe.

Almost all of these activities in our house were conducted in Yiddish which I could speak and write fluently. I have now lost much of this capacity, but when faced by a language problem in various foreign countries I can still muster up enough Yiddish to conduct a conversation when the occasion calls for it. It is a kind of credit card, opening doors wherever Jews might be found. It is also the foundation for my broken German, which is very useful indeed.

Intensely Jewish as my home was, it was never Zionist, a theory and movement totally rejected by my parents' circle. So early on I learned to distinguish ethnicity as a culture from national chauvinism. I have never changed my view of this and have yet to visit Israel or have any truck with Zionism. Rather, my sympathy lies with the Palestinians. My parents were also not religious, although I was obliged to attend Hebrew school after regular school hours. But I had no taste for it and, since I had already been persuaded by my father not to have a Bar Mitzvah, I soon gave it up.

Nevertheless, I became a choirboy in the local synagogue, entirely for pecuniary reasons. I saved up my five shillings a month until it amounted to a total of ten pounds which my father invested in his business, only to lose it all when he went bankrupt. Four years' work was in vain.

Mother's theatrical talent was matched by her poetry. When she was not rehearsing for a play, she was reciting some of her poetry and she lived in a world of dramatic enthusiasm. Later in life, when she was about 70, she took to oil painting, exhibiting a wonderful sense of colour. She soon became a well-known artist, exhibiting in galleries and exciting much favourable comment. My father was also seldom out of the press for some public activity or other. And so it came to be understood in the family that a commitment to society was a necessary part of our existence. All that remained for me, as I grew up, was to identify my own particular cause.

However, I had a problem with the obsession with Yiddish and the Jewish way of life that surrounded me. When I was about ten years old I began resenting all these old fogies who persistently intruded into our home, squabbling at the tops of their voices about some Jewish issue or other, and which increasingly seemed irrelevant to the world I encountered outside the walls of our home. None of my school friends, who came from more assimilated families, could relate to these issues in any way. Our visitors quarreled about pre-revolutionary Russian politics, about Trotsky versus Lenin, about Jews in Russia and much else, which became increasingly alienating to me. As I grew older, I thought the cult of Jewishness futile, representing a fading past, beyond recapture – a lost cause drowning in extravagant sentiment.

My rebellion against Jewishness and any religious identity was a watershed. It freed me from the confines imposed by a narrow community, from the straitjacket of tradition, and from the restricted horizons of an inherited world-view. Within me there grew a certain independence of spirit, even a cheekiness, often verging on thumbing one's nose at authority, which sometimes led me into trouble.

I have always cherished the independent spirit and the freedom of action it gave me. As I reached adulthood and joined the movement, I found that many of the other white comrades displayed a similar rebelliousness – we were all outcasts among our social and familial relations. This was in strange contrast with the outlook and style of the older generation of African comrades who, no matter how militant and revolutionary their politics, they were, in my eyes at least, hobbled by their deference to tradition and custom. As an atheist, I thought their deference to religion inhibited their understanding of social processes and acted as a kind of 'opium', in Lenin's phrase, lulling their militancy. Another factor was the straitjacket of tradition in aspects like marriage where choice of partner was constrained by the requirement to marry within the clan in the rural areas.

I understood that my own rebellion against the system served to isolate me within my white environment while their rebellion against the apartheid system made them heroes in theirs. I felt that in order to accomplish my freedom, I had to rebel systematically – to reject all my inherited values – whereas as long as they retained the values and ethos of their traditions, they could be rebellious but admired. Indeed the most successful of our African leaders have been those who breathed and best articulated the traditions, hopes and fears of their people and who desisted from being seen as idiosyncratic individualists who adopted unacceptable European norms.

Of course, sometimes African youth created its own values which had little to do with tradition. Indeed, the 1976 generation of young Soweto rebels, for instance, rejected the caution of their elders and generated a very different kind of defiance of authority which actually lifted the liberation struggle to a new plane, though at a terrible cost. Even now, some of that generation exhibit an element of defiance which is absent in older comrades. Their gutsy approach to politics opens the way for a new vision, new ways of doing things, and I admire that even if I also see its dangers.

The contrast of attitude and style between cadres in the movement has always fascinated me, partly because these kinds of differences are generally handled with great delicacy in our movement. It is almost as if we had all taken a conscious decision – which has of course never happened – that we should respect each other in our diversity of background and culture, as long as we gave genuine commitment to the cause.

My thoughts go back to one of my old favourites, Greenwood Ngotyana, who was my close partner in the Congress Movement in Cape Town after I had removed myself from white society and become a full-time official. Greenwood was born in the Ciskei and spent his youth as a herd boy in the hills. He first saw a white person at close range when he was almost fully grown. It happened when he had just finished three months of isolation in the hills where he was circumcised and initiated into his warrior group. As he tended his father's cattle near a main road, he saw what he described as a very pale man with long white hair hanging into his eyes. He fled from the apparition and only came to terms with white people when sheer necessity forced him to migrate to Cape Town.

It was always difficult to distinguish legend from reality with Greenwood since he was a raconteur of great relish. He told stories about his first job as a garage attendant who reacted to rude customers by withdrawing air from their tyres instead of pumping it in, or, when it was raining, of merely pressing the pump's air button to make a swish, and then with an 'alright, baas', waving the car away.

Greenwood had little English when he came to Cape Town, but he was remarkably intelligent and within a few years he was drawn into the ANC and the trade union movement, where he became secretary of the African Railway Workers Union. He advanced rapidly and developed a considerable public persona, with a three-piece suit to match, becoming a major figure in the ANC and the Communist Party.

We were thrown together, first in trade union work and then continuously in the campaign for the Congress of the People (COP), picked up again in Chapter 2. We travelled extensively throughout the Western Cape, into many nooks and crannies, holding meetings in small huts or in the open air, calling for support for the Congress and our struggle. I came to love Greenwood, one of the most lively, emotional and exuberant characters I have known.

Yet I remained puzzled by a certain hankering for respectability and his residual conservatism and conformity to tradition, as when he returned home to marry a girl chosen by his family about which I would chastise him delicately to avoid his taking offence. But Cape Town lost this wonderful comrade when he was endorsed out after his release from the Treason Trial in 1957, and he was eventually restricted to the Tsomo area of the Transkei.

I have often observed since then how leaders like Moses Kotane, Walter Sisulu and others exercised a certain caution in their public life about being seen to break with traditional values, thus retaining their place in African society. By contrast, I was seen and treated like a rebel by my own people, at times even excoriated by the family, and came to accept that my beliefs gave me both freedom and exclusion.

But to go back to my youth and why I broke with so many white conventions. This had much to do with the idiosyncratic character of my parents' circle. They were by no means ordinary South Africans. Their circle included many progressives, socialists, hybrid communists and more than a few eccentrics – individualists one and all. Their 'togetherness' was rooted in their foreignness, but there was also a measure of common ground – cultural and political – though on hearing their constant bickering and disputes, one would not have believed it.

My mother collected funds for *The Guardian*, a Communist Party newspaper in print since 1937. They were enormously proud of the achievements of Sam Kahn, the first communist MP, and when Soviet sailors visited Cape Town harbour during the Second World War, some of the crew were invited home for food and drinks and many sentimental reminiscences in Russian. On such occasions my mother mingled nostalgic tears with Russian songs and her heart went out to these sailors as they went back to their ship.

I absorbed this libertarian atmosphere, though at a distance, for I could not be part of their world. It was unreal, alien and could never win my adherence though, insofar as their discussions touched South Africa, I made the necessary connections. I disliked the colour bar, but believed, with my parents, that change would have to come slowly if we were to escape catastrophe.

However, I became acquainted with Marx, Engels and Lenin when I was about 16 through the books in our house, and although my father was far from being a revolutionary or communist, Marxism was not an alien creed and was accorded a certain degree of awe and respect. So one can say that I was actually socialised into left politics though it was some years before my commitment became serious.

My father's financial situation improved during the war and I was moved out of a working-class high school to the snobbish SA College High School where everyone wore a silly uniform, including a straw boater in summer. I disliked the atmosphere but enjoyed the rugby, which gave ample scope for the release of my abundant physical aggression. I was captain of the under 16s but I found the teaching orthodox and dreary, and my studies limped along. I enjoyed rambling on Table Mountain and started a mountain club the members of which went rock climbing every Sunday, leaving my mother distraught. I was also good at maths and so was easily persuaded to choose cadastral surveying as my career path, much against my parents' wishes. They preferred the respectability of law or medicine.

At the end of the war, recession hit the country and my father's business went into liquidation. We smuggled leather out of the factory at night as a hedge against need, and we witnessed the horror of a public auction of our house. We were saved from eviction by our friends who bought the house on our behalf, landing my father with lifelong debts that he assiduously repaid.

But he had enough funds to pay for my university tuition and I continued at Cape Town University in the Engineering Department. And then I fell in love with a French-speaking Belgian student who came from the Congo. Our affair was overwhelming and, despite total opposition from my family, lasted several years. It ended, however, when her Catholic parents learned of our relationship and barred her return to South Africa. The experience no doubt reinforced my opposition to ethnic and religious exclusivity.

My girlfriend broadened my outlook and taught me French but increased the gulf between myself and my circle of friends and family. I came to question the narrow confines of engineering and the parochialism of my fellow students, began attending lectures in the Department of Philosophy and joined the Students Socialist Party (SSP).

I should explain that this was after the war when the university allowed a good number of ex-servicemen to become students, bringing with them a greater maturity and a more advanced knowledge of politics than was the norm at the university. There was also a growing democratic spirit in the country stemming from wartime anti-fascist sentiment and the legitimacy of the Soviet Union and all it stood for. So, a vigorous group of Marxists of many shades came together in the SSP to hold debates, lectures and demonstrations, rapidly becoming the most visible student group on campus. The leaders were an intimidating array of prominent personalities like Lionel Forman, who was already a well-known intellectual, Cassim Amra of the Indian Congress, former Air Force Lieutenant Robin Blatchford, and Simon Zukas, who became secretary-general of the liberation movement in Northern Rhodesia, achieving world renown when he was detained and deported to the UK. Initially, I was totally lost in this esoteric circle of heavy socialist theoretical discourse, but I was soon absorbed and became chairman in my last year of university.

But a streak of liberal ideology stayed with me and I avoided joining the Communist Party despite many invitations. Perhaps my continuing interest in philosophy was an obstacle. Plato and Aristotle fascinated me. Perhaps I was also constrained by being the only open leftist in the Engineering Department. My ex-soldier fellow students often ribbed me with remarks about carrying a bomb in my bag and I became known as 'Benny the Bolshy'.

The left was remarkably lively in Cape Town those days; it was the Left Bank of South Africa. There was the dominant figure of Professor Jack Simons who lectured brilliantly on Marxist philosophy. There were Jack and Leslie Cope, critic and artist respectively; Harry Snitcher, an advocate and one-time chairman of the Communist Party; and many other intellectual whites who gave lectures and seminars, maintaining a high level of cultural and social activities for a broad constituency of leftists. My involvement grew and I was about to join the Communist Party when I had to leave for Rhodesia to do my professional articles as a surveyor.

LIFE WITH COLONIAL FRONTIERSMEN

If Cape Town introduced me to Marxism, Bulawayo made me a revolutionary in the sense that I lost all hope of a gradualist transition in the white colonial structures in southern Africa. My change of heart was facilitated by the fact that I was lifted out of my cozy middle-class home and environment, and transported into the sloth of a working-class boarding house for lumpen white immigrants from Britain and South Africa. Being a total learner in the practical work of surveying, my firm Richardson and Henry paid me £20 a month, which was just enough to pay for board and lodging in a shared room. My roommate was a young salesman, quite clean and presentable, but most of the other lodgers were tough railway workers who seemed indifferent to the filthy conditions of the toilets and the other facilities. My neighbour was a big-bellied, gin-drinking woman who was embroiled in daily fights with her husband, often landing up in a heap on the veranda where all could view the scene. And so I was inducted into the hard world of earning my own bread and surviving among the lumpen flotsam of colonial society.

Fortunately, I was to spend a great deal of time in the countryside, under canvas or living with client farmers, and so I was able to shake off the depression of the slum and the irritations of my pukka sahib employer. Richardson believed in throwing trainees in at the deep end, so on my very first day I was given a truck, a set of survey instruments and a group of 'boys' who were to be permanently attached to me. Their 'boss boy', Thomas, was a Nyasa who had a warm, engaging personality and a kindly disposition so we became friends from the start. He spoke little English and I had to learn Fanagalo, a colloquial version of Ndebele, right away.

I needed Thomas's help badly. While I could use a theodolite, and could read maps and do computations, I knew little of practical work. Fortunately Thomas was used to trainees and, being a perfectly capable field worker himself, he guided me through the first few weeks until I learned the ropes. If he had been taught mapping and how to read a theodolite he would have made a brilliant surveyor. Even then he could use binoculars and manipulate the steel measuring tape (while not being able to actually read it), and his intuitive grasp of what was going on was excellent.

I was determined to make friends with my 'boys' and they responded well enough. Richardson saw me at work and warned me not to get too friendly with them, and that if anyone became difficult I was to take him alone into the bush and thrash him. I was not to leave any marks since the 'boy' was bound to report me to the Native Commissioner (a British civil servant since Rhodesia was still a colony), who would fine me if there was any corroborative evidence.

Even with my mountaineering and camping background, the job was tough and extremely demanding. Mostly we camped out, rose well before dawn to drive to the base of some mountain, climbed for some hours and set up the theodolite for observations until the sun created too much shimmer for decent observing. We then descended to the truck, moved to some other area and spent the middle of the day measuring mile after mile of lines cut through the bush or along some roadway. In the afternoon we once again climbed a mountain to complete another set of observations in the cool of late afternoon.

I could not have managed without Thomas who was always on hand to correct my orientation, lead me infallibly back to the car en route to which I would have become hopelessly lost, and advise on a host of other matters. He was also the cheerleader and organiser of the team of six who accompanied me from Bulawayo plus the other casual workers usually seconded to me by the local farmer. All these men were needed to cut lines through the miles of bush we had to survey and the tops of mountains and hills for triangulation by theodolite. Thomas tore into tree cutting with extraordinary zip. He was narrow-waisted but very broad-shouldered and could wield a large axe with great dexterity, laying about him with consummate ease.

In the evenings Thomas would cook me some rice or potatoes to which I added canned meat. The men ate communally from the sparse rations I gave them weekly. These consisted of a two-pound jam tin of mealie meal per day each, flavoured by two shillings' worth of offal per week which they bought when passing a butcher. Failure to provide this meat was certain to generate serious discontent and I sometimes travelled long distances to ensure its supply. The men appeared not to resent my comparatively luxurious diet, which generally included bread, jam and tea. Every evening we sat around the campfire chatting in Fanagalo.

While I grew ever closer to the men, I was increasingly alienated by Richardson and the settler farmers I worked for. One of them was Ian Smith who later became prime minister. He had a veneer of decent behaviour but his real persona was that of a frontiersman just like the rest. Richardson was a heavy beer drinker and wherever we went together he tried to draw me into his drinking bouts with sometimes drastic effects. Yet, he was enormously fit and could walk for miles without any sign of fatigue and he was a very able surveyor. But he was a dreadful racist, totally colonial in his attitude towards the men, paying them rock-bottom wages for very hard work.

But it was the farmers who upset me most and it was my contact with them that gradually changed me from a dilettante socialist into a revolutionary. When I stayed in their homes I was expected to join in the talk and beer drinking in the evenings and on Sundays which inevitably turned around how terrible the 'boys' were. They delighted in exchanging reminiscences about how they beat them up, lashed them and even shot at them if they turned 'bolshy'. It was more than my job and skin were worth to disagree and I had to nod and murmur assent to all this rabid viciousness which turned my stomach. This was frontier racism at its worst.

On my return to Bulawayo from one of these excursions, I made enquiries about African resistance. But where to start since my world was so remote from theirs? Naively, I went to a Bulawayo township to ask for the trade union offices, which I thought might be working legally and openly. I drew a blank everywhere and soon realised that no one would trust a white stranger.

An opportunity to make some contact with politics came in a

quite unexpected form. A friend told me about a meeting to be held in the town hall to discuss Rhodesia's relations with Britain. The meeting was to be chaired by the Mayor of Bulawayo and addressed by a Councillor Ollie from Salisbury. So, I decided to attend. The hall was packed with several thousand white Rhodesians who responded enthusiastically to the nastiest racism I had ever heard. Ollie, who would have fitted in with the Ku Klux Klan, jeered at the 'niggers' who were not good enough to be his servants. He was followed by the chairman who explained that it was time for Southern Rhodesia to demand dominion status, which should be accorded within the next ten years, and proposed a motion accordingly

Flushed with almost uncontrollable anger, I rose to move an amendment to the effect that progress toward greater autonomy should be conditional on granting trade union rights to Africans. My speech was heard in total silence and when I called for a seconder, none appeared. I sat down, shaking. When the meeting ended, my friend advised that we leave the hall quickly in case people were waiting to beat us up outside. As we left hastily, I was approached by several people – a priest, a civil servant and others – who said they would have seconded my motion but for their jobs. I realised the futility of my intervention but was pleased to have made some move to protest against the viciousness around me.

I had no further opportunity to express political opposition there and I had to bide my time until my return to Cape Town where I immediately approached several old friends about joining the Communist Party. I was astounded to learn that it had been dissolved by the Central Committee just prior to being declared unlawful in June 1950, and couldn't believe that no remaining structures had been left behind. The decision to disband was not taken lightly, and it was not unanimous. Some had argued that as the party had operated openly and was obviously infiltrated, it could not transform itself into a clandestine organisation. Only Bill Andrews and Michael Harmel formally opposed this decision. Some members believed that the dissolution was only a manoeuvre and that the party would be immediately reconstituted underground. This did not actually happen for some time and when it did the decision to disband was condemned. The new party leadership observed that this was the only party in history which did not make provision for immediate reorganisation. The membership had not been consulted about the dissolution and there was a widespread feeling of betrayal.

Some of the leaders who held a reformist view of South African politics, hoping to make inroads within the existing system, now realised that a wholly new situation had arisen and decided to drop out of politics altogether. However, within two years people like Michael Harmel, Dr Yusuf Dadoo and Moses Kotane began the difficult task of creating a new party apparatus under the noses of the Special Branch. They did the job so well that throughout the following eight years of its clandestine existence neither the police nor other members of the movement were aware of its existence.

At the same time, within the ANC there was a growing militancy and a tendency to reject the whole system, placing the drive towards national liberation as the main issue for black people. But strands of gradualist and reformist thinking remained throughout the movement and the two lines continued side by side for some time.

Most of these concerns passed me by, however, as I became involved in my profession. At first I threw myself into the work but soon realised that I disliked the minutiae of town surveying and especially the commercialism associated with the profession.

I sought contacts with people like Brian Bunting, Fred Carneson and Alex La Guma at the offices of *The Guardian* weekly, which was then undergoing serious harassment from the police. Dr Malan's government was consolidating its power by means of harsh legislation and police action.

Some of the younger activists of the left formed the Modern Youth Society (MYS), which was non-racial and which held debates, organised study groups and socials, and I joined in. Most of the members were white or coloured while a few Africans also joined including a few from as far afield as South West Africa, Northern Rhodesia and Nyasaland. One of these was Herman Andimba Toivo Ya Toivo, who later became secretary-general of the South West African People's Organisation (Swapo) and Minister of Mines in Namibia.

We were delighted that these few individuals should want to learn something about politics within our ranks and we felt sure that they would make use of whatever they learned when they returned home. Our expectations were not unrealistic. Many years later the SA Broadcasting Corporation alleged that I was Toivo's mentor and the real founder of Swapo. This served the regime's purpose of attributing any manifestation of African mobilisation as being the work of 'white communists' in South Africa. Another member was Nephas Tembo who became a cabinet minister in Zambia under Kaunda. Although a modest little organisation, MYS served as a good training ground for young cadres and spawned people like Albie Sachs and Dennis Goldberg, who both became prominent in the movement.

I was also invited to join a Marxist study class run by Jack Simons, which soon expanded to become the Africa Club where we held regular lectures and discussion meetings under the watchful eye of the Special Branch who monitored all who came to the building. The Club soon became a centre of gravity of the left and recruitment for the movement.

It is difficult to recapture the mood of that time but I recall the increasing anxiety that filled us as the intentions of the state became clearer. We now had a government elected by a minority of a minority, constituted by a relatively small redoubt of white Afrikaners who had not really expected to come to power but who were now in full command of a state that had always been undemocratic and based on coercion with a minimum of consent.

For blacks, the system never bothered to hide its brutal nature, but for whites there had been a major pretence at upholding a parliamentary democracy. Every deviation from democracy and the rule of law was justified as a requirement for stability. Now there was a small band of isolated whites held together by a thin skin of conviction, but lacking the warmth and solidarity of township cohesion, for whom the prospect of state violence was cause for considerable alarm. At stake were social rejection, future career, financial uncertainty, continuing intimidation and ultimate arrest. Many of our group slipped away to follow the path of convention and orthodoxy. For those who stayed the prospects were bleak for there was no prospect that we would triumph, that liberation was anything but a freedom song. Even the slogan of the day, 'Freedom In Our Lifetime', meant a long postponement. And we were so young.

In the coming months it became apparent that our anxieties were more than warranted.

THE DEFIANCE CAMPAIGN

Although the country had witnessed various forms of mass action by Labour, township residents, rural people and others in which the ANC had played a major role, by 1951 it could not yet be said that the ANC was a mass movement itself. And most of the mass actions had a distinctly local character and focused on some specific issue. What was clearly needed was some campaign which would unify the movement nationally, raise the level of militancy and bring about concerted mass action according to some plan.

This need was met by the proposal made on 29 July 1951 to instigate a Defiance Campaign at a joint conference of the ANC and South African Indian Congress. A Joint Planning Council (JPC) was set up consisting of Dr James Moroka, Walter Sisulu, JB Marks, Yusuf Dadoo, and Yusuf Cachalia. Although the two organisations had collaborated before, there were new issues to be sorted out. First there was the question of the role of individual communists in the struggle, and second, there was the issue of how to co-operate with non-African organisations.

The National Minded Block in the ANC took a conservative, exclusivist position, while Nelson Mandela, Oliver Tambo and Walter Sisulu, who came from the Congress Youth League, were steadily moving away from a narrow Africanism and anti-communism to a more open position. However, the realisation that the illegalisation of the Communist Party in 1950 was only the thin end of the wedge, and that repression was bound to increase for all opponents of the regime, helped to concentrate minds into a new spirit of unity in action.

The JPC decided that a Defiance Campaign would be launched by trained volunteers who would contravene selected laws and regulations. This was not to be seen as a kind of Gandhian passive resistance, but was intended to raise the level of resistance by means of mass action. While initially defiance would be by small groups, it would escalate to take on a mass character across the country. The proposal was endorsed by the annual conference of the ANC in Bloemfontein on 15-17 December 1951 in the form of the 'Defiance of Unjust Laws Campaign'. The president of the ANC wrote to Prime Minister Malan warning him of their intention and on 26 June 1952 the campaign was launched in the main urban centres on the Witwatersrand and Port Elizabeth, the strongholds of ANC power.

But defiance soon spread elsewhere. In Boksburg 50 volunteers walked through the township gates without permits and were soon arrested. By August the campaign had spread to East London, Uitenhage, the West Rand, Cape Town, Grahamstown, Pretoria and Vereeniging. By 26 August, 20 leaders, including JB Marks, Nelson Mandela and Yusuf Dadoo were on trial in Johannesburg under the *Suppression of Communism Act* and another 15 in Port Elizabeth. By 2 September, 500 resisters had been arrested in 24 centres. By mid-October, every major centre in the country as well as many rural areas had seen some sort of defiance. Nearly 2 000 had volunteered in Port Elizabeth alone.

There was plenty of drama in Cape Town too, including within our own small circle. A group of four members of MYS led by Albie Sachs and including Mary Butcher sat down on a Blacks Only bench in the Cape Town Post Office in October 1952. Of the four, the participation of Mary was perhaps the most remarkable. She came from a totally apolitical Natal family who were dedicated Christian Scientists but who were otherwise typical English colonials. But on her arrival at the University of Cape Town, Mary had been drawn into the movement and joined the staff of *The Guardian* on graduation. From there she was soon thrust into a prominent position and subsequently banned. We eventually got married, but that for later.

At first, the group of 'defiers' was ignored, even though it was surrounded by several dozen supporters who tried to explain to the officials that they should take note of what was happening. At last a senior official approached Albie who explained with much gravitas that this was defiance of an unjust law. The official also tried to ignore the group but a small crowd had gathered and there was quite a stir in the post-office entrance hall. Eventually the police arrived and when they also failed to get the group to disperse, the 'defiers' were arrested to cheers from our group of bystanders, now substantially reinforced by inquisitive shoppers. The group was held in the main police station for some five miserable hours and then released on bail. I was unable to take part as I had already arranged to take a post-graduate course in London and was due to leave a month later. I felt dispirited about my role as a mere onlooker but there was no going back on my decision.

The campaign gathered momentum, riots broke out in Port Elizabeth on 18 October, in Johannesburg on 3 November and in East London on 10 November and there were a number of casualties though this was not the movement's intention. The state reacted vigorously, imposing bans and curfews, which made open organisation difficult. The *Criminal Laws Amendment Act* threatened drastic punitive action including lashes for 'protest by way of defiance'.

The movement licked its wounds and the campaign was closed down. Approximately 8 500 individuals had defied apartheid laws and regulations; 100 000 people had joined the ANC. The state resorted to administrative measures as well and 52 black leaders in the Eastern Cape alone were banned from attending meetings. Mandela received a nine-month suspended sentence and was confined to Johannesburg.

The campaign changed the image of the ANC from a rather moderate organisation led by eminently 'respectable' professionals to a mass-based militant liberation movement. There were important lessons too, the main one being that there were limits to the use of non-violent resistance as a tactic. But some leaders felt that the main deficiency had been that the action had been too fragmented and that any future campaign actions would have to be simultaneous and nationwide. It was also realised that new organisational structures were needed to cater for the diverse racial groups. The Congress of Democrats (COD) was formed as a white partner to the alliance of the African National Congress and the SA Indian Congress on 10 October 1953. Subsequently the

South African Coloured People's Organisation (SACPO) also linked up and then the SA Congress of Trade Unions (SACTU) also joined.

The COD emerged as a rival to the Liberal Party, which came into being on 8 May 1953. The Liberal Party stood for a non-racial franchise with property and educational qualifications, while the COD advocated universal franchise from the start and was an integral part of the Congress Movement.

But I missed all these developments having left South Africa in December 1952 to register for a post-graduate diploma in town planning at the University of London. Having realised that surveying would not sustain my interest, I thought that the related field of town planning would be a creative alternative.

LONDON

Living in London was at first enthralling. Here was the centre of the universe where the news was red-hot, where one could choose from any number of exciting events and where one could see in the flesh so many of the great names I had read about in the *New Statesman* and other journals. There was also so much choice in terms of culture, theatre and the arts that I intended to taste it all. It was not long, however, before I realised that most of it was beyond my means, and that the political personalities like Kingsley Martin of the *New Statesman* or Dick Crossman of the Labour Party were rather shallow showmen without many principles or real commitment to socialism. I went to the House of Commons to witness a debate on the colour bar, which I found quite intriguing, only to be told afterwards by Solly Sachs, the veteran SA trade unionist, that the reason the debate did not get to a vote was because both Labour and the Conservatives had agreed to talk it out so that neither side would be committed for the future. And so began my disenchantment with the Labour left and I now understood what Marx meant by 'parliamentary cretinism' when he warned about the Labour movement getting absorbed in futile debating as an alternative to concentrating on building working-class organisation.

I was desperately short of money and took a job at one of the huge mass-catering restaurants near Trafalgar Square, carrying trays of cakes from lorries parked at the back entrance. I confess that I was rather embarrassed to put on the white coat and apron worn by the labourers, but I was also intrigued to be working with a group of mostly Irish temporary workers. It was my first taste of actual working-class life. I then got a job at Battersea Polytechnic as a part-time evening lecturer in civil engineering which I was able to combine with a terribly tedious job as a records clerk in a large engineering factory. It was there that I learned just how vacuous was the life of white-collar workers who were absorbed in the trash they read in the daily gutter press, where the Queen's jaunts were given priority above all other news. All this was humbling for a novice at the workplace and someone from a white middle-class background in South Africa.

I lived in a drafty room in a boarding house near Kilburn High Road where I was underfed and permanently cold. My only solace was a group of three Irish working-class girls who lived immediately above me, one of whom became my lover and who occasionally took me to an Irish party in one of their special pubs in London.

I joined the Communist Party of Great Britain, and was also placed in a special South African branch headed by Vella Pillay and MD Naidoo, two South Africans who had settled in England. Our group met under the benign supervision of Idris Cox, a veteran communist with much experience of the Third World. I was appointed secretary of the South African contingent for the Third World Youth Festival to be held in Bucharest in 1953 and soon had to look after Walter Sisulu, Duma Nokwe, Alfred Hutchinson, Paul Joseph and several others who came over from South Africa for the festival.

I also joined the local branch of the Communist Party in Nottinghill Gate and met many fine British comrades whose total commitment I greatly admired, especially since there seemed no prospect of advance for the party in the context of Britain's stodgy politics. In contrast to the slogging work in the party, the Labour Party seemed driven by careerism. The communists were proscribed from participating in the Labour Movement but at many factories they established a firm base with the party carrying influence way beyond its numbers. These were lessons I absorbed and resolved to take home with me to South Africa where political protest consisted much more of periodic campaigns than steady organisational and educational work. I thought we had much to learn from the steady consistency of a party branch in London where the emphasis was on producing loyal, lifelong cadres who would not slip away when things got tough. It was also vital that communists should not be excluded from the broader Labour and Democratic Movement.

With the arrival of the leaders from South Africa for the Bucharest Festival there was a lot to do and we soon had a contingent of 30 including South Africans working in Europe. At Bucharest, Walter and Duma were given VIP treatment and made a tremendous impression everywhere they went. Africa had not yet established itself as a force in the international arena, so these eminent South Africans were a relatively new and intriguing addition. We had several formal meetings with other delegations, of which the Chinese was particularly memorable, and a wholly new international spectrum opened up before us. We were also given talks by the Rumanian cadre responsible for us on the difficulties they were experiencing in establishing a new society based on socialist principles. His remarks have remained both an inspiration and a warning to me ever since. All in all, I was enormously excited by the sweep of the world movement for socialism and totally won over to the cause of communism.

At the end of the festival I made my way to France for a spell of hitchhiking and a couple of weeks as a farm labourer, and then back to London for the journey back home in December 1953. I had had enough of Europe and of talking about the problems of South Africa at a distance and was yearning to return to the reality and the struggle at home.

CHAPTER TWO

FULL-TIME ACTIVIST

Europe had been an enriching experience, but I tired of it and of the loneliness. Coming back to Cape Town warmed the soul, and I admit to revelling in the comfort of my parents' lovely home in Camps Bay with its glorious sea view and long sunny afternoons. I was also made very welcome by my old Cape Town comrades, though I immediately became aware of the tension they were under. The political environment had deteriorated while I was away, and many leaders had been banned from attending meetings and penalised in other ways. Many had been in prison.

By contrast, my family lived in a cozy ghetto of family and friends and seemed unaffected by the political turbulence in the black townships. The master-servant relationships which governed my family and hometown friends' lives created a seemingly impenetrable curtain around them so that the struggles of black people seemed to be happening in a foreign country. I imagine that the persecution of the Jews in Germany was similarly shut out by the great majority of Germans who had a clear idea of what was happening – after all it was all so public – yet they were able to shut it out and keep on with their own lives.

Of course this wall between white and black was heavily reinforced by residential segregation. My parents' home in Camps Bay was then, as now, part of a bourgeois suburb where blacks were present only as domestic workers. And so I moved between two worlds – that of a non-racial movement in the grip of deep tensions and the racially exploitative, luxurious lifestyle of white South Africa.

I have to admit that it was extremely difficult to straddle the psychological divide between black and white and it took years before I could shake off the influences of white elitism. Even as I later forged deep, warm relationships with black comrades, a gap remained. It was unspoken, even accepted, and most comrades appreciated that we were building a new solidarity in the midst of severe divisions which cast their influences everywhere and on everyone, and that we all had to make a supreme effort in overcoming them. This was most easily done through practical activity.

My isolation within my own family and their immediate environment as a consequence of my associations in the movement rapidly became apparent. At home I could not discuss my new political identity, nor comment freely about the dramatic events around me. I slipped into an uneasy silence with my parents and family. Among my comrades I made a virtue of necessity and sometimes boasted that I was now a traitor to my race, class and religion. Sometimes I recalled the exchange between Soviet Ambassador Molotov and British Labour leader Aneurin Bevan. When the latter accused Molotov of having bourgeois origins, Molotov replied: 'Yes, we are both traitors to our class.'

I came to accept the inevitability of my isolation as a progressive white South African. However, I envied the experiences of my black comrades. Even in exile I had marvelled at the deep nostalgia for home articulated by African comrades. They missed the richness of township life, the deeply social and cultural life they led there, compared with the arid existence of life among the English. I too had been homesick, but for me there was none of the social solidarity of township life. It is something I have missed through all the years in the movement and it warmed my heart to see how it sustained many, despite the hardships of daily life.

And so, since this chapter is about my conversion into a full-time functionary of the movement, it is useful to bear in mind the way my activities were shaped by my personal origins and environment. Even as I became deeply enmeshed in the daily work of the trade union movement and the ANC, I remained confined to the social milieu of white society and its associated suburban existence. Even if I wished to change that, the law ensured that I would remain ensconced in that environment.

The Cape Town to which I returned had undoubtedly changed. The Defiance Campaign had politicised people a great deal, and the harsh measures used by the police had increased bitterness within the movement and in the townships. The *Criminal Law Amendment Act* passed in the wake of the killing of a nun and the stabbing of a police major in the Eastern Cape threatened lashings and prison for a breach of the law, no matter how minor, if it was carried out 'by way of protest against any law'. Thus putting up a political poster could lead to a lengthy jail sentence if it referred to protest of any kind. The movement had to find a new strategy to continue mass mobilisation without directly flouting the law. Also, despite the improved coherence within the movement, nationally there remained significant regional differences.

Johannesburg had become the locus of the national leadership of Tambo, Sisulu and Mandela, among others, with the ANC as the dominant organisation reflecting their stature but also reflecting the fact that Africans, who predominated in Johannesburg, had become the leading force in the struggle against apartheid. In Durban, the Indian Congress predominated, while in Port Elizabeth, Govan Mbeki and Raymond Mhlaba led a large and militant ANC. In Cape Town, however, the ANC had no equivalent leaders, being both a much smaller organisation and with Africans numbering about 100 000 compared to 300 000 coloured people. Also, many Africans in the Cape were in fact migrant workers from the Transkei and had their roots there.

While the movement had solid roots in the trade unions, most of their members were coloured workers who had not yet begun to identify with the Congress Movement. The ANC allowed only Africans to join, since it was originally formed to unite the African tribes of South Africa. Its membership consisted of largely migrant workers with only a small component of urbanised and educated members. On the other hand there was a significant group of white comrades clustered in *The Guardian* but associated with leading communists like Sam Kahn, Brian Bunting, Fred Carneson, Jack Simons and Ray Alexander. These factors gave the Western Cape a markedly different character from the other major centres. Some of these factors remain problematic even today.

Cape Town was also distinguished by a liberal tradition which blurred the edges of colour oppression. Discrimination was abundant, but among the general public the coloureds were seen as less alien than the majority of Africans who were mainly rural migrant workers from the Transkei. But within the movement there was an easy mixing between the races and comradeship was easily established. *The Guardian* required voluntary sellers to go out into the black community every weekend and this was an important element in introducing mixed racial groups into the movement.

Additionally, before its banning, the Communist Party had its national headquarters in Cape Town, and had been proactive in fostering non-racialism as a cardinal aspect of its policy and practices. Indeed, it was probably the only fully non-racial organisation in the country at the time. Nevertheless, it was apparent that in Cape Town, whites had a disproportionally dominant position in the movement to a degree not seen elsewhere, causing some resentment among an Africanist grouping in the ANC. Sam Kahn, for example, who represented Africans on a separate voters' roll in parliament, was an outstanding MP often in the news. Ray Alexander was the undoubted leader of the leftist trade unions, Jack Simons gave brilliant lectures on a range of intellectual and cultural issues, Brian Bunting and Fred Carneson exercised much political influence, and writers and artists like Jack Cope and Gregoire Boonzaier gave a uniquely cultural character to the movement in Cape Town.

However, my first port of entry back into the movement was the Modern Youth Society (MYS) and its secretary, Mary Butcher, with whom I had kept in touch during my stay in Europe. Mary's role had changed from a rather carefree student member of MYS who was slowly shedding her Christian Science slightly upper-class Natal background to take a prominent place in the movement. She was one of the few who were prepared to step into the shoes of the leadership as tier after tier was banned and forced out of office. She had become a reporter for *The Guardian* and was therefore centrally placed for political work. Emerging as a public speaker, secretary of numerous organisations, and a reference point for the press had taken its toll on the young girl I had previously known, in particular the banning order which had been placed on her just a few weeks prior to my return. She had lost weight but was bearing up bravely under all the stress.

We began going to meetings together and despite the cultural gulf between us – she came from the private-school, horse-riding brigade which I disliked – nature's chemistry soon overcame these obstacles. But I was living with my parents who smelled a rat. They rapidly intervened, protesting that a 'nice Jewish boy' could not become involved with a Christian because 'it would never work'. Being now part of a closely-knit political circle, we sought advice and took a 'collective decision' that we should get married soonest, before the family made my life sheer hell.

To do so, I had to abscond from home, a humiliating experience at the age of 26, get hastily married at a registry office in town, and join Mary at her flat nearby. To their credit, my parents immediately reconciled themselves to the situation and accepted Mary into the family without further ado.

Our relationship was strongly reinforced by our deep commitment to the movement. From the first we both understood that our personal lives would be subordinate to our political work. No doubt we took ourselves too seriously but that was the spirit of the times. For instance, on the very night of our marriage, we both attended a MYS meeting where I was scheduled to speak on Colonial Youth Day, and it was only the next day that we were able to escape for a two-day honeymoon at Gordon's Bay.

While all this was underway, I first took on some work as a surveyor and spent several months laying out the Cape Town foreshore. I then decided to open a private practice as a surveyor, though this was aborted before I could really establish myself. Mary was receiving a monthly allowance from her parents and we decided that I should offer myself for full-time work in the movement. After consultations with Bunting and others it was decided that I should go into the trade union movement as secretary of a new Metal Workers Union. Thus, within a few short months of my return to South Africa, I had married, was deeply involved in trade union work and an early target for Special Branch attention. The days of dilettantism were over.

Mary and I often discussed where all this was leading and its implications for our starting a family. We read the literature of the international revolutionary movement including the memoirs of Krupskaya, Lenin's wife, for guidance on how revolutionaries should conduct their personal lives. Her advice was that it was important that they should lead as normal a life as possible. We knew that the future would be uncertain and dangerous, that we could expect severe treatment by the regime and that children would be a serious encumbrance. But we decided that it would be best to lead a normal married life and we had three sons: Fred on 22 February 1955, Ivan on 7 August 1956, and Neil on 16 November 1958. No doubt they all paid a heavy price for being born into the turmoil that was ours, but perhaps it was also a solid basis for the very close relationship we have developed and share even to the present.

Both our family backgrounds contrasted vividly with our new life. Mary's parents were from old, established Natal families, while my parents had moved up the social scale from the poverty they had known on their arrival in South Africa. My older brother, Hillel, was an architect, while Sol was manager of my father's leather-goods factory. I had been brought up in a conventional Jewish environment, had been a Boy Scout, and had shared the aspirations of my middle-class peers. The future had been laid out for me as a respectable professional serving the white community in Cape Town.

Yet, there were differences of substance between my upbringing and those of my friends. My parents were atheists and anti-fascists who had been very active in support of the Soviet Union during the second world war, despite their reservations about anti-Semitism and the Stalinist crimes in that country. My brother Hillel had joined the Communist Party while a student and I recall his having donned a leather jacket and gloves for the fights with the fascists on the Johannesburg City Hall steps. Our house in Cape Town was a frequent venue for left-wingers of all kinds and socialism was a common talking point. And so it was that I absorbed a left-wing culture, developed a rebellious streak and independence of mind which brought me into frequent conflict with my more conventional friends. It also prepared me for my future role as a white dissident, at odds with the community and in constant conflict with the regime.

ARENAS OF STRUGGLE

Life as a trade unionist was tough. Since I was to start a new union, there was much fieldwork to be done. Fortunately, I teamed up with Archie Sibeko who had taken over Greenwood's

African Railway Workers Union and who agreed to set up the African Metal Workers Union in parallel with my coloured union. This arrangement was the norm in Cape Town since African workers could not belong to a registered union and it was considered advantageous to register the coloured union for the formal recognition and negotiating opportunities this gave.

Archie and I worked from the same office, regularly going together to various industrial areas where we held factory meetings, generally without permission, and which were often interrupted by the arrival of the Special Branch. We soon realised that they either followed us from our office, since we always used my car, or they relied on informants at the factories, either management or white supervisors, who phoned them as soon as we appeared. A kind of cat-and-mouse game ensued as the police tried to catch us holding a meeting on the pavement or in the cloakrooms which were both unlawful.

My difficulties were many. It was not easy for black workers to come to trust a white person and I spoke little Xhosa. How I wished for the anonymity of a black skin! Archie's presence was essential. Also, there was little that we could actually do for the workers once they joined the union because the channels to the Labour Department were largely closed to us. Furthermore, the constant police presence made workers shy of us, so we had to resort to dodging the police tail by driving down side streets and then holding short, sharp meetings at the back of the factories where we were out of sight.

The system of separate unions for Africans and coloureds also caused much resentment. Much as we tried to run the unions as one, it was often apparent that the law forced us to give coloureds priority over Africans, for example, in negotiations or even in making representations. Only coloured workers could apply for a Conciliation Board, even if the Africans were more militant or even in the majority in a particular plant. These issues caused tension at our meetings and made us feel that we were reinforcing apartheid structures. Archie and I became exponents of deregistration and the merging of all workers within one industry though this was contrary to the prevailing line.

However, I soon came to realise that I was not cast in the mould of a natural conciliator and found the casework boring. I was hankering for a more political role. But I was also not ready for the opening offered me in the shape of a seat in parliament as a successor to Brian Bunting and Ray Alexander who were both prohibited from holding this office. I was still eligible because I had not been a member of the Communist Party.

I declined the offer, flattering though it was, because I felt wholly unready to be the sole progressive in a parliament consisting of some of the worst exponents of apartheid. Instead, I took on the job of election agent for Len Lee-Warden who was chosen in my place, and since he was banned from addressing meetings, the onus fell on me. I campaigned flat out for his election, which he won. I addressed dozens of meetings on his behalf, which gave me much-needed experience. Through this exposure I became one of the established political leaders in the Western Cape. When I saw what the task of confronting white power in parliament involved I was glad I had declined. Bunting had been a rather dull speaker who suffered greatly from the isolation and hostility he encountered in parliament. Len suffered similarly and had difficulty completing his speeches.

One evening, Athol Thorn approached me with an astonishing proposal. He revealed that the Communist Party had been reconstituted while I was abroad and he asked me to join. I was placed in a group with three others and from then on we met covertly in a car once a month. We drove around Cape Town's suburbs discussing our work in the mass movement, each reporting on our activities, which were then analysed in considerable detail by the group until a decision was reached. On occasion there were documents from the Central Committee or the District Committee, which we read by parking under a street light. Immediately thereafter we burned the documents.

Security was stringent and we made no references to the existence of the party anywhere outside of our group. We were also extremely careful not to allow any indication of a common purpose between us at any of the broader meetings we attended. I soon learned that it was easy for a small group like ours to exert much influence in the mass movement without giving away our existence. While following a general line, we were allowed sufficient flexibility to enable us to participate creatively in these discussions, even to the point of disagreements, as long as these did not go against the fundamental position we sought. We also respected the views of non-party people and supported them on merit. It was a highly effective mode of operation though obviously undemocratic and open to gross abuse. This danger was frequently discussed and it was a cardinal rule that, constituting a highly disciplined and coherent caucus in the broader movement, we should not be sectarian and we should at all times respect the views and roles of non-party people.

At this time the party was very small, possibly numbering less than a hundred members throughout the country. Yet, since we recruited only influential people, and since we traversed the whole movement and had leaders in top positions, the party was able to influence the policy of the Congress Movement considerably while at the same time avoiding any tendency towards establishing hegemony.

PARALLEL SITES OF STRUGGLE

The movement was now operating across three sites of struggle. First, there was the public level, which was the terrain of *The Guardian* and the Congress Alliance consisting of the five Congresses – African, Indian, coloured, white and the trade unions. Next lay the twilight zone where semi-legal activities such as planning meetings involving banned persons and confidential documents were discussed. Finally, there was the level of deep cover where the Communist Party operated.

Each had its role, with the first constantly striving to keep open as much public space as possible for protest and mobilisation. *The Guardian*, for example, was always straining the boundaries of legality by publishing stories that were subject to banning orders and having to defend these in court. The trade unions were also often close to unlawful conduct with strikes and other actions. Banned persons were constantly hauled before the courts for breaking the terms of their banning orders. We won many of these actions since our extremely able and politically driven lawyers were able to find loopholes in the legislation and the prosecution was rather inept. Our policy was to take a chance with the law, though within certain limits. At the same time, the regime was constantly tightening up legislation and circumscribing our activities.

In parliament, Sam Kahn performed enormous feats to expose the injustices and cruelty of apartheid and publicise the struggles against it. His efforts received much press coverage, and he was undoubtedly the most outstanding personality of the Western Cape across all political lines. Being an MP he was also able to give support to the grievances articulated by the residents' associations in the African townships, which constituted another layer of struggle. These associations, later known as civics, were genuine grass-roots organisations, often led by ANC or party cadres, primarily concerned with daily issues affecting the people. They were meant to be largely non-political, but they were nevertheless mobilised in support of the election campaigns of progressive African representatives like Sam Kahn for parliament and the Cape Provincial Council which were generally led by Greenwood.

Greenwood was also very close to Johnson Ngwevela, ANC and party leader in the Langa location, the largest in the Cape at that time, and the base for all sectors of the movement. With its orderly rows of small brick houses inhabited by long-standing African residents who qualified to remain in the area by virtue of ten years' presence and having employment, this was the elite township of Cape Town. Dora Tamana, on the other hand, though also a 'qualified resident', lived in a shack among the sand dunes in Retreat. There she established a rock-solid base among the regular residents as well as among the flotsam of migrants who were to be found in all the informal settlements.

Greenwood was also extremely adept at handling the constant battles between African nationalists, liberals and the communists within the ANC. A recurring bone of contention was the support of the left for white African representatives in parliament or the Cape Provincial Council (only whites were allowed to do so by law). The nationalists would point to the national policy of the ANC on the boycott of institutions of separate development such as Bantu councils which were set up by the regime in the African reserves and were largely regarded as 'toy telephones'. But the left persisted in using the opportunities provided for African representatives, which provided a political platform for our policies. It was also an official channel for taking up people's grievances such as pass law problems and residence permits with state officials.

However, some ANC members continued to regard such work as collaborating with the system. The matter was brought to a head with the arrival of TE Tshunungwa, a senior figure in the ANC nationally. Although he seemed to be very cordial towards the left in Cape Town, he spent many evenings in clandestine meetings with the nationalist group in the ANC in the bachelor flats in Langa where he lambasted the left for its excessive influence in Cape Town.

PARTY AFFAIRS

In mid-1954 I was informed that I had been selected by the Party District Committee to attend a clandestine party conference. I joined a delegation consisting of Bunting, Carneson and Ngotyana, which drove to Johannesburg where we were taken to a factory on the outskirts of the city. It was a weekend, and the large shed made of corrugated iron was deserted, but tables had been set up for about 20 people and braziers lit to keep us warm.

It was a bleak environment, which only reinforced the feeling that this was a rather special occasion where top-level communists met in secret. Yusuf Dadoo, whom I knew only faintly, was in the chair, and sitting around the table were such well-known personalities as Moses Kotane, JB Marks, Michael Harmel, Rusty Bernstein, Ruth First and Joe Slovo, among others. Dadoo led off the discussion with a formal report on the international situation but the meeting soon came to life when Harmel, the undoubted analytical brain of the movement, took over. The debate ranged right across all aspects of the struggle and I was enthralled to be present. I also realised that Cape Town was a minor player on the national stage and that the contributions of our delegation were sometimes off course.

Moses Kotane was a dominant figure exhibiting decades of experience. He displayed great wisdom and a profound analytical power, challenging loose formulations, questioning here and there with a vigorous style. One of the main items was a draft party programme which we had previously discussed in our party units in Cape Town and which was subsequently seen as providing guidance to the movement as a whole, including the Freedom Charter.

The party had by now settled into the policies which were adopted when it was reconstituted in 1953. During the previous decade of legal activity there had been two contending policy strands. One, led by Kotane and Dadoo, sought to give priority to the struggle against colour oppression and for national liberation, while the other more conventional line was led by Andrews and other more traditionally oriented communists. At the last legal conference of the party, two political resolutions had been tabled reflecting these strands and both were passed.

The essence of the differences lay in a disagreement about the relationship between the National Democratic Revolution and the Socialist Revolution and how this affected the role of the ANC. The ANC had previously been seen as a bourgeois-type organisation within which communists could operate and even hold senior positions but whose ultimate role was in doubt. This was strengthened by the avowed anti-communism of some of its key figures like Nelson Mandela, Walter Sisulu and Oliver Tambo. By contrast the party was seen as the classical vehicle of anti-capitalism and as the leader of the working class. The international situation was also an important factor in that the South African Party closely identified with the Soviet Union while the ANC had no clear position.

However, the party's view on the ANC changed when the *Suppression of Communism Act* was passed because the ANC took part in vigorous protests against the banning of the party. Also, when the party disbanded, many members increased their participation in ANC affairs, with many rising to positions of considerable prominence and influence. Hence, when the party was reconstituted, it was well equipped to serve as a kind of think tank and ginger group operating within the mass movement. The party had the theoretical and organisational coherence which was lacking in the ANC, which was composed of many diverse political perspectives.

Having defined its role, the party leaders, especially Kotane, displayed an impressive virtuosity in straddling the different arms of the movement. Kotane worked with nationalists and anti-communists so subtly and sensitively that he became one of the most influential figures in the whole movement, highly respected even by non-communists like Luthuli and Tambo. Not all party leaders had the same skill, and for some it remained a kind of select group where they could discuss Marxist ideas and the experiences of the World Communist Movement in cozy isolation.

However, people like Kotane were able to introduce party policy into the ANC and win acceptance for its positions while at the same time conveying the moods and attitudes within the ANC to the party so that its positions could be modified accordingly. He was therefore a harmoniser between the party as vanguard and the ANC as leader of the mass movement so that perspectives converged and difficulties were ironed out.

At the same time, the party was highly successful in protecting its security and no one outside its ranks had the faintest inkling about its existence. This was to be a major bone of contention once the party emerged into the public domain because people like Helen Joseph felt betrayed at having been kept in ignorance all those years about a small group meeting and deciding policy outside of the committees in which she operated.

Secrecy was the norm within the party itself. Recruiting was done with extreme care, and members knew only those in their own cells. Even at higher levels there were cutouts so that few, if anyone, knew the entire membership. While members were obliged to attend cell meetings, their main job was to work effectively in the mass movement.

Despite the growing cohesion of the movement nationally, each of the main centres had special characteristics. Cape Town tended to be sectarian and work in the national movement was hampered by the insistence on class perspectives within that movement. Marxist study classes were the norm while *The Guardian* sustained a pro-Soviet posture with dogged determination. Bunting argued that it was his editorial duty to present such positions, which reflected the majority view in the mass movement, and no one challenged this openly.

Although the party worked skilfully and with much flexibility within the national movement, in its own structures and thought it was very orthodox in identifying totally and uncritically with Soviet positions. Even the Stalin revelations failed to change this although many were temporarily shaken in their idealisation of Stalin and his legacy. The publication in Britain's *Guardian* of Krushchev's famous denunciation of Stalin at the twentieth party congress was a watershed. At first there was total disbelief and rejection of *The Guardian's* version. It was said to be yet another smear by Western journalists who had for decades published false accusations about life in the Soviet Union. But then the Italian party leader, Palmiro Togliatti (Ercoli) launched an attack on Stalinism, and an official Soviet paper published extracts of speeches made at the same congress by various lesser Soviet leaders which echoed many of Krushchev's allegations. Confirmation came soon after and the party was thrown into confusion.

In my party group some members were obliged to acknowledge that the claims made in Brian Bunting's booklet, *Life is More Joyous*, an account of his experiences in the Soviet Union, were substantially unfounded. All of us had accepted uncritically the propaganda we had been fed about the Soviet Union, and most of us averred that never again would we take the Soviets at face value. Yet in exile, Brian took on a post as TASS correspondent in London and soon reverted to his blind allegiance and defence at all costs of Soviet policies and conditions on every occasion. His editorship of the *African Communist* over many decades was marked by an almost religious devoutness towards the Soviets. But Brian was by no means alone in reverting speedily to orthodoxy; the whole party followed suit in not wanting to see wrongdoing, and it took another 30 years and the total collapse of Eastern Europe before the same crisis of confidence was repeated.

Another crisis of belief was brought down on our heads when Soviet tanks crushed the Hungarian uprising. The issue was debated widely in the whole world movement and we could not escape the disillusionment and resignations it brought even within our ranks. A private meeting of party members and supporters was called to discuss the affair and Fred Carneson argued that Hungary had been the home of reaction for decades. It was only the Soviet forces that led to their overthrow and the installation of a progressive but weak administration. He admitted that many ordinary workers had participated in the rebellion but argued that the working class may also be wrong at certain historical junctures, and the party and its ally, the Soviet Union, was right to defend the government.

I must own up to my own blind acceptance of pro-Soviet positions, which I acquired in London and as a result of my experiences at the World Youth Festival, where the World Communist Movement seemed impregnable. We felt that we were part of a chain of power that was rapidly encircling capitalism and that must soon establish socialism as the world system. In this context skepticism about some of its pillars was difficult to sustain. In our Cape Town party cells where it was difficult to hold any open discussion due to our makeshift meetings and the absence of critical literature, it was nearly impossible to sustain any but a simplistic blind faith in the justice of our cause.

While the party and its supporters were preoccupied with these events, the ANC was more concerned with the internal situation. The Defiance Campaign had built a solid platform for further struggle, and it was urgent that means should be found to give it expression.

THE CONGRESS OF THE PEOPLE

A proposal to hold a Congress of the People (COP) was put to the joint executives of the ANC, SAIC, SACPO and SACOD, meeting together in Tongaat, Natal on 21 March 1954. Chief Luthuli presided. The four sponsoring organisations were represented equally for the first time, marking a new point of departure for the Congress Alliance. It was understood, however, that the ANC would play the leading role and this no doubt placated the more nationalist elements for whom this new structure posed some difficulty.

The meeting agreed to launch a campaign to collect 'demands' from the people throughout the country at the grass-roots level, which would then constitute the basis for a Freedom Charter to be adopted at the COP. The formal launch was made at the Cape Provincial Conference of the ANC on 8 May 1954 with the publication of a poetic statement, the 'Call to the Congress of the People', drafted by Rusty Bernstein.

Soon after, national and regional Action Councils were formed, and then local committees throughout the country. The campaign got going speedily, despite the banning of Chief Luthuli, who was confined to the Lower Tugela for two years, and the forced resignation of Walter Sisulu from the ANC, who was then replaced by Oliver Tambo as secretary-general. Other bannings followed.

Other campaigns were also set in motion. The Western Areas Removal Campaign in Johannesburg was one of the most vital of these. This centred on the people of Sophiatown who were threatened with forced removal from an area they clung to dearly. There was a high degree of mobilisation and tension rose to fever pitch, but all public meetings were banned in Johannesburg to silence public protest. The police organised some 4 000 armed personnel with hundreds of trucks so that resistance was impossible. The incident, however, left a bitter memory.

The trade union movement was another site of intense struggle. White and black workers were being increasingly polarised, leading to the dissolution of the left-of-centre Trades and Labour Council and the formation of the rightist SA Trade Union Council. The left was weakened by the banning of leading personalities under the *Suppression of Communism Act* and the *Industrial Conciliation Act*. This excluded Africans from direct affiliation to registered trade unions, forcing the establishment of parallel unions in the same industry. In response 19 oppositionist unions formed a new co-ordinating body in 1955 called the SA Congress of Trade Unions which soon joined the Congress Alliance as a fifth partner.

Evaton in the Transvaal was the site for a mass boycott of buses to protest against increased fares, a frequent issue in the Transvaal. The police organised criminal gangs to attack boycotters in what amounted to a precursor of future tactics. The schools also became centres of protest and in December 1954 the ANC's national conference called an indefinite boycott of schools in protest against the introduction of Verwoerd's Bantu Education system. This measure imposed inferior education on blacks as well as the mandatory introduction of Afrikaans as a subject even though the great majority of Africans had no previous exposure to Afrikaans, which was in any case seen as the language of the oppressor.

Meanwhile, campaigning had started for the COP. In the Cape efforts were made to bring in a wide range of coloured personalities and a meeting was convened of a large number of organisations under the chairmanship of Dr Dick van der Ross, a leading coloured intellectual. Working together proved difficult since the Congress Alliance held rather different views on how to conduct a mass campaign. The moderates departed, and those remaining formed a local Action Council with Greenwood Ngotyana as the principal organiser and myself as number two.

We speedily became an effective team and developed a close mutual affection. Our task was to involve the vast network of organisations and groups throughout the Western Cape. We held hundreds of meetings, many in remote corners of the region, often relying on the rurally based Food and Canning Workers Union for assistance. We visited Ceres, Wolsley, Mossel Bay and Gansbaai, stopping off at little hamlets and villages where the union had African and coloured members who worked seasonally in canning factories, rather like the workers in John Steinbeck's *Grapes of Wrath*.

We were followed everywhere by the Special Branch and managed to shake them off on only a few occasions. They relentlessly followed us in pairs, sat in on our meetings, took notes of speeches and hovered in the background everywhere. We never became accustomed to their presence, but they did not deflect us from the tasks of the Congress of the People. Once the 'Call to the People' was issued in the form of a leaflet, we saturated the Western Cape with copies. We then went back to all the villages, held meetings and asked the people to offer their demands for inserting into the draft Freedom Charter.

Greenwood and I, sometimes accompanied by others, went out for three or four days at a time in the countryside, meeting people at the grass-roots level everywhere. It was possibly the most democratic and grass-roots-orientated campaign ever mounted in the region. One incident stands out as representative of the campaign. Two of us drove out to a coloured village deep in the countryside in Kraaifontein where somebody remembered a group of coloured farm labourers who had once been active in the Communist Party. We arrived at a cluster of shacks hidden in a group of trees, way out from the main roads. We sought out an old man known to my companion and told him that we would like to speak to the people about the Congress of the People.

A meeting was soon brought together which we addressed. At the end of our speeches, an old man spoke out with deep emotion and indignation. He produced a tin box which had been buried in the ground and which contained some membership cards of the old Communist Party. He said that the worst experience of his life had occurred in 1950 when a representative of the party had come to the village to tell them that the party had been dissolved in the face of government legislation. Since then, the village had been totally out of contact. He demanded an explanation for the dissolution of the party.

We replied that we were not representing the party, but the Congress Alliance and that we had come to hear their demands to be inscribed into the Freedom Charter. They then talked for several hours about their terrible conditions, the floods they were subjected to in winter, the sandy wastes, the absence of roads, the broken-down huts and the struggle to get seasonal jobs in the surrounding farms and distant factories. Their living conditions were atrocious. Malnutrition was clearly visible and water provision was poor since they had to draw water from a polluted well. In addition, they were harassed by the local authority.

We visited many such villages in the depths of the Western Cape countryside. Our team of speakers was often multi-racial – African, coloured and white – since we were trying to present an image of a new unity against apartheid. George Peake was a frequent participant in these trips and later became president of the SACPO. During these trips, we visited several vineyards where we met coloured farm labourers who were living in shacks and who were victims of the 'tot' system. They were paid a very small salary and fed as much as 12 tots of wine a day in lieu of wages. As a result, drunkenness was widespread and they suffered sclerosis of the liver and malnutrition. For me, who had been brought up in the comfortable white suburbs of the Cape, it was an eye-opener.

One trip ended in disaster and was a turning point in my ever-greater involvement in the struggle. The Western Cape Action Council received an invitation early in 1955 to a meeting in George, a modest town roughly equidistant from Cape Town, Port Elizabeth and Queenstown – the three action centres for the Cape Province. The invitation letter was signed by TE Tshunungwa, national organiser for the National Action Council in Johannesburg, and was the first intimation that a national structure was being created around the campaign. We were advised to send a delegation of our own to meet with two others from the other centres to discuss the campaign and create a Cape Provincial Action Council. We were aware of certain conflicts between Johannesburg and Queenstown, which represented a narrower stream of African nationalism. We also suspected that the attempt to create a new leading committee for the Cape Province, which covered a very large geographic area, had more to do with efforts to curb the left than with advancing the campaign. Tshunungwa was well known as a nationalist militant somewhat at odds with the left-leaning leadership of the powerful movement centred in Port Elizabeth. But we could not refuse to go, so we set out on the long drive to George in my car.

A telegram from Tshunungwa asked that we should meet up under a large tree at the junction to a turnoff from the main road just outside the town leading to the African township. We were to arrive exactly at 7 p.m. on Friday evening. We arrived as instructed, rather keyed up, and were heading out of town when I noticed a car parked in a side street switch on its headlights and fall in behind us at a distance. I had developed a special sensitivity to being followed. I could sense a police car instinctively and immediately knew that this was trouble. Many years later, when I arrived in Nairobi as an exile, it was many months before I could force myself to stop looking in my rearview mirror, ever expecting to see the Special Branch on my tail.

I was cruising at about 60 miles per hour and told my companions of my suspicions. We debated anxiously whether to try to turn off the main road as one of them knew a farmhouse where there was a friend. But before we could take a decision the car following put on great speed, overtook us and then spun in front of the car forcing me to screech to a halt. Three burly men burst out of the car, surrounded us and opened our doors. 'Come on, Turok, out, and remember I'm armed,' said the one at my door, holding his hand to his armpit.

It was the first time that the police had threatened me with a gun and the first time they behaved in so menacing a manner. Being far from Cape Town, in a dark road outside a small Afrikaans town, on work that though not strictly illegal, was nevertheless covert, left me with a hole in the pit of my stomach. The other policemen dragged my passengers out of the car and were forcing them into another car that had pulled up. A policeman got into the back seat of my car and told me to drive to the police station.

I was taken into the 'European' entrance and saw some 20 Africans huddled in the African section of the charge office – obviously the other delegations from Queenstown and Port Elizabeth. It was a complete sweep of the whole conference. It was only later that I discovered that we had chosen the weekend when the Cape Nationalist Party was holding its annual conference in George, which was to be attended by the prime minister and therefore came under close police security. They had intercepted Tshunungwa's telegram and were lying in wait for us. After some hours I was informed that I would be charged under the *Road Transportation Act* with carrying passengers for reward which was illegal. Bail was refused. At 1.00 a.m. I was finally allowed to phone Hymie Bernadt, an attorney close to the movement, who gave me the name and number of a local attorney in George and who I woke up. He promised to see me in the morning and I was then led to the lockup.

The cell was occupied by a man lying on a mat, covered by two blankets. An empty mat awaited me and I lay down, trying to shield my eyes from the penetrating glare from the bulb in the ceiling. There was no prospect of sleep. Even when I grew drowsy, I was woken with a start by the lifting of the peephole cover every hour or so. It was also fiercely cold. Finally, I dragged the second blanket off the body of the stinking drunk next to me, curled up and got some sleep.

In the morning the attorney arrived, shocked that a 'gentleman' like me should have had to spend a night in a cell, angry that they had deprived me of bail and at the petty charge under which I was being held. It was beyond his experience for an 'educated white person' to be treated in this way. He arranged for me to be released on £25 bail and took me off to a nearby hotel where, paradoxically, I was able to observe at close quarters the delegates to the conference that was responsible for my arrest. There were many well-built suited farmers, but it was the flashy young lawyer types buzzing around the hotel who were obviously the most active group.

I could not get the attorney to show the same solicitousness towards my African comrades as he had shown to me. The police stubbornly refused them bail. So, while I stayed in the hotel for two days they held their meeting in jail, making all the necessary decisions to move the campaign forward. We were finally united in court, where two drivers were acquitted for lack of evidence while one was fined because one of his passengers had inadvertently admitted that he had paid for two gallons of petrol.

But our reunion was tremendous. I was overwhelmed by their concern for me. It was the first time some of them had encountered a white man who had suffered prison for the cause, and I was very proud when they informed me that Tshunungwa had nominated me for vice chairman of the Cape Provincial Action Council which had been duly constituted in jail. I was, however, never able to take up office since the council was never able to meet. But it was a fine gesture. Tshunungwa subsequently came to Cape Town to assist us in our campaign and we got along very well despite his anti-white reputation. He would refer to me as the 'lion of the south' which was a takeoff of Prime Minister Strijdom who was known as the 'Lion of the North'.

THE FREEDOM CHARTER

Our campaign to collect demands for insertion in the Freedom Charter met with solid support throughout the Cape. The demands were usually written down on bits of paper and then sent to the National Action Council in Johannesburg. Some of the demands were sent in by ANC branches, particularly where these were well organised, as at Worcester. The demands were simple and direct, reflecting points made by grass-roots people.

A set of demands was also prepared by SACPO and other organisations, such as trade unions, so the demands came to reflect the organised sections of the movement as well as the grass roots.

In the Cape Town Action Council, in addition to the Congress representatives, trade unionists and the Liberal Party were also represented in the early stages of the campaign. The Liberal Party representatives, Gibson and Hjul resisted the calls for 'one person one vote', but they were in a minority and in due course left the campaign.

In due course, I was invited by the National Action Council in Johannesburg to be one of the ten keynote speakers at the Congress of the People to be held on 25/26 June 1955. We set about organising lorries and buses for the various delegates from the Western Cape and all roads seemed to lead to Johannesburg. There were three keynote speakers selected from the Western Cape, including George Peake, who was to chair one of the sessions, and Sonia Bunting, chosen to speak about the clause on Peace. Fortunately, the four of us drove up to Johannesburg in a car. Other groups of delegates who travelled in lorries and buses were less fortunate as they were stopped by the police en route. This kind of harassment was repeated across the country and many delegations never made it to the conference.

PRE-CONFERENCE MEETING

When we arrived in Johannesburg, we were each allocated to accommodation with a comrade, in my case Michael Harmel, a senior leader of the Communist Party. I had prepared my speech on the Economic Clause (Clause 4) based on the idea that the wealth of the country should be largely controlled by the people as a whole. This was in line with discussions in the party and Congress meetings in the Cape. It also reflected my own theoretical views, the insight I had gained in my trade union work and my contacts with the migrant workers in the fruit industry and vineyards. It was clear to me that the economy was in the hands of a privileged white class of owners.

On the Friday evening prior to the congress we were taken to a meeting where a draft Freedom Charter was placed before us. The charter had been drawn up by a group of banned leaders within the National Action Council on the basis of the demands which had been submitted throughout the country, but they were unable to be present to provide guidance. On examining the clause on which I had to speak, I felt that it would not adequately reflect my own understanding of what the congress was supposed to achieve in the demands put before us in the campaign. I therefore drafted an amendment, stressing that the commanding heights of the economy should be in public ownership. My amendment was seconded by Billy Nair, a trade unionist from Durban, and was accepted by the meeting.

When I returned to Michael Harmel's house and reported this change, he was taken aback. The draft had clearly been carefully crafted by the most senior leaders of the movement, but I defended my change as being in line with the National Democratic Revolution of the Congress Movement. Harmel accepted that the alteration was within the general spirit of the charter.

Reflecting on this affair, it was brought home to me that the Cape was perhaps pursuing a rather narrower political line than that of the national leadership in Johannesburg. Indeed, I came to appreciate that we did not, in Cape Town, have the kind of African Nationalist personalities found in Johannesburg and, indeed, in other major centres in the country. Cape Town had a more leftist perspective, partly because of the important role of communists and partly because *The Guardian* paper held an important position within the movement. Brian Bunting, the editor, still unflinching in the defence of international communist positions, at the same time gave full coverage to the struggles of the Congress Movement as a whole.

All this meant that Cape Town was rather to the left of the Congress Movement nationally. My own intervention, therefore, on the Freedom Charter, and my speech to the Congress of the People, reflected this. A copy of the speech does not exist, but a policeman's record introduced in the subsequent Treason Trial reports that I had condemned the mines as the basis for cheap labour in South Africa, robbing the people of the country's wealth. I pointed out that gold mining was a monopolistic industry, and that the large manufacturing industries were based on low wages and owned by an oppressive class of bosses. I called for the ownership of the mines to be transferred to the ownership of the people and for committees of workers to run these industries. I also called for the banks to be run by the people. My speech was followed by Billy Nair, who had seconded my amendment the previous evening and who went on to attack capitalism's exploitation of the people and argued that the industries, land, big business and the mines should be owned by all the people in the country. Our speeches were met with enthusiasm and we felt that we had struck the correct note.

The congress was one of the most remarkable events in the history of the movement. It was attended by 3 700 delegates, including 320 Indians, 230 coloureds and 112 whites and there were about 10 000 observers and bystanders outside the fenced enclosure. The conference was held on an open field where a platform had been erected and where planks had been placed on bricks in an amphitheatre for seating the delegates. Many other participants had been held up by police roadblocks that had been mounted on all major trunk routes. But those present were certainly representative of the people as a whole, including the different racial groups in South Africa. Rough and ready as the arrangements were, the atmosphere was that of a celebration rather than a conference. There was much jubilation, greetings between friends and spontaneous bursts into popular Congress songs. We all knew that history was being made that weekend and it was a privilege to be there.

There was a large police presence in vans, on horseback and on foot outside the enclosure. There was also a large contingent of the Special Branch who were writing down all the speeches conveyed to the gathering on the loudspeaker system. We were not intimidated, being accustomed to this practice, but we were aware of the presence of an unusually large contingent of police.

On Sunday afternoon at about 3.00 p.m., a posse of police armed with Sten guns entered the enclosure and marched threateningly to the platform. The atmosphere was suddenly electric. First, a hush descended on the gathering as the speeches stopped and the crowd became sullen. Then, the whole meeting rose to its feet and anything might have sparked off a very serious situation. But the crowd burst into the song *Unzima Lomtwalo* ('The Burden Is Heavy') and thereby saved the day. The anger of the audience had been overwhelming and the police could quite easily have been swamped by the crowd, in which case there would have been a massacre.

The police mounted the platform and demanded that the meeting be closed, but the chairperson had the presence of mind to ask that the meeting be allowed to vote on the adoption of the Freedom Charter which was affirmed unanimously.

The meeting was then closed and all participants were instructed to queue at the exits of the enclosure so that they could be searched and names and addresses taken by the police. It was late in the evening before all this could be completed, ending one of the most important events in the history of the country.

CHAPTER THREE

ON TRIAL FOR TREASON

I return to the previous chapters' account of my background and how I got involved in the movement and how very different backgrounds could lead to comradeship in the same movement. I return, too, to these encounters which sometimes revealed some puzzlement and even disbelief from African comrades that someone like me should have become so committed to the struggle. Trying now to set out the reasons why the struggle has been the dominant force in my existence almost all my life may help my own understanding of it all.

While a student my extramural reading led me to Marxism and I became aware that all over the world, people of my class had joined the struggle for socialism and communism. And that although Marxism was a theory about the liberation of the working class and oppressed people, middle-class intellectuals had played a seminal part in both developing the theory but also in practical work. Lenin came from a middle-class family, as did Mao Tse-Tung, Che Guevara and Castro.

So it was clear to me that race and class origin were by no means barriers to a commitment to socialism. Furthermore, these names may now be of only historical interest, but for us they were the height of political inspiration, even romance. We hero-worshipped these people and placed them on the highest of pedestals. If this point seems overemphasised, it is not in order to claim any special virtue for having joined the movement, but to argue that ideology is a very important factor in commitment. Of course, in identifying with these people I was also becoming an internationalist, a process reinforced by my association with the Communist Party. Being a part of the international communist movement coincided with my youth – we were so certain of the victory of the world revolution!

But I was also driven to get involved in the movement by the growth of fascism in the country. Given my exposure to Europe during my period abroad and what I had learned about fascism there, I was sensitive to the parallels at home. What made it all the more acute was the blatant identification of leading elements of the Nationalist Party with Hitler Germany and Nazism. Coupled with that were the deterioration of race relations and the increase in racial domination. I had a nauseated feeling that we were on a slippery slope to a crude, racially divided society and that one had to do something to stop it.

There was a kind of inevitability in the process. I doubt whether there was any single event or separate decision which led to my being absorbed in the movement, but subconsciously I knew that I must either deliberately and abruptly break off my involvement or go along with the tide. And it was becoming increasingly difficult to break off openly without earning the censure of my comrades.

The more I got involved, the more I was impressed by the maturity and wisdom of the leadership of the movement and in particular of the ANC. I came to appreciate this during my work for the Congress of the People and it was strongly reinforced during the Treason Trial, described later in this chapter. I saw that the leaders were cautious but determined. Also, they were not a small clique of self-serving politicians, but genuine national leaders of a broad national movement, which by now had a mass character, and I wanted to be part of this historically important experience.

Finally, I suppose that my own character was also responsible. A spirited young rebel and increasingly an enthusiast for what I believed in, I put an enormous amount of energy into my work and gained much in return. I acquired new skills and grew in insight even as I went about addressing meetings, sitting in committee and arguing about policy. I am afraid that these characteristics have remained with me ever since and it is not seldom that people have commented on my 'energy' and on my being 'an enthusiast'. Coupled with a degree of individualism, these qualities have sometimes landed me in hot water, as we shall see.

Looking back, there can be no doubt that the Congress of the People in June 1955 was a turning point for the country, and it was decisive for me as well. The COP was a very high-profile event, much publicised everywhere, with the press giving it front-page treatment and, for the first time, I was given considerable public exposure. The behaviour of the police at the COP had been startling. Everyone in that huge crowd must have felt an icy fear as the posse of police stood there facing the crowd with their Sten guns. It was the kind of confrontation that has led to a massacre in other places and other countries. We avoided that by a hair's breadth and when all of the spectators were searched and had our names taken at the end of it, I knew that I was now a marked man. But, most important of all, I felt for the first time that I had joined a mass struggle that I had not previously had the feel of. Here was the real thing – the physical presence of the masses and the armed police ready to fire. It was exhilarating, frightening and full of drama.

Of course I had read about many of the earlier mass actions of the movement such as the miners' strike of 1946 and the police attacks on workers. Indeed, all the leaders could tell about their experiences with the brutal state machine, which were also part of our regular reading in *The Guardian* and in the various books which were part of our political education. But my personal experiences were rather limited to individual police harassment and here was something quite new, more akin to the behaviour of Nazi storm troopers.

On my return to Cape Town from the COP, I went back to my trade union work with a deeper sense of purpose, being now able to fit it all into the national pattern of resistance. My experience with the Boston Bag Workers Union was salutary. Boston Bag was a factory employing some 110 coloured women, mostly under 21, who were machinists sewing cloth into various kinds of bags for flour and similar commodities. A group of them came to our office to ask for assistance in a dispute with their employer over wages and work conditions. After consulting Ray Alexander on tactics, I went out to the factory and met with some of the leaders on a sand dune near the premises.

They told us of harsh conditions imposed by aggressive overseers and very low pay by a management operating a system that ensured that there should be a continuous turnover of staff in order to keep wages low. No sooner had a worker reached a higher level of seniority than she would be sacked. Most of the girls had only recently left school and were paid a pittance. I attempted to negotiate with the employers, but they refused to speak to me or to recognise the union and the only course was to petition the Labour Department for a conciliation board under the *Industrial Conciliation Act*. We collected the signatures of the workers required for this petition, but before the process could develop, some incident in the factory sparked off a strike and most of the workers walked out.

There were demonstrations in the street outside the factory and picketing in the face of the usual harassment by the police. Here too, the Special Branch was in evidence at all times and intensified their surveillance of our office. For the first time, I appreciated just how central and difficult is the role of a trade union official. The workers' jobs were in my hands and the tension was considerable. But the strike ended with an agreement between management and the union; we even won stop-order facilities and recognition rights.

A similar strike followed at Lystra Zip Factory, though it began differently. The employers phoned the office saying they could no longer control the very young (16 to 20-year-old) Malay girls they employed and anarchy prevailed on the shop floor. I visited the factory, met with the workers and found that they were, justifiably, totally contemptuous of the owners and managers who were clearly not competent to run a factory. The employer was a genial man who wanted a quiet life along with good profits and the two were incompatible. We immediately went into a series of meetings where the workers proposed a restructuring of the work process to avoid the bottlenecks in production. The young Malay girls also insisted on their right to go to the toilet and to have breaks as workers in other factories did. The management was obdurate and suddenly became nasty. A strike ensued but this too was settled and an agreement and recognition followed.

Another strike two months later was much more difficult. A timber factory in Retreat manufacturing fruit boxes came to our notice through the ANC in the area. Conditions in the factory were appalling, pay was very low and the African workers, who were in a majority, found the situation unacceptable. Archie Sibeko and I met with the workers, set up a new Timber Workers Union which was structured on parallel lines, with Sibeko being responsible for the unregistered African Union while I was responsible for the coloured workers who were allowed to register with their union. We enrolled most of the workers into the union, they paid two shillings a month subs, and several meetings were called. We decided to again petition for a conciliation board and obtained the signatures of the coloured workers for this purpose. This aroused considerable resentment among the African workers who felt that the union was bypassing them only to satisfy some spurious law which they knew nothing about. They also objected to having two unions and could not follow the explanations we gave them.

However, we soon had enough signatures to petition for a conciliation board, which actually met at the Labour Department offices. Sibeko was strongly opposed to any discrimination in negotiations and insisted on attending the board as an observer even though, as an African, he was excluded by law.

No agreement could be reached and we called the workers out on strike. On the morning of the strike, a large posse of police was outside the factory and arrested several dozen workers whose mood was high, and we prepared to defend them in the courts. Bail was granted and we worked out a defence with Attorney Sam Kahn that succeeded on a technicality.

By now the workers were thoroughly aroused, keen to use their newfound strength. To our dismay they declared that they were no longer interested in the few shillings increase we had proposed, but wanted retribution, some of them proposing that they burn down the factory. We naturally opposed this and explained the necessity for a long struggle in which workers' power would steadily grow to a wider confrontation with the capitalist class as a whole, but it took some doing. I felt that the lesson was that in South Africa, where class oppression is so severe, black and workers' power might be exercised in a revolutionary rather than a reformist way and that this might affect the approach of the whole movement.

Absorbed as I became in these union struggles, I also had

responsibilities in the wider political field. The Congress organisations had worked well together during the COP and there was an understanding that new institutional arrangements were needed to cement our unity. The National Action Council of the COP was replaced by the National Consultative Committee with representation from each of the five Congress organisations and this became the Congress Alliance in August 1955.

The movement seemed to be at a loss on how to capitalise on the COP and proposed a 'One Million Signature Campaign' which came as an anti-climax. Perhaps the proposal was only intended as a holding operation while we sorted out the hesitations within the ANC about the adoption of the Freedom Charter. Although the Charter had been adopted at the COP, Chief Luthuli and Professor ZK Matthews argued that it was not binding on the ANC, which had to consider it separately, and a national conference was called. Some leaders of the ANC were clearly anxious to retain the independent existence of the ANC within the Alliance. They argued that only the ANC itself could issue directives to ANC branches and that this requirement could not be ignored by the new Alliance structures. They also expressed reservations about the lectures which were used throughout the country as part of the COP campaign on the grounds that they had a Marxist orientation.

In the debates about broad policy for the ANC and the Alliance Chief Luthuli argued against a narrow conception of nationalism and urged 'an all-inclusive African Nationalism embracing all people ... regardless of their racial and geographical origin who resided in Africa and paid their undivided loyalty and allegiance to Africa'. This was in line with the approach taken in the Freedom Charter, namely that South Africa belongs to all who live in it, black and white. But there were some important reservations about the economic clause and questions were posed as to whether the clause might bring our opponents to label the charter 'socialist', indicating undue influence by communists. My amendments to the effect that the commanding heights of the economy 'should be transferred to the ownership of the people as a whole' became a hot issue which was canvassed in the movement's journals such as *Fighting Talk* and *Liberation* with Michael Harmel arguing that the charter was not a socialist document.

In the end, Luthuli and others were convinced about the acceptability of the language in the charter and it was adopted by the ANC at a special Orlando meeting on the Easter weekend of 31 March 1956. The final version of the economic section read: 'THE PEOPLE SHALL SHARE IN THE COUNTRY'S WEALTH. The national wealth of our country, the heritage of all South Africans, shall be restored to the people. The mineral wealth beneath the soil, the banks and monopoly industry shall be transferred to the ownership of the people as a whole. All other industries and trades shall be controlled to assist the wellbeing of the people. All people shall have equal rights to trade where they choose, to manufacture and to enter all trades, crafts and professions.'

On 30 April 1956 the Minister of Justice warned of forthcoming arrests for high treason and on 5 December the harsh reality was brought home to me when two members of the Special Branch knocked on our front door at 3.00 in the morning and produced a warrant for my arrest on a charge of high treason. I think I had been too preoccupied with the day-to-day activities to have actually absorbed official warnings and the warrant pushed under my nose was a total surprise. I laughed at the police and felt rather light-hearted about the whole affair. But they were serious enough and searched the house meticulously, discovering a pile of papers hidden among clothing in a wardrobe including, to my chagrin, a translation of the Freedom Charter by the famous Afrikaans poet, Uys Krige, in his own handwriting. This was a serious lapse on my part which returned to haunt me when the document was presented in court, since Krige had never identified himself with the ANC or any leftist tendencies.

After the search, I telephoned Sam Kahn seeking legal advice. He was jocular about it all and told me that I would soon meet quite a number of friends at the central police station. Indeed, when I arrived there I found some ten comrades of all races gathered in the charge office, somewhat nonplussed, but in high spirits. We were then placed in police vans and driven to a military airport where we were put on a small military plane and flown to Pretoria. The immensity of the situation then dawned upon us. Several people were ill on the plane, perhaps from tension, but also from the buffeting we all got in the hard, cushionless seats.

Arriving at a military airport in Pretoria, we were transported to Johannesburg in wire-meshed vans and then, passing through Hillbrow, we saw newspaper posters proclaiming in large letters 'National Treason Arrests' and we realised the scale of what was happening. On arrival at the Fort Prison, whites were separated from blacks and we found ourselves in the company of Rusty Bernstein, Joe Slovo and other comrades from all over South Africa. We learned that Chief Luthuli, Nelson Mandela, Walter Sisulu and dozens of other leaders from across the country were being held in the black sections of the Fort.

In the dismal confines of the prison, we were placed three in a cell, sleeping on mats on the concrete floor. We were allowed to sit in a small exercise yard, and soon dozens of newspapers and large quantities of food flooded in. The world outside had exploded in spontaneous support of those arrested and for the next two weeks we were short of nothing except freedom. The story of the Treason Trial has been told many times and at some length, so there is no need for me to go over familiar ground. However, the effect of the trial on my political development and personal future was enormous. Locked up with the most prominent personalities of the movement, sitting through the proceedings in the drill hall during the preparatory examination, being bombarded day after day with evidence and speeches we had all made over the years and receiving press publicity as never before – all this gave one a sense that history was being made on a grand scale.

Bishop Ambrose Reeves organised a defence committee and bail for all the accused was soon fixed on the basis of sureties by some very prominent public figures. I was invited to stay with Rusty and Hilda Bernstein throughout the proceedings. We travelled to court in a chartered bus and were looked after handsomely by the support committees that sprang up. The Bernsteins were kindness itself throughout my stay, which was often lonely, especially as the court proceedings were exhausting.

Some of the evidence caused alarm. The speech by Robert Resha threatened violence, and we knew that the state meant business. We were a total of 156 accused, of whom 104 were Africans, some 20 white, 20 Indian and eight coloured. All tendencies of the

Congress were represented and the ideological foundations of the movement were to be challenged in the proceedings.

The legal battle was very dramatic. We had some of the top lawyers in the country defending us and the most effective and aggressive cross-examiner in the country, Vernon Berrange, decimated police witnesses in rapid succession. The magistrate remained relatively calm, though there were many stormy scenes, including a trial-within-the-trial for contempt of court. The preliminary examination, which had begun on 2 January 1957, continued for some nine months with our having to attend court almost daily. At the end of it, a prima facie case was found to exist and we were committed for trial in the Supreme Court.

On 17 December 1957, charges were dropped against 65 of the accused, including Chief Luthuli and Oliver Tambo, but I found myself among the 90 referred to the Supreme Court.

CAPE PROVINCIAL COUNCIL

During this period, the representative of the Africans for the Western Cape in the Cape Provincial Council died. I was asked to stand and agreed to do so, not knowing what awaited me. Two other candidates, including Gibson of the Liberal Party, first put their names forward too, but withdrew on the grounds that they did not wish to oppose someone facing a charge of treason. I was then elected unopposed and became the Western Cape representative for Africans on the Cape Provincial Council.

It was difficult at first to take the Provincial Council seriously, given my preoccupation with the Treason Trial. In the context of the trial, the council seemed to be irrelevant and a farce. The council meetings were held in a rather august building that served as the headquarters of the Provincial Administration, which was responsible for such matters as education, health, roads and, to some extent, African townships in the whole of the Cape Province. The council met for a total of only three or four weeks a year, usually in two or three sessions, so it was very much a 'rubber stamp' body pretending to be a parliament. Nevertheless, one was expected to behave like a parliamentarian and make appropriate speeches using the jargon of parliamentary procedure and assisting constituents in the same way.

Being an MPC gave me access to all official departments and personnel. Most importantly, I could now intervene with the managers of the African townships in the Western Cape in cases of deportation, permits, workers' rights, housing and so on. I took these up quite seriously, following the long trend set down by previous African representatives in parliament and the Provincial Council, and a great deal remained to be done. However, I was able to do my work only in bursts during the trial recesses.

The Western Cape did not have as large a permanent settlement of Africans as other areas. It was largely a migratory population with no rights and subject to constant harassment by the Native Affairs Department. Thus a constant stream of cases needed attention, many coming to me through the trade union officials who took advantage of my powers to take up individual cases. Archie Sibeko, who was then the secretary of the African Railway Workers Union, brought me numerous migrant railway workers who lived in hostels, thereby strengthening his union. I learned a great deal about the day-to-day life of a migrant worker and was reasonably successful in saving many individuals from deportation. I also had many confrontations with township officials and police and learned of their barbaric attitudes first hand. Government policy was to keep the number of Africans in the Western Cape to a minimum and, furthermore, to keep them moving so that no one gained the right of residence in the area through qualifying under the ten-year rule.

All this casework held some interest and gave satisfaction, but the chamber itself brought nothing but torture. Although reasonably experienced as a public speaker as a result of the Congress meetings, I had little gift for the debating style required in the chamber. Furthermore, I had an intense dislike of the formality required and, indeed, I refused to use the word 'honourable' in referring to members of the House. This was partly in line with the general posture of the movement in Cape Town. For instance, Bunting refused to have anything to do with Nationalist Party members in parliament and kept largely to himself. I think he paid a price for this in his own further isolation and it probably affected his performance as well, since operating within a system entails conforming to some extent.

In any event, my very first speeches entrenched my isolation. One speech focused on the Freedom Charter and called for the universal franchise in the Cape. The outcome was that my fellow African representative, Bunny Curran, a Liberal Party member from the Eastern Cape, dissociated himself from me and asked the Speaker to move him from the double bench we shared. He also made a statement to *Die Burger*, the leading Cape Nationalist newspaper, to the effect that he disagreed totally with my position and would henceforth have nothing to do with me. On one occasion, a Nationalist Party member came to my bench during a break and asked whether I was really serious in advocating 'votes for natives'. When I showed him that I was indeed serious, he said: 'My God, we are going to hang you.'

Each speech, therefore, involved considerable trauma. Congress had not yet developed policies on such matters as hospitals, education and roads and I had difficulty developing positions on my own. Another difficulty stemmed from the overwhelming hostility of the House, which significantly intensified an already trying experience. My job was not to persuade the House, but rather to reach the press, which had been permanently installed above the Speaker's chair, and so I directed my speeches to them. But it led to sleepless nights in anticipation and I am not sure that I succeeded very well. For one thing, being absorbed in the Treason Trial and remote from Cape Town, it was difficult to do the necessary research on the local issues dealt with in the council. Also, I had no time to familiarise myself with the complex parliamentary procedure. The United Party opposition, while not as hostile as the Nationalists, gave me no advice at all, nor did they inform me about their tactics. Consequently, as a particular debate unfolded, I was left in total ignorance about how amendments would emerge and when voting would take place. So, I resorted to finding the odd issue on which I could make a speech about the place of Africans in our society, hoping that the press would find my comments interesting. I had some satisfaction at the end of it all when I made my final speech in 1960, after five years of serving in the council, to find that *Die*

Burger wrote it up at length, saying that I was a man who would make a mark in the future.

My period in the Provincial Council was brought to an end when the government abolished the legislation providing for African representation in parliament and the council, so I was the last of the African representatives in that House.

My activities in the Provincial Council had one very unfortunate side effect. My brother, Hillel, had just established himself as an architect in Cape Town and, like all other architects, was seeking government work. With each provocative speech I made, his hopes of getting such commissions faded. When he lost two large contracts from the Cape Provincial Administration, our relationship deteriorated seriously. He and my parents tried to bring great pressure on me to tone down my speeches and my activities, but by then I was far too committed to take heed. Family relationships became very strained and, in any case, I found myself wholly out of sympathy with the concerns and lifestyle that my family adopted. My father and brothers were, by then, rather well off, lived in comfortable homes and were thoroughly white South Africans in their attitudes. By mid-1957 Mary and I found ourselves alienated from them and, since the Treason Trial was expected to go on for years, we decided to move to Johannesburg. We rented a small house in Bellevue East where she and the children joined me and a new life began.

LIFE IN JOHANNESBURG

A new phase began in the Treason Trial. With the preparatory hearing over, we were now summoned to the Supreme Court in Pretoria. Beginning in August 1958, all 91 of us had to attend the daily proceedings presided over by Justice Franz Rumpff and located in what had previously been a synagogue. This was a far more congenial environment than the drill hall and the atmosphere was much less strained, but we all had to make the daily one-hour trip each way by bus between Johannesburg and Pretoria, which was tiring on top of the long days in court. Our defence team was magnificent, consisting of Issy Maisels, the top Queen's Counsel in the country, Bram Fischer and many others.

The Crown had brought in Oswald Pirow, who had been a leading political figure of the right in earlier days, to head its team. The charges were serious and there were times when we thought that a conviction and hanging were real possibilities.

But the prosecution had overreached itself in framing the indictment. By charging us with treason, which necessarily involves an intention of violent overthrow of the state, they went too far. Furthermore, in bringing so many people together under one charge and seeking to marshal such a vast quantity of documents and speeches, they overreached in another regard, and consequently failed to bring the charges into a coherent pattern. Our defence team decimated the indictment on several occasions, which was then reframed and brought back to court. The prosecution was then forced to divide the 90 accused into three batches of 30, suspending the prosecution of the two second groups, where I was located, until the charges against the first batch were completed. I was, therefore, ultimately released from attending court and was able to get on with my new job. It was not until 19 January 1959 that the Treason Trial of the first group of 30, which included Helen Joseph, Kathy (Ahmed) Kathrada, Duma Nokwe, Nelson Mandela, and Walter Sisulu, finally began. The case proceeded on and off, with a long break during the 1960 state of emergency when the accused were detained until they were finally acquitted on 29 March 1961.

The crux of the case against us emerged slowly through all the legal argument. The issue was whether or not the ANC was pursuing a policy that was fundamentally violent. The essence of the crime of high treason, according to Oswald Pirow, was 'hostile intent'. But this intent was not easily proven for an organisation that had used non-violent methods. However, the prosecution argued that in the context of the South African system the demand for universal franchise and full equality as set out in the Freedom Charter would 'necessarily involve the overthrow of the state by violence'. They insisted that 'in any case, the accused must have known that the course of action pursued by them would inevitably result in a violent collision with the state resulting in its subversion'.

The argument then extended to assert that the movement was

part of an international communist-inspired effort working for the violent overthrow of governments throughout the non-communist world. The issue of communism was used, therefore, to give an international perspective to Congress and make more convincing the existence of a conspiracy. The state was then obliged to deal with ideological aspects of Congress policy, alleging that it was fundamentally communist. The accused were said to be 'inspired by communist fanaticism, Bantu nationalism and racial hatred in various degrees'. The evidence of the state on these matters often produced the light relief badly needed by the accused.

It was clear that this claim of involvement in an international conspiracy could not be made to stick. The expert evidence introduced by Professor Andrew Murray, for example (who had taught me philosophy and was a good Platonist but a hopeless Marxist), revealed the poverty of the theoretical underpinning of the state case. On our side we had some brilliant lawyers, of whom only Bram Fischer was a Marxist. Maisels was a liberal without a feeling for ideology, but this did not constrain his tenacious cross-examination of expert witnesses. With a rather dry style he produced a 'not guilty' verdict. The court ruled that the prosecution had not proved that the ANC was a communist movement or that the Freedom Charter envisaged a communist society. Nor had it been proved that the party members had infiltrated into the ranks of the ANC after the banning and become executive leaders. Instead, it had been shown that the ANC allowed both communist and non-communist to become members on condition that they sustained ANC policy. Several leaders of the ANC had been communists for a long time.

This finding was of immense importance for the ANC and remains an important consideration today. Despite serious allegations against men like Sisulu and Mandela about communist sympathy and, even in some cases, membership, it had not been possible to sustain the case that the ANC was a communist organisation. This was a powerful endorsement of party policy that insisted that communists should not try to turn the ANC into a communist organisation even if there were particular issues on which communists might press a particular stance. Essentially, it was vital that the role of the ANC in the struggle remained that of a national liberation movement able to unite the broadest section of the oppressed against white domination.

The trial had dragged on and on. The daily attendance in court was a form of torture. Despite generally high spirits and convivial relationships, fatigue sometimes proved overwhelming, but it had its positive side. First, 156 people of enormously diverse backgrounds were brought together to share the iron-mesh enclosure in the drill hall in the opening stages of the preparatory examination and then during the long days of the hearings. The battles of the lawyers with incompetent police witnesses and with the steely, cold magistrate brought us together in a political, but also social union. We became familiar with people whose names were known internationally and appreciated their personal qualities under stress. We learnt far more about each other under these conditions than would have occurred in years of normal contact – something I discovered in prison later on. And a particular kind of warmth emerges which enriches the human spirit and lasts for a long time. There is no equivalent in ordinary life.

Chief Luthuli, the leader of Congress and spokesman for the accused, made a profound impression on everyone. His gravitas and naturally royal bearing combined with a simplicity that was endearing. It was he who led the accused in their representations and negotiations with the defence team and he did so with a dignity that sustained morale enormously. At no stage did we feel ourselves to be criminals, no matter the conditions under which we were held, nor the indignities to which the court and the police tried to subject us. We may have been on trial legally, but we were by no means cowed or subordinate in court. Luthuli was not one for mingling overmuch with the other accused. At the same time he did not stand apart; there was simply a natural distance between he and the rest. But he was cordial with us and readily approachable. Next to him was Moses Kotane, the general secretary of the Communist Party and senior member of the executive of the ANC. Moses had been a truck driver as a young man and came to the party early on, attracted by its non-racial character and its class identity.

He was a man of the people and remained so all his life. He lived in Alexandra Township, was an avid patron of the local soccer club and was known to everyone in the streets. At the height of the dominance of criminal gangs in the township when the streets became very dangerous, especially at night, Moses still had the freedom to move and meet with whomever he wished.

During the trial, Moses enjoyed interacting with other accused. He could be fun. At the same time, one knew that there were distinct limits to familiarity with him. Beneath the jocularity he was a very sensitive person in his human relationships, and he could be rather changeable too. He could be joking and totally without reserve, but he could also be blunt and abrasive. At times, he seemed to be bullying and uncaring about how he handled people. If he offended you, he could nevertheless take your arm, lead you off for a stroll and regain your friendship and confidence. He had tremendous charm when he wanted to use it and deep insight into how others thought and felt.

It was during the tough moments of the trial when particular bits of evidence seemed to be overwhelming that Moses would be most solicitous of others. Most intriguing about Moses was his intellect. Although he'd had little formal education, he was enormously punctilious about the use of language, penetrating in his observations and a formidable opponent in debate. He did not bother to develop a 'personality'. He had a confidence rooted in considerable self-esteem that had grown as he jousted with many educated intellectuals. At times he seemed rather ponderous, particularly in taking decisions, but he was really canvassing all the options in his mind. When he finally settled on a course of action his arguments were clear, penetrating and compelling.

I have never seen Moses address a public meeting although I have been in many committee meetings with him. I am told his style was calm, factual and restrained. He preferred to rely on argument rather than charisma. Among the accused, Moses's opinion was, perhaps, the most weighty of all. Other accused told me that when the black prisoners were in the Fort in the first two weeks after the arrests, Luthuli talked most with Moses, and the two made up a leadership triumvirate with Professor Matthews. They were treated with great deference by other prisoners and were not expected to get in line with the others for food; it was brought to them. The accused also held lectures and seminars in which Moses took a leading part, exhibiting political insight and experience superior to anyone else's.

During the trial recesses a great deal of legal consultation took place. Lawyers from among the accused were drawn into the formulation of defence strategy, which often involved deciding how to tackle individual witnesses and also how to approach the magistrate himself. One of the accused most deeply involved was Oliver Tambo who was a practising solicitor in partnership with Nelson Mandela. He was a rather reserved and remote man who rarely mingled with the accused in an informal way. His modesty may have been due to his humble origins as the son of a peasant farmer, but there was something more – he was uncomfortable with intimacy and was reserved without being haughty. He had a reputation for being very clever and his academic record was indeed outstanding. I thought him aloof at times and he was one of the accused to whom I never became close. This was partly because he was very busy maintaining the law firm and dashed off to the office as soon as the court was adjourned. But he was highly respected and certainly accepted as one of the key leaders among the accused.

The contrast with Nelson Mandela was considerable. Nelson was a tall, strapping man of fine physique, light on his toes and quick to smile. It was strange how he combined a wonderfully natural charisma, which was not forced in any way nor 'put on', with a youthful, easy-going 'hail fellow, well met' style which was unbelievably charming. Nelson was one of the boys. Approachable, kind, considerate and, above all, a popular leader. When I came to work with him later on at committee level, I came to appreciate his toughness and self-discipline that helped to explain his extraordinary survival in prison.

During the preparatory examination, Joe Slovo not only stood accused but also acted as one of the defence team at the lawyers' bench, a duality that the magistrate found hard to accept. He was a young advocate, relatively junior at the bar, but because of his deep knowledge of the movement, an important member of the defence team. Joe had some moments in the case when he was at the forefront of the tense battle in the courtroom. On one occasion a shouting match ensued between Joe and the magistrate over a point of procedure. The magistrate sought to cite him for contempt of court. In the ensuing trial-within-a-trial, Joe showed his legal ability and his inner strength, refusing to bend a knee in the face of what looked like a stern judgement. But the legal team defended Joe and the matter fell away.

Joe was always well informed about how the case was proceeding and both knowledgeable and insightful about how the defence would argue its case. He was very accessible and ready to pass on these insights to the accused. This was a great help in overcoming nerves since we felt involved as participants instead of mere victims.

Since he was locked up with the whites accused in the Fort, I got to know Joe well during those two weeks. He could be full of fun and had a capacity to recall endless jokes picked up at the Bar. He had a little ditty that we all sang:

My baadjie, my baadjie, my baadjie,
My baadjie, my collar and my tiejie,
If you wanna go to heaven when you dietjie,
You must have a collar and a tiejie.
(My jacket, my collar and tie, etc.)

But as the trial proceeded and I made Johannesburg my home, I found that Joe enjoyed a certain elitist lifestyle that caused resentment among the lesser mortals in the movement. He and Ruth First moved in a select circle and were somewhat insensitive to the effect this had on their relationship with rank-and-file members. The dinner parties at their well-appointed home were rather exclusive and there came a time when Mary and I declined invitations to their parties. At the same time they were both deeply committed and were able to mix equally with any cadres anywhere. Joe was undoubtedly extremely able, but life at the Bar seemed to have a bad effect on him and diminished his political outlook. Consequently, I did not warm to him then and even less so later on in exile. Nor did I anticipate that he would become one of the most powerful figures in the movement in the 1980s.

Among the accused there were many diverse personalities and political leanings. What is one to say of Temba Mqota from Port Elizabeth who could, notwithstanding sharing with his non-

African comrades all the stresses of the trial, nevertheless, say to me over lunch in the church garden in Pretoria where all was friendliness and Christian grace, that he objected to my presence – a white man sitting with him in a joint trial of the Congress cause? I was shocked and said, 'You tell me this at a time when we are both facing the hangman's noose?' But he adamantly maintained that his 'position is irrevocable'. In exile, he later joined the Group of Eight, which was expelled from the ANC for pursuing a separatist Africanist policy disruptive to the Congress Movement.

Life was an extraordinary blend of the trivial and the dramatic. We travelled backwards and forwards from Johannesburg in a bus where Resha often emerged as a delightful personality. Resha was then 40 years old and an important personality in the ANC, being volunteer-in-chief in the Western Areas Campaign against the removal of the African community from what was then a mixed-race area.

The need to unwind at the end of a day in court was a challenge to everyone. Robert would lead the bus in song or crack jokes about going to visit domestic workers in the white areas and 'eating dog's meat' which was said to be perfectly edible. Resha had worked in the mines as a young man and became a freelance journalist later on. An attractive personality, friendly and warm in his personal relations, he was yet a profoundly committed African nationalist and a dangerous opponent of the regime. Resha had deep roots in the townships in Johannesburg and it was said that the *tsotsis* (young toughs) of Sophiatown were loyal to him and would follow his leadership at all times. I often met him in London in later years and never experienced the slightest personal antagonism or conflict although we know that he remained committed to a somewhat narrow African nationalism which did not, however, constrain his role as one of our top international workers.

As the trial proceeded, the accused were not excluded from other punitive actions. The secretary of the Congress of Democrats, Yetta Barenbladt, was among those who were banned under the *Suppression of Communism Act*. I was pleased to be asked to take over as national secretary since I was now firmly stuck in Johannesburg for the duration of the trial. I was soon introduced to the inner circles of the Congress leadership and entered upon the most fascinating period of my political life. My salary was a princely £20 a month, which was my total income since the £60 a month from the Provincial Council was handed to the COD.

Installed in an office of the COD in Fox Street, I soon obtained the services of Shanti Naidoo as my secretary. The national executive of the COD was chaired by Piet Beyleveld who had been a member of the Labour Party. Although he was a valuable person in the context of the movement at that time his name will be forever tarnished by his turning state witness in several trials in 1963. For Beyleveld cracked soon after his arrest and his evidence played some part in convicting some of the key personalities in the movement. Other members of the National Executive of the COD included Helen Joseph who played such a powerful part in so many campaigns and then became an outstanding symbol of defiance while under house arrest.

There was also a Johannesburg Regional Committee of the COD that was very active. The role of the COD was to influence whites in favour of the Congress Movement and to accept the Freedom Charter. It was a stony path and we encountered a great deal of hostility. Meanwhile the Liberal Party, which had at first adopted a qualified-franchise policy (amended later to universal franchise), had more appeal for whites who found the Congresses too radical. Paradoxically, the Liberal Party was able to use its non-racial membership as a draw card against the separation we practised in the Congresses, even though our commitment to the end of white rule was ultimately so much greater.

The COD also suffered for being branded early on as a communist front simply because many of its prominent members had been members of the Communist Party. This was an allegation that people like Helen Joseph refuted since she distanced herself from communist ideals and extolled straightforward democratic principles. She resisted ideological debates and was more concerned with action than theory. Small though it was, the COD was energetic and efficient. It became involved in many campaigns among white people throughout the country, but its most important contribution was clearly in the work of the Congress Movement as a whole and in the working committees that were established in all the regions.

CONGRESS SECRETARIAT

I was soon drafted to the secretariat of the Congress Alliance and became its administrative secretary in 1958. Its members were Walter Sisulu, Duma Nokwe, who was the general secretary of the ANC and secretary of the Joint Congress Executives, which constituted the formal head of the Alliance, Yusuf Dadoo from the South African Indian Congress, George Peake from the South African Coloured Peoples' Organisation and Leslie Masina from the South African Congress of Trade Unions. Piet Beyleveld represented the COD.

Other members who alternated on the committee were Yusuf Cachalia and Leon Levy. The secretariat soon became a major focus for my work. Beyleveld soon fell away due to the pressure of his commercial work and I came to represent the COD as well as serving as secretary. We were soon meeting frequently, sometimes on a daily basis. I came to know and love Walter, appreciating more and more his qualities of leadership, political acumen, deep insight and sensitivity to the public mood of the day. He sensed, better than anyone else did, how the masses felt on particular issues. He often carried us and set the pace. The achievements and style of the ANC and the Congress Movement owe a great deal to him.

Nokwe was a different kind of person. Highly intelligent, the first African advocate in South Africa, gifted with great theoretical capacity, he brought a particular kind of confidence to the ANC and our work. Yusuf Dadoo who flourished in mass meetings and conferences was, by then, a rather isolated person, badly affected by his banning from the SAIC and out of touch with the day-to-day work of the movement. The trade union representatives on the secretariat brought with them some of the narrowness of trade unionism and also a certain chip-on-the-shoulder about being the least favoured organisation of the Alliance. The Congress Alliance was very broad in its politics and people like Luthuli and others resisted, in a subtle sort of way, any attempts to introduce sectarian concepts into the movement and to focus on the working class in particular. They were determined to maintain the national dimension of the struggle in the forefront. The Communist Party

CERES TOGRYERS MUSEUM

Museums vir 'n beter lewe

Museums for a better life

History of Ceres

Stock farmers crossed the Witzenberg mountain range as early as 1727 to establish themselves in the Ceres Valley. The accessibility of the area was greatly improved during 1848 when Andrew Geddes Bain built the Michells Pass and Ceres Village was established on Saturday 21 July 1849.

The first erven were surveyed after the opening of the pass and the town Ceres, named after the Roman Goddess of Corn was officially given municipal status on 3 November 1864.

In the subsequent development in Ceres the focus was turned to the development in local agriculture. The deciduous fruit production was boosted only after the completion of the railway line to Wolseley in 1912.

The name "Togryers" (Transport riders) originated from the very big influence that the transport riders had on the development of Ceres. The completion of Michells Pass in 1848 made the town accessible to wagons, and within time one of the main routes to the diamond fields went through Ceres.

The visitor to the museum can learn more about the natural history of the area, the first inhabitans and their lifestyle as well as the establishment of Ceres. Other exhibits include the destructive earthquake of 1969, a collection of wagons and many more displays.

DID YOU KNOW......

- Ceres is one of the ous fruit and vege districts in South A
- The mountains a capped in winter ar casions the snow enough to be reache
- According to the towns in hierarchy, fied as the second town in the Breed next to Worcester

HET JY GEWEET ....

- Ceres is een van tevrugte produserer Suid-Afrika.
- Ceres het soms sw slae gedurende die w
- Ceres is geklassifisee belangrikste dorp in

our own small contribution to the erosion of apartheid. Most intriguing of all were the parties that we held from time to time at our house. During the Treason Trial, there were occasions when, either to celebrate a particular event or to raise funds, our house was chosen as the venue for a Congress party. Of course, it was unlawful to serve liquor to our guests, most of whom were black, so we could anticipate that the police would be in evidence sooner or later. We developed a technique of keeping the drinks in a walk-in wardrobe in Fred's bedroom and served the drinks in paper cups. Sure enough, the police would arrive at midnight or thereabouts and surround the house, whereupon those Africans who did not have passes would dash over the back wall into a field nearby or escape into a side street while those still inside the house would dispose of their paper cups in the kitchen rubbish bin and the wardrobe was locked before the police could enter. On such occasions there was much laughter and good humour and the police never managed to bring a charge against us on the grounds of a breach in the liquor laws, but they did often arrest Africans without passes and drag them off to the police cells nearby.

Of course we had our critics, ultra-leftists and 'blackists' who ridiculed us for our middle-class lifestyle in the face of professed dedication to the struggle for liberation. No doubt we did not fully cope with this contradiction between the personal and the political, to use a contemporary phrase. No doubt we did not fully overcome the prejudices of white society we had absorbed and, no doubt, our black comrades found us inadequate as rebels against race discrimination. True, personal lifestyle was very far from the political in a formal sense and yet who could say that our actual commitment was deficient given the whole of the circumstances? I recall a young white woman member of the Liberal Party who declared that she did not want to be a beneficiary of white privilege and would not go to a white cinema or travel on a whites-only bus. She took to her bicycle and could be seen pedalling furiously from Orange Grove to the centre of the city. We thought such gestures futile. We went to cinemas, used the white transport system and our children attended a white school. This was part of our belief that we had to lead as normal a life as possible while giving all our energies to the struggle. In retrospect, it was the correct approach and we were able to survive as rational, reasonable human beings throughout this very stressful period.

What made our situation particularly difficult was that we were operating politically at three different levels as mentioned earlier in less detail. First there was the Congress of Democrats which was legal and above board. Although I was banned from attending meetings in 1955 and therefore could not attend official gatherings of the organisation, I was able to receive journalists and other visitors, and I became very much a public figure in Johannesburg.

Then there was the semi-legal work with other banned people like Sisulu and Nokwe on the secretariat of the Alliance, which required quite different semi-clandestine methods of work. And then there was the wholly secret work in the party, especially when I became a member of the secretariat of the Johannesburg District Committee. In the office of the COD, my job was to work with the many young white newcomers to the movement who used the offices as a base for branch work in Johannesburg. There was a bustling, friendly spirit in the office and we churned out thousands of leaflets and posters for the numerous placard demonstrations at the Johannesburg City Hall and elsewhere.

By this time, Mary had become chairperson of the Johannesburg COD and was totally immersed in its work, so home life and work were dedicated to leaflets and banners and endless meetings discussing the many campaigns. I particularly enjoyed producing *Counter Attack*, a duplicated newssheet for COD, which dealt with policy and campaigning. We agonised a great deal about the role of COD. The organisation was only some 300 strong throughout the country – a pygmy next to the 100 000-odd of the ANC. Recruiting was difficult and our members came to us singly. Each one was prized and welcomed with open arms.

Of course, the odd security agent also joined. One young man who was very unconvincing was followed from the office and finally visited at his home where he was confronted with being an agent. He was extremely nervous and, on leaving, we saw him reach for the telephone through the glass front door of his house. That was enough to confirm for us that he was reporting to his minder. We also had suspicions about Oosthuizen, an Afrikaner journalist who joined us, but whose background was incongruous for a member of COD. Try as he might, he was never wholly accepted and was therefore not fully integrated into COD. This weighed heavily on his mind, especially as he was also having similar problems with his family. One day he put his head in a gas oven and put an end to his misery, leaving us feeling terribly guilty.

Marius Schoon was another problem case. A graduate of Stellenbosch University, born of true Afrikaans parents and retaining a strong love for Afrikaans culture, he had come to us through his rejection of the white bourgeois lifestyle. We thought that he was a bit of a hippy and too fond of partying, in fact a bit of a 'joller'. While Marius was accepted as a bona fide COD member, he was not allowed to join MK when it was formed. In desperation, Marius set up a sabotage team of three and attempted to blow up a police station in Hillbrow. But one of his team was an informer, so he was arrested and sentenced to ten years' imprisonment. When he finally joined our group in Pretoria Prison, we both reflected ruefully on the lengths to which he had to go to prove himself a genuine member of Congress.

The secretariat of the Alliance steadily moved toward becoming a kind of steering committee of the movement. As the campaigns followed each other, so we were obliged to meet more frequently, a favourite venue being the home of Goolam Pahad, the father of both Essop Pahad, later a minister, and Aziz Pahad, later a deputy minister in Mbeki's government. Amina Pahad, wife of Goolam, was the best curry cook in the movement and our committee would go there for lunch, thereby avoiding a breach of our banning orders on attending gatherings and yet enjoying a fabulous lunch. Sometimes we met at the home of Yusuf Dadoo who was no mean cook and who greatly enjoyed preparing our lunch himself.

At these meetings, Sisulu invariably ran the show while I was responsible for correspondence and some drafting of documents. Sometimes I would meet him briefly in a café in Fordsburg or he would come to our office. He was an unlikely person to hold so senior a position. Outwardly very ordinary in appearance, of mixed ancestry and mild in manner he was first a labourer in a

Johannesburg dairy and then worked on a gold mine on the Witwatersrand Reef. He also worked as a kitchen boy in East London and in several factories. At the same time, he studied privately to improve his education. But his real development came with membership of the ANC which he joined in 1940, becoming a founder of the ANC Youth League and secretary-general of the ANC from 1949-1954, until he was banned. While he had strong anti-white feelings as a young man, Walter overcame them and he was a delightful colleague to work with. In many ways my contacts with him were the most rewarding of all, deepening my commitment to the struggle. His strength was a profound wisdom, total integrity and a deep understanding of the masses. He showed no concern whatever for establishing a public image, nor would he seek publicity. I saw my role as a support to him. I drafted papers for him and was a kind of personal assistant. He was the ideal practical activist politician and was the dynamic kingpin of the whole movement at this time.

During this period, we often met with Moses Kotane who seemed to be feeling the strain of the Treason Trial and of the extraordinary tensions to which we were subjected in dodging the Special Branch. Moses seemed to be tired, sometimes falling asleep at meetings of the Joint Executives, and he seemed to be content to play a back-seat role. In part, this was by design since he, as the most senior figure among the communists, did not wish to take on too high a profile in Congress decision-making. The contrast between the two was striking. Whereas Walter's judgments were based on a wisdom rooted in experience and insight into the masses, Moses's relied more on a profound political and theoretical understanding. The decisions taken at these meetings were critical for setting the pace and direction of the whole movement. There was a degree of flexibility in the membership of the committee as the component organisations sent different people to represent them. The bannings also made meeting very difficult and various individuals were often unable to shake off police surveillance. So, despite our efforts to work consistently, decisions were sometimes taken in haste. Documents were drafted in restaurants and cafés and the directives got out to the organisations in a fairly haphazard manner.

I had many problems trying to protect documentation and would often carry with me totally secret party documents. I found hiding places in my car, secreting the paperwork inside the leather of the seats, in the dashboard, or even in a bottle tied under the undercarriage. There were also confidential documents of the Congress and of the COD. I often attended up to five meetings a day, each in a different place and with a different level of security. It was probably the most intense period in my life.

The national executives of the different Congresses met in a variety of clandestine locations too. Contact was person-to-person or through a coded message on the telephone. Meetings were often cut short because of the arrival of police in the neighbourhood. Yet it was remarkable that the police did not have an informer at the senior level, so we could be quite bold in our movements. This did not stop the state from banning leaders and cadres around the country, banning public meetings and arresting people under a variety of security-related laws. All this imposed a style of work on us that constrained proper democratic procedures, and I suppose the movement paid a price for this. It also meant that the rank and file was not adequately consulted and I heard from Mary often enough that they felt left out and sometimes bewildered by decisions taken in remote places.

The role of the secretariat and the meetings of the joint executives were an essential part of the smooth operation of the Congress Alliance. Each organisation had its own structure, constitution, membership and traditions. The Indian Congress, for example, which had been founded by Mahatma Gandhi at the beginning of the twentieth century, was set up to defend the interests of people of Indian origin. The ANC was, of course, designed to unite all Africans, irrespective of tribe and class. The COD was a whites-only organisation and yet we were supposed to campaign together in a coherent way without merging our identities. There was also the problem of containing SACTU within the Alliance. This was not only exclusively a trade union movement, but also clearly represented working-class interests and this within a movement in which the use of class analysis or class categories could be divisive. Congress policies were couched in national terms and democratic language which, at this time, was different from the class approach of SACTU.

These problems came to the surface in the 'Pound a Day' Campaign proposed by SACTU. I was asked to draft a campaign document for the secretariat with Sisulu standing over my shoulder, monitoring the choice of language used. SACTU was often dissatisfied with the way worker issues were handled by us. There was a strong feeling that working-class interests were not given sufficient recognition and that there was an unspoken bias against trade unionism on the part of some leaders for ideological reasons. SACTU was therefore a bit ambivalent in its relations with the secretariat, and we, in turn, were not entirely satisfied with the representatives from SACTU who were, on the whole, junior to or less experienced than those from the older Congresses. There can be no doubt that even the communists of the movement were restrained in the choice of language in speeches or documents about the political role of the working class and the special class interests of workers. The lack of enthusiasm for purely worker issues showed up in the 'Pound a Day' campaign and the dragging of feet on the part of the leadership was evident in the Johannesburg Campaign Committee, chaired by working-class and communist veteran, JB Marks with myself as secretary.

We tried to encourage activists and leaders to go into the industrial areas of Johannesburg to create factory committees. However, even though we urged that this was part of the process of strengthening both industrial and political organisation at the factory level, we were not very successful. SACTU itself was partly to blame for the dissonance within the Alliance in that it was workerist and economistic in its approach and hesitant to give the Alliance politics the kind of prominence needed.

As tensions grew around the country, the Alliance called a 'Stay at Home' for 26 June 1957. The 'Stay at Home' model of general strike in South Africa requires some explanation. In terms of the *Industrial Conciliation Act*, Africans were not recognised as 'workers with legal powers to strike for economic gain' even though they were allowed to strike for other reasons unrelated to conditions of work. We made frequent use of this anomaly. We were able to call upon workers to stay at home in protest against some law or in support of any demand, so general strikes were conducted in this way. The 'Stay at Home' formula meant that the focus of action was in the residential areas and not at workplaces. This disarmed the substantial body of skilled white workers, supervisors and managers who had easy access to the police and called upon them at the first sign of industrial action. It was difficult to sustain a strike in the factory areas, whereas in the townships it was relatively easy to generate a sense of solidarity. Picketing could be carried out in the streets, at bus stations and railway stations. In some cases, there was a certain excess of zeal on the part of tough young cadres who intimidated people at transport depots and, in some cases, targeted scabs returning at the end of the day.

THE PARTY

Meanwhile, the party was carrying on its own kind of work in its own way. The Johannesburg District Committee met at least monthly and discussed at length the various campaigns of the movement. From there, documents were drafted and the line was conveyed through the party groups to the various arms of the movement. The party was undoubtedly a vanguard of a kind and sought to maintain a high level of theoretical analysis and policy. While each member had to account for his or her actions *and* role within the party and the mass movement, the party was less concerned with the detailed work of individuals than with the development of policy. Indeed, there was a certain flexibility in implementation and individuals, including leaders, were allowed a measure of autonomy and discretion in the way party policy was introduced in the mass movement.

Party members were not allowed to form caucuses within committees of the mass movement and members were able to disagree with each other in debate. This meant that our work was both creative and safe in that party members' identities were not revealed from the positions members took or in the way they voted. Furthermore, full account had to be taken of the positions and perspectives of non-members within the mass movement so that men like Luthuli and Matthews were not constrained in making contributions to the formation of policy.

One of our duties as members was to advance the theoretical knowledge of Marxism within the party itself and outside it. I was responsible for a group of four Africans from Alexandra Township, which included people like Florence Mposho who became the leader of the women's section of the ANC in exile. She was of thoroughly working-class origin, as were other members of the group, and we had many study sessions on Marxist theory after we had finished our Congress business.

Other study classes were held for non-party people mainly as a mechanism for recruitment to the party. I conducted a class on dialectical materialism with Alfred Nzo and Tom Nkobi, both full-time officials of the ANC in Johannesburg. Security considerations meant that we would meet in my car on a bi-weekly basis, each propping up a copy of Maurice Cornforth's book on the subject, which could be hastily referred to under a street light as needed. Nzo proved an apt student, able to quickly grasp the subtleties of dialectics, and I enjoyed our sessions. In all these activities we operated on the 'need-to-know' principle so one could arrange a variety of group meetings without being asked awkward questions by comrades about what was going on.

TRIAL FATIGUE

Despite the rising tensions in the country, the closing years of the 1950s saw a certain element of fatigue entering into our work. In part, this was due to the drained energies from the Treason Trial, where the top leaders were preoccupied with fighting the treason charges and which also induced a certain preoccupation with legalisms brought on by the constant exposure to legal arguments in court. Every person on trial became a sea lawyer, expert in court procedure and fine points of legal defence. Somehow, militancy was sapped and energy ebbed. At the same time, the Africanist wing in the ANC was increasingly restless, stimulated in part by the aggressive approach of the government under Dr Verwoerd. He said: 'We will use an iron hand with regard to mixed gatherings aimed at undermining the government's apartheid policy.'

Legislation became ever more repressive, imposing even further racial discrimination throughout the country. Verwoerd introduced the Bantustan scheme designed to divide up the country, with reservations set aside for Africans, while leaving 87 per cent of the country for white ownership and occupation, thus removing any prospect of African citizenship outside the bantustans. The Bantu authorities were essentially instruments of repression and it was evident Verwoerd's claims that Africans were on the road to self-government was bogus.

It was also a period when African women became increasingly militant, especially in the rural areas. The initiative was taken by the Federation of South African Women (Fedsaw), established on 17 April 1954, and which soon took up the issue of passes for women. The government was moving to the imposition of passes for women which would lead to pass raids with all their hazards for vulnerable women. On 9 August 1956 Fedsaw organised a mass demonstration of 20 000 women from all over the country to present a petition at the Union Buildings in Pretoria. Soon confrontations between women and authorities became increasingly violent and women burned their passes. There were serious incidents in Lichtenburg and in Standerton, where an entire location went on strike, ending in a baton charge and the arrest of 914 women, and in Nelspruit where there was an almost total strike.

In October 1958, white Johannesburg housewives were informed that their African women servants had to report to pass offices. This led to large protests by African women from Sophiatown and Alexandra, with women marching to the centre of Johannesburg, and during the last ten days of October, 2 000 women courted arrest and 1 200 were jailed in the Fort, many of them with babies. In 1959 a crowd of 2 000 women was broken up by police in Durban following rioting and the burning of beer halls. There were mass protests at Harding on 21 July 1959 against forced use of dipping tanks and so-called betterment schemes. However, the ANC did not take sufficient notice of these protests, nor was the ANC Women's League given the kind of encouragement that would have galvanised women more effectively across the country.

THE POTATO BOYCOTT

Ruth First, then the Johannesburg editor of *The Guardian*, wrote an exposé called the 'Farm Labour Scandal' about African pass offenders who were hired out from prisons to work on various potato farms where they were treated like animals. Their clothes were taken away and they were dressed in sacks and accommodated in huts. They were forced to work at gunpoint and under the supervision of men carrying whips from morning to night, digging out potatoes with their bare hands. Ruth's stories about these conditions made a profound impression and on 30 May 1959 Robert Resha announced a boycott of potatoes as a protest. The boycott proved remarkably successful and in the following three months a huge mountain of potatoes accumulated throughout the Transvaal. The boycott was supported by African workers even though it was their staple food, but feelings on the issue of farm labour were running very high. After three months the boycott was called off, having generated enormous publicity about this pernicious scheme.

I worked with Ruth on various committees and in various capacities. She inspired a certain awe because of her high intelligence and forceful personality. Indeed, most of us were intimidated by this bundle of energy; even in apparent repose, she was like a compressed spring. But I discovered another side to Ruth when she asked me to drive her to the far reaches of the northwestern Cape to seek out a chief who had been confined to a remote region and seemingly had been forgotten. Ruth and I drove hundreds of miles in her car to the sandy wastes of the northwestern Cape and I found her to be a vulnerable and warm person with a fine sense of humour beneath the brittle exterior. We were an odd couple in that vast sea of sand with hardly a soul in sight, particularly as Ruth was dressed in her normal smart city clothes, high heels and permed hair. Every hour or so she would take out a moist tissue and cleanse her face of the heavy dust which penetrated the car despite all the windows being kept firmly shut. At one point we found petrol dripping out of the petrol tank which had been punctured by a stone. The prospect of being stuck without petrol in that desert was daunting until I found that some soap could block up the hole.

After travelling many hours and following many false trails, some local people directed us to a remote grass hut compound where we found the chief and two of his entourage in what looked very much like an oasis in a desert. When we explained who we were, he was delighted to give an account of his miserable experiences. The huts were some ten miles from the nearest store, where they could spend their meagre allowance meted out by the authorities. Otherwise, they were not allowed to leave the compound where their only activity was to try to grow some vegetables in this very inhospitable soil. Their totally isolated and harsh existence moved us profoundly.

Ruth wrote up the story on our return and it made a considerable impact. From that time, my relations with Ruth were very different and when she threw a tantrum or was bossy, I understood that this was only one aspect of her character and a kind of defence for a woman who was making a powerful impact in what was basically a man's world.

THE PAN-AFRICANIST CONGRESS (PAC)

The frustrations of the end of the decade when mass campaigning was faltering under the weight of repression created a climate favourable for the Africanists in the ANC. At various meetings the call was increasingly heard for the formation of a purely African movement. This was partly due to a belief that Africans should not associate with other races in their liberation. 'Africa for the Africans' was the slogan elsewhere on the continent and the Africanists believed that they had to join the trend. The Africanists alleged that the leadership of the ANC was being influenced by non-Africans and, in particular, by white communists. It was indeed the case that people like Michael Harmel, Rusty Bernstein, Ruth First, Joe Slovo and others were very influential in the movement, but the claims of the Africanists were grossly overstated. In any case, these white comrades were exceptionally talented and their roles were due to merit, not skin colour. Nor could it be said that men like Luthuli, Kotane and Sisulu would accept subordination or that their sense of self-worth could be undermined.

The ANC insisted that the Congress Alliance did not involve the subordination of the ANC but this did not prevent the Africanists from breaking away in April 1959 to form the Pan-Africanist Congress. The PAC stated that it objected to the

Freedom Charter, which gave all races equal rights in the country, and they also objected to the influence of communists and 'communist ideas within the Congress Movement'. Ironically, this did not prevent the PAC from establishing cordial relations with the white-led Liberal Party, nor did it stand in the way of cordial relations with the United States embassy. An important meeting of the PAC took place in the offices of the United States Information Office in Johannesburg. All attempts thereafter to include the PAC in united action were rebuffed. The PAC grew rapidly, developing a national organisational structure and drawing large crowds at meetings and demonstrations.

But the unfolding of events took everyone by surprise.

Parents Harry and Rachel Turok and sons, Hillel, Ben and Sol. Cape Town, 1945.

Right: Mary, Ben Turok's wife, taken while her husband was imprisoned for his role in a sabotage attempt on the Rissik Street Post Office. During this period, she was subjected to constant harassment by the Special Branch.

Below: Rissik Street Post Office, Johannesburg, which Turok was accused of attempting to sabotage. *(Sunday Times)*

Rachel Turok (Ben's mother), and sons Hillel, Ben and Sol *(seated)*. Latvia 1930.

Below: Turok graduated from the University of Cape Town in 1950 with a Bachelor of Science degree in Engineering.

Right: A youthful Ben Turok as a student at SA College High School, Cape Town. 1943.

Bottom: Ben Turok *(standing extreme right)* was a member of SA College High School's under 16 rugby team in 1942.

JB Marks, leader of the Mine Workers Union, Communist Party and the ANC, 1961. *(Sunday Times Archives)*

Sam Kahn, Communist Party MP and 'Native Representative' in parliament, c1951. *(Sunday Times Archives)*

Ben seated *(second from left)* next to Sonia Bunting (wife of Brian Bunting) on the speakers' platform at the Congress of the People.

Above left: Justice Albie Sachs, currently a Constitutional Court judge, pictured here ✳1963. Always an outspoken opponent of apartheid, he was constantly in conflict with the authorities and was consequently jailed under the ninety-day detention laws.
(Sunday Times Archives)

Above right: Bram Fischer QC, a member of the legal defence team at the Treason Trial of 1956. In 1966 he was found guilty of sabotage and the promotion of revolutionary activities, and was sentenced to life imprisonment. *(Eli Weinberg/ Sunday Times Archives)*

Below: Turok with Fred Carneson and Albert Luthuli in Cape Town, 1957.

Photographer Eli Weinberg obtained permission to photograph in Joubert Park, Johannesburg, all 156 members of the Congress Alliance, who had been charged with and acquitted of treason. The permission was subsequently withdrawn. Weinberg took separate groups and made up this well-known composite of the entire group as if they had been photographed collectively. *(Sunday Times Archives)*

The Congress of the People held in Kliptown in 1955. The objective of this landmark meeting was to draft a charter for a non-racial democratic future (The Freedom Charter).

Ben Turok while serving as 'Native Representative' on behalf of the Cape Provincial Council, leading a delegation to the Pass Office in Langa Township, Cape Town, in 1957.

Activists Adelaide Joseph and Mary Turok on their release on bail after having been charged with furthering the objectives of the ANC. Johannesburg 1962.

Mary Turok with Fred, Neil and Ivan, taken while Ben was in prison, 1964.

Right: Rusty and Hilda Bernstein with their daughter Toni and son-in-law Ivan Strasburg, leaving the high court in Johannesburg, 1964.
(Sunday Times)

Below: The discussion group of the Journal of African Marxists. Manchester 1985.

Right: The late Walter Sisulu and Ahmed Kathrada,1959. Both were later convicted during the Treason Trial and sentenced to lifetime imprisonment on Robben Island. *(Sunday Times Archives)*

Below: Entrance to the Fort in Hillbrow, Johannesburg, the prison where treason accused were detained while awaiting trial. *(Sunday Times)*

Above left: Brian Bunting, prominent activist and editor of *The Guardian,* a communist newspaper founded in 1937.
(Sunday Times Archives)

Above right: Joe Matthews, senior Inkatha Freedom Party leader, at a press conference in Cape Town in 1994.
(Robert Botha/Sunday Times)

Left: Activist Ruth First, wife of Joe Slovo, with daughters Gillian and Robyn, 1961.
(Colin Edwards/Sunday Times Archives)

Above: Oliver Tambo, the then president of the ANC, with Thabo Mbeki at the Five Freedoms Forum held in Lusaka in 1989.
(Sunday Times)

Right: Ben with Walter Sisulu in Sauer Street, Johannesburg, on his return to South Africa in 1990.

Top: Nelson Mandela and Joe Slovo at an SA Communist Party rally in Johannesburg in 1990. *(Robert Botha/Sunday Times)*

Bottom: Ahmed Kathrada, Nelson Mandela and Walter Sisulu at the 49th ANC Congress held in Bloemfontein in 1994. *(Sunday Times)*

Above: Ben Turok at the Open University in England, 1985. He joined the staff as a part-time Social Studies tutor in 1972 and continued to teach there on and off and in various capacities until 1986.

Below: Helen Joseph, top Congress of Democrats and Women's Federation leader, commemorates the women's march on the Union Buildings in Pretoria in 1986.
(Daniel Simon/Sunday Times)

Top: Ben with members of the board of the Institute for African Alternatives (IFAA) after meeting Salim Salim, secretary-general of the Organisation of African Unity (OAU) outside their headquarters in Addis Ababa in 1988.

Bottom: Ben Turok with Prof Bade Onimode, chairperson of the Institute for African Alternatives outside their Nigerian offices in Ibadan in 1989.

CHAPTER FOUR

LIFE UNDERGROUND

The Treason Trial clearly marked a totally new chapter in the struggle. Not only did it demarcate far more clearly the divide between the state and the movement, but it also brought out the importance of individuals in the struggle. The writings of Lenin and above all Plekhanov on the role of individual leaders in political struggle show how the personality of a leader is shaped by and in turn shapes a struggle. The emphasis in Marxist literature is always on the social groups or classes, on social conditions and the political environment without, however, devaluing the contribution of leaders.

I go along with this position in general, but my experience of the Treason Trial was that the significance of individual talent, and individual blemishes or weaknesses, could become very significant at certain moments. I say this because it is the tradition in the ANC to call up the collective as the source of all wisdom and authority in decision-making. This is a very important principle and most of us have to a significant degree subordinated our individual impulses to the collective in the belief that this is both democratic and sound. Yet when I look back on this whole period that I am describing, I cannot but be struck by the importance of personality and character.

Some individuals, for instance, seem to be preoccupied with status and individual power. At the extreme, this manifests itself in careerism and opportunism that can be a blight on any organisation. But even in its more subtle forms it can become a serious burden on a political organ. Of course, we all have our moments of gratification or disappointment when we win or lose an election to office of any kind. You tell yourself: 'I would love to be the chairperson of that committee' and then find that you are passed over. Of course it is disappointing and personal ambition is hard to suppress. But when it goes beyond that in some individuals, and it often does, it becomes a problem. We see this particularly strongly now that we are a parliamentary democracy where personal ambition is associated with real material advantages and where rivalry can become nasty. But it is there at the grass-roots level, too, and I know that even at branch level rivalry can be unpleasant and divisive.

And yet, as I was saying, personal qualities and achievements are important. For instance, I prize very highly my role in the Congress of the People and the Treason Trial. To be at the centre of things, when history is being made, has a special kind of thrill which remains with you forever. As many know, the Freedom Charter is still referred to in the ANC as the cornerstone of all policy. Even recently, when Thabo Mbeki made his announcement of victory in the second election on 2 June 1999 he quoted the charter in saying that South Africa belongs to all who live in it, black and white. This is a principle we have sustained through all the years of bitterness and divisiveness as a people. It reminds us that the ANC is not a political party and is even more than a national liberation movement: it is an expression of a people's aspiration. I am reminded of this even now as I read the draft preface to the 2002 edition of *Strategy and Tactics* presented to the December 2002 national conference of the ANC which states: 'But ours is more than just a national liberation struggle because it places the interests of the poor and the role of the working class at the centre of its theory and practice.'

So it has always been important that the leaders of the ANC should be seen to be an expression of that spirit and there is no doubt that Chief Luthuli, Oliver Tambo and Nelson Mandela were such personalities. Mbeki is preparing himself for the same role. It is a difficult one because we are such a diverse people, with massive inequalities and differing cultures, so to somehow become the symbol of that mosaic requires special qualities and vision.

I have always been overwhelmed at the magnificent breadth of vision to emerge from our African townships. Of course there are lots of 'blackists' and ultra-leftists, but in the main the townships have manifested enormous vision about the shape of our future

South Africa. How people who live in severe poverty and hardship can continue to uphold the best values of non-racialism and democracy is beyond me. And yet it has always been like that, and it is what has sustained me through all the years of travail.

In the 1950s, as we prepared for the Congress of the People, we became conscious of the need for this kind of vision. The Call to the People of South Africa, which preceded the COP, was written in pure poetry that made a dramatic impact way beyond that of an ordinary political manifesto. And that is why when we called on the masses to submit their written demands, they did so in their thousands – on scraps of rough paper and in proper documents. And so the Freedom Charter is a document for all and for all time.

But I digress. The point of this little intervention is to stress the role of personal qualities in leadership, something that we grew to appreciate as things got tougher as we all knew they were bound to do. Throughout the Treason Trial and then on into the underground and in prison, we were all pushed to use our last resources of courage and resilience. Bombast, heroics and such-like characteristics are of little value in a people's struggle. Unfortunately, the present political scene, with its fruits of office and its party politics, does lend itself to posturing. This is why younger comrades have to be inducted into the wholesome traditions of the ANC so that our movement does not become polluted by careerism and opportunism.

A final point on this matter of personality. As the situation deteriorated in the late 1950s, as we moved towards more desperate measures and methods of struggle, we also had to constantly remind ourselves that it would be a long haul, testing our endurance and patience to the limit. This remains relevant today. There are no quick fixes when the problems are so great and those who lack the tenacity and sheer grit to stay the course should not be placed in positions of leadership. For myself, without undue modesty, I think that I proved my stamina and some toughness of spirit in my mountaineering and in surveying. I also did not shirk making hard decisions in my personal life, my marriage and joining the struggle and so on. But I have no doubt that each new crisis in the political arena in which I found myself forced me to face very difficult situations with the appropriate demeanour. I am not saying that I succeeded, but that is what I had to try to do.

But let me pass on to the next chapter that deals with events that I alone can recapture because my comrades of this period have all passed away. This impels me to recount the events of 1960, a turning point in our struggle.

It was a crisp, clear, sunny day, typical of the Transvaal highveld with its rolling grass plains of intangible distance. Mary, our three children and I were driving in our station wagon and approaching the end of that long haul from Cape Town to Johannesburg. On my trips to Cape Town to attend the Cape Provincial Council it had become standard practice that we should leave in the mid-afternoon, drive through the night, stop at a hotel in the early morning for breakfast and a short sleep and then drive on to reach home in the early afternoon. This way the children slept through the night on a mattress in the back of the station wagon, could then have something to eat to take the edge off the journey and play in the back until we reached home.

And so it was that we were driving past Sharpeville when we came upon convoys of armed police in trucks, alert and upright as though on their way to war, interspersed with convoys of screaming ambulances tearing down the national road. We counted dozens. Here and there small groups of armed police directed traffic and cleared blockages. There was an urgency in the air and we knew that something calamitous had happened, but we had no idea what it was. We were not allowed to stop and could not ask the reason for all the activity. It was only on our arrival in Johannesburg that we heard the news on the radio that dozens had been shot and many more wounded in a demonstration at Sharpeville. Since then, Sharpeville has become one of the most symbolic events in South Africa's liberation struggle. It was to ignite the anger of millions of oppressed and those with a conscience in South Africa and around the world. I need to go back a little to explain this momentous disaster.

In 1959, while the Treason Trial seemed to be coming to a climax, claiming the full attention of the leadership, there emerged a campaign based in Alexandra Township called 'African Women Against Passes'. Very soon, hundreds of women were being arrested and held in jail in Johannesburg. While the leadership was kept fully informed, it was not in control of the protest.

The issue was raised at several meetings of the Alliance Secretariat as the scale of the arrests was becoming a matter of concern. Some 900 women were in prison and more were pouring in with no end in sight. A particular concern was that some of the women were pressing for bail to be arranged by the ANC. Walter Sisulu said that there was no way the movement could raise the money required to bail out all of these women and that the organisers should calm them and persuade them to hang on until arrangements could be made. But the amounts required for bail escalated to a point where the protest was becoming an embarrassment to the leadership, so the idea arose that the women should be persuaded that they could not all be defended and that, indeed, their being in prison had raised the level of significance of their protest. This was how the slogan 'No Bail, No Defence, No Fine' came to be built into ANC thinking in the anti-pass struggle.

Claims have been made that the slogan was, in fact, proposed to the PAC at a conference on 31 May 1959. I have no knowledge of this, but am aware that the PAC issued a leaflet headlined 'Passes Must Go Now. No Bail, No Defence, No Fine' in early 1960. The decision to embark on a campaign around these slogans was formally taken at a PAC conference on 19-20 December 1959. Whether the slogan was borrowed from the PAC or not is not certain, nor is it really material. What I do recall is that the women's campaign had forced upon the secretariat the realisation that a new defiance campaign would bring far more volunteers into the action than ever before and that the legal processes to which we had become accustomed could not be ensured.

Sisulu urged that a new approach be put before the people, namely that arrest would mean imprisonment and that people should be prepared to defend themselves without lawyers and serve their sentences if necessary. Sisulu drafted a document, which I typed in five copies, and we circulated one to each of the provinces for adoption. It was essential that top security be maintained and that the plan should not leak to the press or anyone else. However, we hit a snag in that questions were being raised by the Natal leadership who wanted explanations about a number of aspects. So, instead of pressing on urgently to meet the rising sense of frustration and of crisis in the country, we delayed implementation while the concerns were sorted out.

The leadership – harassed by the exigencies of the trial, frustrated by their inability to dedicate themselves fully to the political needs of the day, aware that attendance at public meetings had fallen off seriously and that there was a rising tide of complaints, particularly among the youth, about the need for guns rather than leaflets – were to some extent immobilised. Sisulu, more than anyone else, was sensitive to this new mood and he was very worried about it. He had hoped that the new defiance campaign would awaken and give direction to resistance once more. But Natal delayed and we lost the initiative. However, at the December 1959 conference, the ANC resolved to launch an Anti-pass Campaign on 31 March 1961. Almost simultaneously, the PAC decided to launch their campaign around the same slogans before that date. On 4 March, their leader, Robert Sobukwe, sent his instructions to all branches to prepare for action. On 16 March he wrote to Major General Rademeyer, Commissioner of Police, to inform him that the PAC would carry out a 'sustained, disciplined, non-violent campaign' and that its members would present themselves for arrest on Monday, 21 March 1961.

The PAC was highly sensitive to the mood in the country and responsive in a strategic way. Sobukwe sensed that a climax was in the offing and adopted a pose of 'heroic leadership'. Thus it was that Sobukwe, Potlako Leballo and other PAC leaders, together with 150 volunteers, presented themselves at Orlando Police Station for arrest. In Durban, Port Elizabeth and East London nothing happened, but at Sharpeville, some 35 miles south of Johannesburg, a crowd of some 5 000 gathered at the police station, apparently in response to a rumour that a police official would address the crowd. There was some pushing and shoving as the crowd pressed against the fence and the jittery police opened fire. There was a bloodbath with 69 people dead, mostly shot in the back, and 180 wounded.

The PAC was well organised in the area and the local cadres carried out an effective mobilisation campaign, disrupting public transport and cutting telephone wires on the eve of the action.

The inhabitants were seething with anger at liquor raids by the police, rent extortion by the local council, removals and other local issues.

The shootings at Sharpeville were totally unexpected but raised the temperature across the country. So, although the Anti-pass Campaign of the PAC floundered, large crowds participated in protests. Taken as a whole, however, the PAC Anti-pass Campaign was stillborn, even though the country was stunned, many whites panicked and the gun shops did a roaring trade. Internationally, there were protests everywhere. In Cape Town, there was a massive 'Stay at Home' and in Vereeniging there was large-scale absenteeism.

The ANC reacted speedily and Luthuli called for Monday 28 March to be observed throughout the country as a day of mourning, which took the form of a 'Stay at Home'. Extraordinarily, the government too was shocked by what it had done and on 26 March, pass arrests were temporarily suspended. Luthuli, capturing the mood in the country, burned his pass on the same day and urged all Africans to do the same. Suddenly, the country seemed to be ungovernable. Huge demonstrations flared up in many areas with serious riots in Johannesburg. In Cape Town, 50 000 people gathered at the PAC-organised funerals on 28 March. On Wednesday, 30 March, the government declared a state of emergency. All the Treason trialists were rearrested and on Thursday 31 March nearly 2 000 political activists around the country were picked up.

SAFE HOUSE

Most of my time was now spent in the various movement offices getting leaflets printed and organising protests everywhere. It was an extraordinary situation in which events seemed to be unfolding unpredictably. We all sensed that it was a moment of immense significance and that a momentous clash was about to happen. The Special Branch was very active and we knew that all the offices were under continuous observation. On Wednesday 30 March, Jack Hodgson told me at the COD office that there was a great deal of activity around police headquarters. That night at around midnight he came to our house and said that there had been a telephone call from Durban to the effect that there were large numbers of police cars gathered at Special Branch headquarters and that similar activities had been reported in other centres. The advice was that people should leave home in case of mass arrests. The information caused me little surprise. Mass arrests were in the air, and so I packed a small suitcase and Mary drove me to a house in Observatory where I had, a few days earlier, warned an old school friend, Ralph Sepal, that I might soon be asking for sanctuary. I knocked on the door at almost exactly midnight and asked the hosts for asylum for a few days. They were surprised but welcoming, and so it was that I spent my first night – one of many – at their home. Two hours later the Special Branch arrived at my house, furious to find that I had fled. They searched everywhere, even in the ceiling, and warned Mary they were determined to catch me.

My safe house became a centre for the underground. Within a day or two, Yusuf Dadoo arrived as did Michael Harmel, Moses Kotane and several others. Suddenly, I was thrust into the midst of the top leadership of the party at a time when the whole country was gripped in a paroxysm of panic. Violence on a large scale swept through Soweto where municipal buildings were set alight. In Durban there were huge processions and in Cape Town large crowds marched in the city centre on an unprecedented scale. In Durban police opened fire on thousands of demonstrators and there were outbreaks of violence and pass burning in all the major centres. On 8 April the ANC and the PAC were banned.

Our safe house became a hub of planning and campaigning. We were shocked to learn that so few of our leaders around the country had taken the warnings seriously. Many who had been woken at midnight simply turned over and went back to sleep. The consequence was that our small group suddenly became saddled with enormous responsibilities. Our problem was, however, to maintain the secrecy of our base and yet keep in touch with the ANC leadership in Soweto as well as the remaining party cadres throughout the country. For me it was a thrilling experience. I had known Moses and Michael and some of the others quite well, but to be cooped up like this with them 24 hours a day, being privy to their discussions and consulted on decisions to be taken, was an enormous privilege.

Despite the need to maintain top security, meetings had to be held and decisions taken. Wolfie Kodesh became our contact man, visiting us in his 'clean' car, bringing us news about others who had survived and those who had been taken. He also brought us visitors, among whom was Ruth First who had fled to Swaziland with her three children after her husband, Joe, had been arrested. Moses and Michael were anxious for Ruth to stay with us as a member of the leadership core, but she had evidently been badly shaken by the arrests and felt the need to be with her children. I noticed that she was taking sedatives and so her request to go back to Swaziland was reluctantly acceded to. Jack Hodgson, on the other hand, wanted very much to remain with us, but Moses did not feel that he could be useful at this stage and so poor Jack had to go back into exile in Swaziland. It was decided that Yusuf Dadoo should go abroad to join Oliver Tambo on the external diplomatic work. Moses, Michael and myself were thus left as the three core members of the party leadership.

Our existence at that time was not without its humorous aspects. We slept in a back room abutting the garden at the back of the house. We depended on our hosts to alert us to any suspicious movements and any unwanted visitors. When their own friends called, we beat a hasty retreat to sit in our little backroom and, on some occasions, even went out in the garden to sit in the bushes for several hours while their relatives moved around the house unsuspectingly. We had to keep all signs of our presence out of the front lounge, bathroom and the rest of the house, not a little worried that the domestic servant might refer to us among her friends. Our hosts were immensely solicitous of our welfare and kept us supplied with coffee and food. We greatly enjoyed the company of their two boys.

On one occasion, at about 10.00 in the evening, someone arrived and told us of a suspicious-looking car parked in the street outside the house. Since I had become the security officer, I slipped out the back of the house and moved in the shadows to observe the car, taking up a position in the shadow of a tree on the pavement not 20 yards away. There was a long period of inactivity and then, as I moved closer to the car, from the back seat a woman's bare leg was raised in the air, jerking violently. I nearly burst out laughing and went back to report on this 'threat to our security'.

There were times when Moses, Michael and I sat in the garden, drenched by the rain, while our hosts entertained their friends and relatives. They were among those who fully supported the movement and were committed to it, but for one reason or another were unable or unwilling to be fully involved in activity. They were among a network of safe houses through which we could move and survive the intense security net that encompassed the whole country, though none of them had anticipated that they would be called upon to house the party leadership during a state of emergency. Each reacted to the request to house us with a different degree of willingness. Some refused point-blank. Others agreed willingly, delighting in the sense of adventure and excitement we brought with us. Of course, it was dangerous. The police and the government were furious that some top leaders had evaded arrest, although their swoop had succeeded in catching the greater majority of the top and middle-level leadership. The fact that Moses and Michael were safe was because they had long-standing instructions from the Central Committee to get to a safe house when things got too hot. Fortunately, they had followed instructions and so were available to provide leadership when it was most needed.

During the next five months of emergency, we moved to ten different houses, slipping away when we sensed some suspicious activity around the house or when we felt that the domestic servants, who are the inevitable part of white households in Johannesburg, became suspicious or too curious. We were indeed a strange group to be lurking in the backroom of some rich white person's home. There was Moses, then a man of about 60 and an African, Michael, of about the same age, and myself. We sat all day in our backroom reading, writing, chatting or typing. At times we were allowed out into the garden depending on its size and degree of seclusion and depending on whether the servants were around. From time to time our courier would drive up, semi-disguised, and bring us newspapers, letters, information and the odd bit of clothing or whatever else we might need.

Being the youngest of the group and the least experienced, I was delegated to do the correspondence with the different sectors of the movement and to keep the documents as well as maintain our security. This was no easy matter, especially as Michael had absolutely no regard for security. Keeping him within the bounds of the house and garden required constant nagging. He would put on an overcoat and 'go for a walk'. On several occasions, we were sure he had been recognised, but there were no serious breaches of our security. However, one dark night in Yeoville, Michael and I were picked up by a van on a street corner only to find that a police car was in the vicinity. Michael had walked to the meeting place and I was sure he had been identified. But the police car was just a coincidence, apparently, and we were soon safely back in our hideout.

Under normal circumstances Moses was always neatly dressed in flannels, tie and jacket and rather touchy about how people related to him. But now he wore blue overalls, as was common among African gardeners. In my case, since I was often in contact with the media and visitors from overseas political parties I, too, was also normally well dressed. But now I had grown a beard while Michael grew a moustache with which he fiddled constantly and gave us much amusement. The few visitors who came to see us enjoyed ribbing us about our altered appearance.

During the few weeks that Dadoo was with us I got to know him better. He was a great cook, serving up tasty curry and spiced eggs for breakfast. He had an easy manner, free of any tension, and was willing to go along with whatever was decided even if it affected his own fate adversely. He was clearly not suited to a clandestine existence, so his going abroad was a good decision, particularly given his reputation internationally.

Moses was an entirely different character – even more complex than the person I thought I had come to know during the Treason Trial. I rapidly came to appreciate that this rather slow-moving and ponderous person, slightly overweight and who moved so deliberately, was actually a first-class intellect. His manner was very changeable. He could be warm, immensely kind and unreserved in his physical contact with people. He could readily put an arm on your shoulder, showing how he cared. But he could also be irritable and irritating to a degree. There was a flash of temper as well and when it would flare up unexpectedly, he could be quite cruel, not only politically but also personally. But I soon learned to live with it and to appreciate that Moses was almost certainly the most outstanding personality in the movement's history.

Moses Kotane was born in Rustenburg in 1905 to a devout Christian family of Tswana origin and had only a little formal education. He became a keen reader and started work as a photographer's assistant at the age of 17. He joined the ANC in 1928 and the Communist Party in 1929. By 1931 he was a full-time functionary and a trade union organiser. He studied in Moscow for a year in the early 1930s and became general secretary of the party in 1939.

For a man with little formal education, Moses was astonishingly self-confident. Within the party he rubbed shoulders with men who had a university education and who were intellectuals of a high order. Michael Harmel, for instance, had a first-class intellect with wide interests and knowledge in music, literature and politics. He was also an excellent chess player as I found to my cost when he beat me consistently during the long months of seclusion. Moses easily held his own in the numerous exchanges with people like Michael. He was well organised and systematic in everything he did. He would have been an excellent philosophy student. He read documents meticulously, delighting in pointing out flaws in the logic or syntax. He would also have been an excellent teacher and researcher. He rarely used emotive adjectives, depending entirely on cold reason in an argument. Even at mass meetings when he was billed as the star speaker and was expected to raise the temperature and inspire the audience, his approach was slow, factual and explanatory, eschewing rhetoric. And so Moses established a national reputation as a leader of the highest calibre – serious, committed and principled beyond question.

Moses represented that deep contradiction that lies at the heart of African communists in South Africa. It was often hard to tell which was dominant in his make-up – the African nationalist or the international communist. Luthuli, and later Tambo, came to respect Moses and trust his commitment and judgement totally. They saw him as first and foremost a fellow African nationalist and within the leadership of the ANC his loyalty to that organisation was never in doubt. Yet Moses was also the decisive force within the party. Just when I was beginning to think that his nationalism was the main reason for his favouring an ANC position, Moses would come back firmly to positions based on the interests of the party.

This two-sided character can be found in most African communists and, far from being a disadvantage, is a source of strength. Those Africans who did not feel in their bones a nationalist commitment were not thereby better communists since the South African struggle required a dual loyalty, without allowing one or the other to become too dominant.

Despite his penetrating mind, Moses was not a good writer. While he could attack a text rigorously and provide good formulations he could not produce a fluent, interesting text but depended rather on a collective effort. He was also not given to fostering a public image. Moses was a desk man, a sort of backroom committee man, and he disliked pressures placed upon him to perform the public role of leader. Independent-minded as he was, he was all for collective decision-making and even when he disagreed violently with a committee's view, as he did on one critical occasion during this period, he accepted the collective will even when he thought it would lead to disaster.

Despite a certain cantankerous character and a certain bluntness, he could also be extremely sensitive to others. When he wanted to lobby for my support, he would take my arm, walk me into the garden and use great charm. What impressed me most of all were his slow but solid decision-making powers. Here was a man who took decisions with great care, conscious of all the possible outcomes, so he won my total confidence. At the end of the state of emergency and in the following years in Johannesburg and abroad, I always felt that I would follow his lead absolutely.

A wholly different personality was Michael Harmel. While I came to love and respect Moses increasingly throughout our stay, I found Michael to be an uncomfortable partner. Born in 1915 in Johannesburg, he obtained an MA in Economics at Rhodes

University. He joined the party in 1939 and was secretary of the Johannesburg District Committee from 1940-1946. He was a member of the Central Committee from 1941 until 1950 and was one of the two members, with Bill Andrews, who objected to the liquidation of the party, for which his name will be long remembered in the history of the party.

Michael's lifestyle was thoroughly disorganised and haphazard, and he was somewhat unpredictable in his personal relations. During the many months alone with him in the little backroom while we were in hiding, I came to respect his intellect while feeling increasingly uncomfortable in his company. Michael was a totally committed communist and his loyalty and seriousness were absolutely unwavering. His concern for the wider issues of politics and society and his principled adherence to a Marxist philosophy and vision were never in the slightest doubt. And yet, on a human level, he could be cruel with a streak of vindictiveness, particularly towards those who strayed from the party line. No doubt this was a reflection of the Stalinist influence that penetrated so deeply throughout the World Communist Movement during Michael's formative years as a communist. Michael could be unnecessarily fierce and aggressive in dealing with dissidents and this made him rather unpopular.

At the same time, his personal courage and commitment were exemplary and I often had the feeling that he knew no fear, even to the point of recklessness. It was my task to keep Michael's papers hidden, to keep him under cover and guard against any act that might expose our little group. He seemed not to care and while the rest of us were fearful of discovery, this posed no problem to Michael at all. He read voluminously, often late into the night, not waking until mid-morning which made working together awkward. And yet I could not but admire and respect the deep intellect he brought to our work, the vision he exercised in relation to the struggle and the very considerable experience he brought to bear on our activities. Although his main occupation was journalism he was also the principal theorist of the movement and the most learned Marxist of the party – our Lenin, in fact – always original, never working from sterile doctrine.

Michael died in exile in Prague in 1974, deeply depressed,

having been sent there as the Communist Party representative on World Marxist Review, a post generally reserved for retired members of communist parties. In my encounters with him in London in the early 1970s, I found him a changed man, suffering more than most the frustrations and sterility of exile. He should have remained underground at home.

These months in hiding passed slowly. I missed Mary and the children desperately. In many ways things were worse for her. My sudden disappearance left her holding the fort with three small children. Daily police raids and ongoing detentions led her to take the children to Krugersdorp where they stayed with Rabbi Ben Isaacson. She then rented out our house, sent the two older boys to stay with my parents in Cape Town and she and our youngest boy, Neil, moved in with Hymie Rochman and his wife in Yeoville. What was left of COD was a small group consisting of Mary, Pixie and John Benjamin, and Ronnie Kasrils, and they tried to get things going again from a rented office under a nom de plume in Jeppe Street.

Mary bought a large hat and glasses as a partial disguise, but it is difficult to hide a six-footer. The COD group met in various cafés in Hillbrow but it was difficult to get anything off the ground. She then rented a flat in Berea and the boys came back to join her. From time to time Wolfie brought her to spend an evening with me in a secluded place in a car or in another safe house. Rather the same was happening between Nelson and Winnie.

For my part, I tried to keep busy, circumscribed as the situation was. We read newspapers anxiously, we communicated with various parts of the country and even had a visitor from the Communist Party of Great Britain who brought some money and consulted with us on our prospects. Our future was very uncertain and perhaps rather bleak. There was no way of telling how long the state of emergency would last and how long we would be obliged to remain holed up in backrooms in the white suburbs of Johannesburg. We discussed at some length the possibility of leaving the country in order to set up headquarters in a neighbouring country. Our problem was that there were very few senior people remaining outside prison. We were paying the price for those who had disregarded the warnings and stayed put in the comfort of their homes, only to be arrested.

Both Moses and Michael came down against relocating outside the country. They argued that there were several instances in Africa and elsewhere where a leadership had gone into exile and the general experience was that they had been forced to move ever further away from base, becoming remote and isolated from the struggles in their countries. At least we were within easy reach of the various arms of the movement and there was the prospect that, provided we maintained top security, we could survive. Indeed, my own conviction was growing that underground was rather a good place to be. We were slowly establishing ever-improving contact with people in Durban, Port Elizabeth and Cape Town, and the struggles in Johannesburg were becoming increasingly effective. We were able to issue leaflets, conduct underground meetings and yet evade police surveillance.

In a way, I actually felt safer underground than in the offices of the movement where one was always under tension. In the underground there was a tranquillity and a sense of security that enabled one to operate efficiently while at the same time being able to reflect in depth on policies and strategy. The conviction grew within me that the underground was an essential component of the struggle. This feeling was confirmed by an extraordinary expedition in the early months of the emergency.

Contact with Port Elizabeth had only just been re-established, and Moses wanted me to visit our people there in order to re-establish contact on a sound basis. And so I was given a 'clean' car to drive to Port Elizabeth. I left at midnight on the long haul of some 800 miles. But early in the morning, as dawn broke over the flat veld in the Free State, I was overcome by the warmth of the early-morning sun and awoke to find the car bouncing in a field next to the road. I had been driving at about 70 miles per hour and the car was crashing through the rough terrain of sand and rock so that it might easily have overturned. The car came to a standstill and when I inspected the damage it was to find that the front axle seemed to be bent and the wheel touching the fender. I managed to get the car back on the road and fortunately found a garage some ten miles away. I was fearful that if the damage was substantial I would have great difficulty getting back to Johannesburg. Fortunately, a mechanic was able to straighten out the suspension sufficiently for me to continue on my journey.

On arriving at Port Elizabeth I booked into a hotel under a false name. As I was entering my address, a Special Branch officer came to inspect the entry over my shoulder, giving me the fright of my life. Nothing happened and I went to my room where I was soon called for by Tollie Bennun, a white businessman comrade in Port Elizabeth. But as we left my room together there were two Special Branch men standing on the landing eyeing us suspiciously. We walked out of the hotel but decided that I should not return there. It was only later that I discovered that the reason for the Special Branch activity was the attendance by the prime minister, Dr Verwoerd, of a Nationalist Party conference. On such occasions it was routine that all hotel registers were inspected and all visitors monitored.

I had a meeting with Raymond Mhlaba, one of the senior leaders in the area who had been released from detention. Port Elizabeth had for some time been one of the most militant areas in the country, with a large manufacturing base but also with deep roots in the interior. I had had previous contacts with Raymond and Govan Mbeki who were mentioned earlier and were a powerful team. Both of them were subsequently arrested and sentenced to life imprisonment in the Rivonia Trial. I found Raymond to be a reserved, tough personality who inspired confidence. We discussed the rebuilding of the movement in Port Elizabeth and in the Eastern Cape as a whole and he was confident that neither the arrests nor the state of emergency would hinder the restructuring required. After our meeting I drove back to Johannesburg and reported to Moses and Michael.

During the five months of the emergency which ended in August, we moved nine times in order to break any leads that might build up. At one point Michael and I were separated from Moses though we were reunited every few days for meetings, to draft documents, respond to letters and so on. The separation had a bad effect on Moses who seemed to be growing more irritable and nervous in his isolation. Michael and I were confined to one room day and night and were getting on each other's nerves. Almost the only relief from the tedium came when we had visitors.

One of the most welcome of these was Bram Fischer who was living a most extraordinary existence, flitting from his responsibilities to the Treason Trial defence team to visit us in the underground. It was amazing how Bram adapted himself to such different environments with almost no change in his manner. Gentle, exceptionally polite, kindly, never offensive, Bram would visit us and stay to chat over a bottle of whatever drink that he had brought. Bram was already a legend in South Africa, symbolic of the very diverse origins and makeup of the movement. Born in 1908, he came from a distinguished Afrikaans family. His grandfather was prime minister of the Orange River Colony and his father judge president of the Orange Free State Supreme Court. Bram had been an outstanding student, winning a Rhodes scholarship to Oxford from 1931-34. He later joined the Communist Party and became a top barrister in Johannesburg. He was one of the defence lawyers in the Treason Trial and later led the defence in the 1964 Rivonia Trial.

To me, Bram was an enigma. I found it hard to see in this daring visitor the thoroughly respectable pinstripe personality at the Johannesburg Bar who lived in a large home with a garden and substantial swimming pool in one of the most well-heeled suburbs of Johannesburg. I could not see in him the qualities I thought necessary for a leader of the Communist Party. He seemed to be wholly without a commitment to Marxism and seemed to have none of the attributes of the tough organisation men at the top of the movement. Instead, his language and manner were much more those of an upper-class gentleman. I did not yet realise that beneath this amiable exterior there was a toughness and resilience that few appreciated.

Bram was not forceful in the committee, nor would he present a case aggressively. His style was suggestive and subtle, talking round a problem in a slightly preoccupied manner as though he was feeling his way through a maze of possibilities. Apart from his concern for us, he also had the responsibility of caring for those in detention. He would bring us information about individuals in prison, or about how this one's wife was alone without money and how that one was coping inside. He told us how he smuggled a small radio inside a sock to one of the detainees. I soon came to appreciate that this very humane, affable man was actually fearless, made of steel and taking risks all the time. This disarming, innocent-looking man could get away with murder.

Another outstanding quality was Bram's ability to gain the respect of the widest sectors of South African society. He was loved not only in the movement but also in the Christian community, among Afrikaners, liberals and even within the relatively conservative terrain of the Bar itself where he was chairman in Johannesburg for a time. No one would have predicted that Bram would refuse to go into exile, that he would skip bail in January 1965 when he was charged with membership of the Communist Party, that he would go underground and live there in disguise, and finally be sentenced to life imprisonment. In prison he was treated like a traitor and given harsher conditions than anyone else. He had to clean toilets and do a whole range of menial chores which he endured with unfailingly good morale. He died while still a prisoner in 1975.

At one point I noticed that Michael was rather absorbed in his own thoughts. He would sit brooding, somewhat preoccupied. One day he sat down at our typewriter and typed furiously until he had produced a lengthy document which he then put before me. It was a full-scale analysis of the political situation, leading to the conclusion that a new set of conditions existed in the country and thus questioned the character of our own struggle. He argued that in banning the ANC the state had created an entirely new situation, leading inexorably to the necessity of violence. The document came as a shock to me but I immediately realised the validity of the case and he, Moses and I began to discuss it. Moses had some reservations but I think that the general thrust of the argument was acceptable to him.

There was some difficulty in conveying our thinking to others. The ANC had established a committee in Soweto and one of our contacts with them was Ruth Matsowane who visited us on one or two occasions. She was a very impressive person, perhaps rather over-excitable and nervous. Nevertheless she was courageous and perfectly willing to take the risks in her role as a contact person with the leading group in Soweto.

Another contact was Bartholomew Hlapane, known to us as Arthur, whom we saw a great deal. He was a quiet man of middle-level status in the movement but who was chosen to play an important part during this period. However, he broke down under interrogation in 1963 and went on to give evidence against Mandela and others. I had an incredible experience on my own release from prison in 1965. While visiting Ruth Hayman, a solicitor in the centre of Johannesburg, I came face to face with Hlapane as the lift doors opened on the ground floor. He was wearing precisely the kind of khaki coat that I had worn while working clandestinely some years earlier. Hlapane had turned into one of the most notorious traitors of the movement.

THE PARTY EMERGES

There now follows an event that must undoubtedly be seen as historically critical, marking a turning point in the evolution of our struggle. I refer to the announcement of the existence of the Communist Party and the commencement of its independent public activity. Up to that time, the party had effectively operated as a small ginger group, developing policy and ideology within the wider Congress Movement. It was by no means concerned with theory alone, but actively discussed and promoted ideas and proposals for action within Congress. It did so subtly and, on the whole, sensitively, leading by persuasion.

But some party leaders wanted the party to do more than that, and sometime in the middle of the state of emergency, a special meeting of the leadership not in prison was held at our safe house. It was a small meeting of about six or seven people and included Joe Matthews who came especially from Lesotho disguised as an Indian merchant. In the midst of the discussion about the current situation, Michael Harmel raised the question of the party announcing its existence. He argued that with the banning of the ANC and the proscription of legal work, a new situation had arisen in which both the party and the ANC were in the same situation. There was therefore no formal reason for the party to maintain its former secrecy. Michael's statement was totally unexpected and a hush fell over the meeting as each of us digested it.

I saw Moses blanch and sit tight-lipped during Michael's presentation. Others shuffled their feet. After a lengthy pause, comments came and were generally cautious. People were feeling their way around the issue. Someone raised the question of the strength of the government and our own weakness, the danger of a backlash and the harm it might cause to unity within the Congress Alliance. Then Moses launched a strong attack, arguing that this was premature and unnecessary and that it would cause an enormous rift within the ANC. He thought it was wrong to make such a move while leaders were in prison and could not be consulted. Those who were not communists would feel they had been stabbed in the back. I had never experienced such a critical moment in my political life. Here were the two giants with whom I was in continuous contact and whose unity was essential to survival during the emergency and they were clashing over this most fundamental of issues. I wish I could now recall the details of the debate more clearly, but I was too stunned.

At the end of the discussion, each of us was asked for our view. I supported Michael, as did everyone else in the room, leaving Moses isolated and looking very miserable. He shuffled his feet, clasped and unclasped his hands nervously, and seemed to be pressed to the limit of his endurance. But he remained in control, accepted the decision and we moved on to discuss implementation. Michael and I drafted a leaflet that was approved by Moses and handed to our structures in Johannesburg. By this time a printing and distribution system had been set up and within a few weeks the leaflet was being distributed by our units in several parts of the country. Johannesburg was particularly effective. We now knew that the party had the nucleus of an independent system of operation that could also be used by the Congress Alliance. We established contacts with various individuals across the country for this purpose.

One of these was Archie Sibeko who had worked with me in the trade union movement who had evaded arrest and was now leading a clandestine life in the African townships in Cape Town. Archie was hiding out in the roofs of houses in the townships, apparently for several months, moving around and changing his location as we had done, but more vulnerable in the more exposed conditions of African townships.

We made other contacts around the country, gradually extending our network. Among those who worked with us in Johannesburg was Bob Hepple, a law lecturer at the University of Witwatersrand, who was involved in the trade union movement in Johannesburg and edited its weekly paper. He was a highly intelligent and capable man whose involvement in the movement was not known and so he was able to join us in various meetings and discussions. He proved to be extremely reliable and his youthful, fresh face was always welcome when he visited our little group. Bob became increasingly involved in the illegal work but cracked when he was detained. He subsequently gave a statement to the police, which led to his exclusion from the movement.

The emergence of the party gave an enormous lift to our morale, but there were outraged statements from the government once the leaflets were picked up by the press. We also knew that there would be awkward consequences within the movement. People like Helen Joseph who were not party members and who, although not anti-communist, were nevertheless known to have a basically liberal democrat ideology and to be resistant to Marxist doctrines. How would they react? How would the leaders of the Indian Congress and Chief Luthuli himself respond to the provocative act by the party? We did not know and would not find out until after the emergency when 'normal' activity resumed. Subsequently Helen let it be known that she felt a sense of deception in having worked so long with communists who had organised themselves into a party without her knowledge.

Over the years there have been individuals like Tennyson Makiwane and other African nationalists who articulated their opposition to this system of a party within the movement. And so they too attempted to organise factions, meeting separately and pushing for policies of their own, but none of these individual groups managed to sustain their factions, nor were they strong enough to prevent the party operating in its own way. It is probably a system without precedence in the history of national liberation movements and arguably no party has managed to insinuate its presence and influence on such a scale. While the emergence of the party eventually enabled relations with the Alliance to be formalised, it took some years, and arguably this matter has not been solved for all time.

END OF EMERGENCY

As August approached and calm fell over the country, so the government began to release detainees. We were not certain, however, that the emergency would come to an end, bringing to a close our underground existence. So we were not really prepared for 31 August when the emergency was formally ended and the remaining leaders were released. There followed a meeting of our group and the members of the Central Committee living in Johannesburg where Moses spoke about our work in the underground and where people like Bernstein and Slovo spoke with deep appreciation of the work we had done. It was a highly gratifying experience and Moses thereupon informed the meeting that the stewardship of the party was now being handed back to the Central Committee.

The question was raised about the return home of our group which might be problematic since we had launched the party into the open and could be held accountable for this by the state. The meeting concluded that the police would be unlikely to take action on this score. I raised the issue of the security of the movement itself in that there was no knowing how soon the situation in the country might deteriorate again and the leadership once again arrested. I proposed that a roster of the Central Committee be established with three people permanently underground. This would protect the leadership and oblige us to sustain an efficient underground apparatus for the future. I argued that if we all went home, a certain laxity would return and we would be unprepared for the next round of repression. My proposal received some support but there was considerable fatigue around and the desire to return home proved irresistible.

There was also an extended discussion on how the ANC might respond to its new condition of illegality. It was felt that the ANC should not follow the path of the party in 1950 into dissolution but resist any efforts to close it down, continuing to work normally as far as possible. It was thought that the ANC would certainly take this position and that is what happened. The signboards were taken down at ANC offices and letterheads were destroyed, but the same people returned to their offices and the

ANC structure continued functioning as before. Individuals were arrested here and there for wearing ANC badges or speaking in the name of the ANC. But this was grist to the mill since it kept the name of the organisation in the public eye and created an atmosphere of resistance. However, I felt that we ought to have kept some elements of the underground in preparation for the clashes to come. It seemed that some took the suggestion seriously and Ivan Schermbrucker told Mary that it had been decided that I should stay underground. She wept bitterly, saying that she couldn't stand it. It seems that this changed people's minds and I was allowed to go home.

My return home to Mary and the children was wonderful. The boys were ebullient and noisy as ever and we did all we could to make up for all the disruption, especially as we knew that there would be more to come. I went back to my work in the COD offices since it had not been banned and to the Congress secretariat that was now illegal. I became ever closer to Nokwe and Sisulu as we prepared for the next round.

While the urban areas were relatively quiet, resistance had flared in the rural areas, particularly in Pondoland. On 30 November 1960 the government imposed a state of emergency in Eastern Pondoland and other rural districts of the Transkei. This was in response to the development of violent protest in those areas arising from the imposition of taxation and soil conservation measures by reactionary chiefs and headmen. There were riots, the burning of huts and some stoning of white motorists. Tribal officials imposed by the government were murdered and armed resistance started by the 'Hill Committee'. Riot police and armed troops were brought in, there were mass arrests and the whole area was in a state of siege. By January 1961, 4 769 Africans were arrested in Pondoland with 2 000 brought to trial. Over 100 were charged with murder and many others with arson and other serious offences. By the time the Pondoland rebellion was suppressed, it had already lasted nine months and involved 180 000 people, making it the most important of the rural uprisings in the modern period.

The headquarters of the ANC was being briefed about these developments, particularly by Leonard Mdingi, an ANC cadre in Durban. But the situation was serious enough for a decision to send Tom Nkobi, a national organiser of the ANC, down to the area from Johannesburg and I was asked to drive him there. I was then still a member of the provincial council and could legitimately argue that I had constituents living in Pondoland who were migrant workers in Cape Town.

Tom and I drove to Durban, picked up Mdingi and proceeded to Bizana in the heart of Pondoland. There were police roadblocks in several places and armed police were dashing about in Land Rovers. My explanation was accepted and I was allowed to pass through, somewhat to my surprise. It is of course normal in South Africa for a white man to be accompanied by black employees and no questions were asked about the identity of my companions. Pondoland at that time of the year was a dust bowl. As we drove on the untarred roads, clouds of dust hung in the air, lending an eerie mood to the area. A normally rich and lush countryside was dry and brown, deepening our sense of foreboding in this seemingly hostile territory under white military occupation.

I registered at a small run-down hotel, more of a boarding house really, while Tom and Leonard sloped off to make contact with the Hill Committee. At 1 o'clock that night there was a knock on my door and I found Tom and Leonard waiting at the car. We drove to a spot some ten miles away, without lights and as quietly as we could. We arrived at a cluster of grass and mud huts to find four people waiting for us. Two of them were old men with that particular dignity etched on their faces that was a distinguishing characteristic of rural Africans in South Africa. They sat bolt upright and behaved as though they expected to be treated with great respect and deference. With them was a young ANC cadre known to us by reputation and who served as an interpreter.

Tom was naturally the leader of our little delegation and while he understood Xhosa reasonably well, the discussion was conducted in English for my benefit. Tom introduced himself and his role and asked for a briefing about the situation. The elders consulted before each reply. What was conveyed to us by the interpreter was the considered opinion of the whole group and the words were measured. What emerged was that they were the leaders of a kind of guerrilla war waged with ancient weapons once obtained from the Boers and kept secretly over decades.

They told us how the chiefs had imposed the oppressive measures of the government and how the people had risen first in protest and then in armed resistance. There were clashes between the small group of armed tribesmen and the police who arrived first on foot and then in helicopters. But the tribesmen were easily overpowered and the Hill Committee then launched a boycott of the white stores in the small towns of the region as a reprisal. The whole area was tense and anything could happen. They raised an unexpected issue. They wanted to know from Tom whether the ANC was going to give them the arms to take up the fight properly. Tom replied that armed struggle was not ANC policy even though the resistance of the Hill Committee was much admired. He undertook to carry the request back to Johannesburg and see what could be done.

Early in the morning, just before dawn, we drove back to the hotel feeling that we had met the most wonderful group of peasants and that it was time to review our own approach to resistance in the country. On our return to Johannesburg, in my first contact with Walter Sisulu, I reported on our trip and urged that the national executive review their relations with the peasantry and take full account of the potential for rebellion among the rural people based on the experience of the Pondoland revolt. I suggested that some mechanism for affiliating representation from these areas be looked at. Walter replied that there was a rural committee within the national executive and that Port Elizabeth and Durban both had extensive contacts in the rural areas. Nevertheless the point was taken. With hindsight, it seems to me that if the national executive had set about the task of linking itself more closely and directly with the rural areas, the subsequent launch of the armed struggle would have been greatly facilitated. I was asked to write a pamphlet on my visit and did so, but found myself sorely circumscribed, being unable to reveal my contacts with the Hill Committee and what I had learned there.

THE PARTY ON VIOLENCE

Towards the end of 1960, I was asked to assist with the organisation of a special meeting of the party, though I was not told its purpose. I drove a minibus, picked up various individuals and was directed to a large vacant house in a white suburb. We set about preparing the premises for a meeting of some 20 participants who arrived in small groups, having been ferried there in minibuses and cars hired specially for the purpose. Soon there gathered some of the top national leaders of the movement and we set about our business.

It became evident that we were about to review the whole character of our struggle and introduce a new phase that was to change everything. Rusty Bernstein read a document about the need to create an armed force since the old ways of struggle were now so circumscribed, with the state willing to resort to the most extreme forms of repression to defend the system. Rusty then read a resolution, which was adopted without opposition, and the piece of paper was then burned in front of the meeting and the ashes thrown through a trap door in the floor of the room. This rather dramatic procedure served to highlight the seriousness of the decision and we were all sworn to total secrecy. We all knew that we had passed over into a new epoch in the country's history and that the consequences for us, collectively and individually, could be extremely serious.

The issue of violence was also being raised within the ANC at the same time. I was not privy to all these discussions but I knew that there were many contacts on the go. Some of these were to explain why the party had emerged and Moses was sent to Luthuli to ease the way for acceptance of what had happened. Others like Maulvi Cachalia, a leading figure of the Transvaal Congress, were also contacted for the same purpose. But the traditional struggle methods were not immediately discarded.

South Africa was to be declared a Republic on 31 May 1961 and there was widespread opposition to this move. Congress decided that it would be a good moment to put our position across so a decision was taken to call for a national stay-at-home organised by the National Action Council of the joint Congresses. A group of us consisting of Yusuf Cachalia and a few others moved to a safe house. I remember wearing a brown overall and peaked cap of the kind worn by railway workers, which disguised my identity quite effectively. I was told that it was not only necessary to avoid being recognised by one's facial features but that the way one walked could be equally revealing. The long railway coat was very helpful there.

The campaign began, we issued a large amount of publicity and the stay-at-home was very effective on the first day. But we had once again underestimated the determination of the government and the power of the police. On the first day they arrested picketers throughout the African townships and prevented any open organisation. From early in the morning on the second day they went from door to door, threatening anyone staying at home, often forcing people out of their houses. The brutality of the police was marked. They beat people up, in some cases urinated on people in bed, beat up parents in front of their children, compound workers in the mines, docks and railways were taken to work under armed escort and there was widespread harassment. The result was that the second day was less effective and Mandela, who was in hiding, announced to the press that the strike was not as successful as expected because of police intimidation, and he was calling the action off.

MANDELA'S NEW ROLE

In March 1961 the bans placed on Mandela temporarily lapsed and he made a dramatic appearance at the All-In Conference of opposition groups held in Pietermaritzburg on 25-26 March. The object of the conference was to unite the differing tendencies among Africans, but it largely failed in this objective. Mandela emerged as an impassioned speaker. His speech made a great impact and set the scene for his new role as the underground leader of Congress.

Disappearing after the conference, Mandela moved secretly between various safe houses before taking up residence at Lilliesleaf farm in Rivonia, north of Johannesburg, a property rented as an underground headquarters by the movement. In January 1962, he secretly left the country to travel to Algeria, Ghana and various other countries to negotiate for military and diplomatic support. He was away for some months, having been highly successful at winning important commitments from many heads of state who received him as an equal.

While he was in hiding in Johannesburg, I met with him on several occasions at a number of venues. Nelson wore a blue overall with a peaked cap, which was the common uniform for a driver. At one time he lived in a small flat rented from Wolfie Kodesh where he read the works of Clausewitz on theories of war. Nelson was clearly preparing himself to become a military leader. It was quite remarkable how well he took to his confinement. He was keeping fit with weights and skipping rope and his morale was very high. Never upset by minor discomforts – he was sleeping on a folding camp bed in a tiny flat – he was always cheerful and ebullient, a little like a coiled spring, ready for his destiny.

His smile was welcoming and he was outgoing in his manner and kindly in his interest in one's personal problems. I thought that he was unlikely to survive for long in his situation partly because he was so keen to be involved and to meet others. I also thought it rather unfair that the rest of us should be leading a relatively normal life with our families while Nelson was playing out the role of 'symbol from the underground'. But this was what had been decided and I knew that it was only a transitional moment in the struggle when each one of us could once again land up in a similar situation.

THE FOUNDING OF UMKHONTO WE SIZWE (MK)

A few months later I was visited at the COD office by a very excited Jack Hodgson who told me that there were moves to begin a sabotage campaign. Although he was a banned member of the Congress of Democrats, Jack was often involved in other 'special' duties about which he was extraordinarily secretive. He told me that an organisation was being set up to carry out sabotage throughout the country and I was being invited to become a member and lead a unit. My reply was that I was quite agreeable in principle, but I could not see how I could play that kind of role at this time. I was holding three key positions in the COD, on the secretariat and in the party, and I could not see how I could either give up those duties or be effective as a saboteur. In addition, my photograph appeared frequently in the press and I was often recognised in public.

Jack explained that what they had in mind was that we should create units which in the first instance would burgle explosive dumps on the gold mines to acquire the explosives needed for a sabotage campaign. I would have to conduct surveillance of an explosives store on the mines. I expressed my doubts about the wisdom of this, but Jack insisted. I also felt little confidence in Jack who, although the nicest of individuals on a personal level, was not the most effective of comrades. However I agreed and was duly informed that I had been formally recruited and appointed to lead a unit.

During the following weeks Jack came to the office full of enthusiasm for his new role. He showed me glass phials and bits of rubber and other gadgets that he was using to create some equipment, which I thought rather amateurish. By November a national high command of Umkhonto we Sizwe (Spear of the Nation, literally) which came to known simply as MK, had been established and, unknown to me, the first men dispatched overseas apparently to China for military training. In the townships there was a rising clamour for guns to defend people against police repression. But the leadership was convinced that any move to violence had to be controlled and directed by a centralised apparatus that had to speedily acquire the techniques of armed struggle.

MK started as a very small organisation open to all races, thereby marking a major change from the separation of races within the Congress Alliance. A gradual network of regional commands was established whose task it was to set up four-man units to prepare for sabotage. The regional commands were responsible for selecting specific targets, and they were given a certain degree of autonomy for this purpose. Members were instructed to develop their own schemes in the manufacture and use of explosives and encouraged to build a stockpile of bombs.

I was invited to a meeting with Nelson Mandela and Joe Modise to discuss some strategic issues. I was surprised at the choice of Joe for such a difficult role as I had known him during the Treason Trial as one of the young 'Turks' in Soweto, notorious as a youth leader who could resort to tough measures when needed, but who had not shown any special political leadership capacity. My selection was no doubt due to the fact that I had trained as a land surveyor and was probably one of the few members with that kind of know-how. Our discussion was about the need to look at the logistics of South Africa's infrastructure and how it could be disrupted. We acquired a complete set of cadastral maps and I was asked to examine key communication links – road links, railway lines and so on. I concluded that a small group of highly skilled saboteurs could do a great deal of damage by selecting key targets that were critical in linking the major centres of the country. On the other hand, it seemed that there were few areas that offered a safe haven for a group of guerrillas.

I was also involved in the setting up of a broadcast to be made by Walter Sisulu over a mobile radio station announcing the emergence of MK. Rusty Bernstein had assembled a technical group that had acquired a large portable aerial that could transmit from a roving truck so that the signal could not be used to pinpoint the source. My task was a humble one. I had been learning to play a treble recorder during the Treason Trial and I was asked to play *Nkosi Sikelel' iAfrika*, our ANC anthem. We set up the recording equipment in an office for Walter to make his announcement but when my turn came, I was so excited that I fluffed it. I simply could not play the tune accurately, so they had to use a taped version instead.

Elsewhere around the country, preparations for the launch of MK were proceeding at a hectic pace. Harold Strachan, then in Port Elizabeth, was one of the first self-taught experts in explosives. He was a history lecturer at a technical college, but he also had great technical talent. He spent much time in the local library reading books on chemistry, gradually acquiring a set of chemicals which he then made into homemade bombs. He was put under great time pressure by the leadership so that there was insufficient time to study the process seriously, and he was working on a hit-and-miss basis in his own garage. On one occasion he took a bomb to the beach in order to test its explosive powers. It wouldn't go off and he sat at a distance, mesmerised as a group of children approached, heading for the bomb. He was then forced to go up to the bomb itself and kick it to make it explode – but nothing happened. The children passed by and he was left to dismantle the apparatus in a cold sweat. When he was arrested the police found all the evidence they needed as he did not have the resources to work in a safe place.

Similar activity was taking place across the country. I myself was too busy with political work to be involved in the practical preparations, but I knew what was going on and I had formed a four-man unit and identified the Rissik Street Post Office near our office as a suitable target. The post office was an old building, much of its interior made of wood, and on the first floor were located the offices of magistrates who were responsible for the sentencing of Africans under the pass laws so symbolic of apartheid.

I 'cased' the place and thought that it would be an easy matter to place an arson device on top of the phone booths on the ground floor. A colleague inspected the other floors and thought there were other suitable locations upstairs. And so it was that on 15 December 1961 I met with Rusty Bernstein and Jack Hodgson in a restaurant in the centre of Johannesburg, where I was given a parcel containing four canisters normally used for tennis balls. Each canister contained a chemical that would become highly inflammable when in contact with sulphuric acid.

The chemical was normally used in welding in order to burn at a very high temperature. With the canisters were four glass phials filled with sulphuric acid and sealed with a rubber stopper. I was told that it would take eight hours for the sulphuric acid to burn through the rubber so that after the phial was placed in the canister, the acid would ignite the chemical, causing a fierce fire.

We planned to place these canisters in the post office in the late afternoon so that the fire would break out eight hours later, in the middle of the night when the building was empty. Sitting in the restaurant with Rusty and Jack, my stomach was in knots and my hands were clammy. I was not the only one in a total funk. Rusty's hands were shaking uncontrollably and he was embarrassed by it. Jack was rather more buoyant and seemed to be enjoying himself. For him, it seemed more of a prank than a dangerous exercise.

Jack and I left the restaurant to drive to the venue where we would meet my two colleagues in the unit. I found that our mode of transport was Jack's own car, a rather dilapidated little two-seater that was well known not only throughout the movement, but also to the police. This was a total breach of our security rules in that a known car was never to be used for secret work. But there could be no retreat at this stage. I became even more uneasy when Jack asked me to drive because he had certain little jobs to do. As I pulled away from the kerb, Jack began inserting the glass phials into the containers. It was at the intersection of Market and Eloff Streets that calamity struck.

Suddenly, a burst of smoke filled the car and I thought we were about to explode. I brought the car to a halt in the middle of this intersection, the busiest in the whole of Johannesburg, scrambled out of the car and moved away. I was about ten paces off when I realised that Jack had remained in the car, so I went back and got in again. I saw that he had opened his door and kicked the offending canister, which was now emitting thick smoke, into the street. Cool as you like, he bent down and retrieved the canister, leaving the smouldering powder in the street, closed the door and said: 'Get moving.' By that time, however, a traffic cop had appeared at his window, which Jack then opened, and to the question 'What's going on?' he answered, 'Oh, some fireworks have gone off.'

A crowd had gathered, but I managed to start the car and speed off down Market Street, while Jack continued to place the rest of the phials in the other canisters. I urged him to call off the action since our equipment was obviously faulty and since dozens of people had been standing at the street corner waiting to cross over. But Jack insisted that we go ahead and, since he was the senior command, I had to agree. I did not know that my eyebrows had been singed off, my hair burned and my suit filled with dozens of little burn holes. We drove to a parking lot off Market Street to meet our comrades. I had two suitcases in the trunk of the car where I placed the canisters, wrapped in brown paper, being careful to wipe them clean of fingerprints.

Walking up Market Street was a nightmare. I thought the whole world knew I was carrying a bomb and that my fear was visible to all. I also expected the device to explode at any moment, killing me and any passersby. I arrived at the post office in a terrible sweat. I placed the bomb in the predetermined place on top of the telephone kiosk, even though there were people in the post office who might have noticed something. My partners went upstairs and one bomb was placed in the desk of a native commissioner while another was hidden behind the cistern in a toilet. We departed rapidly, each going his own way.

I drove home and Mary immediately asked me what had happened. It was then that I learned that I had been singed by the bomb and my suit ruined. Since the rule of membership was on the 'need to know' principle, she had not known that I was a member of MK and I offered no explanation. I merely took off my suit and took it to the dry cleaners straight away. There was nothing I could do about my singed hair, but I managed to comb it in a way that disguised what had happened.

At about 6.00 p.m. there was a phone call from Benjamin Pogrund, a reporter on the *Rand Daily Mail,* who asked me whether it was indeed I who had been seen by a traffic policeman at the intersection of Market and Eloff Streets running away from a burning car. Imagine my chagrin at having been spotted and reported to the press! I denied it, pointing out that my own car was red, not green and that the witness had been mistaken. Pogrund pressed long and hard, so I knew I had been correctly identified.

That evening, Mary and I went to the cinema in the centre of Johannesburg. My mind was certainly not on the film and afterwards I drove slowly past Rissik Street Post Office to see if anything had happened. Mary asked me what the matter was and I was not able to tell her, but she knew that I was on edge. When she read the newspaper the next day, everything became clear. She was rather resentful at not having known about my MK role and we discussed this. Certainly, she had to pay as high a price as I did. She had previously been left with the children while I was in hiding and she had to face the police when I was away. But our security demanded this kind of balance and she was bound to accept the arrangement.

The next morning the *Rand Daily Mail* carried the story about my having been involved in a strange episode with some explosives in a car, and I decided to consult Rusty and Joe. We decided that I should skip for a few days and see what the police's reaction would be. I went home, packed a suitcase and returned to one of the safe houses we had used during the emergency, feeling rather deflated by what had been intended to be the launching of the armed struggle.

The *Mail* carried several other stories as well. I learned that there had been nationwide action in most of the large centres with bombs and attacks on electricity pylons and other government installations to launch the armed intervention of MK. In Soweto, one man accidentally blew himself up, which was a harsh reminder that armed struggle would bring casualties.

The same evening, 16 December 1961, Walter made his broadcast, setting the whole country on edge. It said:

> Units of Umkhonto we Sizwe today carried out planned attacks against Government installations, particularly those connected with the policy of apartheid and race discrimination.
>
> Umkhonto we Sizwe is a new, independent body, formed by Africans. It includes in its ranks South Africans of all races. It is not connected in any way with a so-called 'Committee for National Liberation' whose existence has been announced in the press. Umkhonto we Sizwe will carry on the struggle for freedom and democracy by new methods, which are necessary to complement the actions of the established national liberation organisations. Umkhonto we Sizwe fully supports the national liberation movement, and our members, jointly and individually, place themselves under the overall political guidance of that movement.
>
> It is, however, well known that the main national liberation organisations in this country have consistently followed a policy of non-violence. They have conducted themselves peaceably at all times, regardless of Government attacks and persecutions upon them, and despite all Government-inspired attempts to provoke them to violence. They have done so because the people prefer peaceful methods of change to achieve their aspirations without the suffering and bitterness of civil war. But the people's patience is not endless.
>
> The time comes in the life of any nation when there remain only two choices: submit or fight. That time has now come to South Africa. We shall not submit and we have no choice but to hit back by all means within our power in defence of our people, our future and our freedom.
>
> The Government has interpreted the peacefulness of the movement as weakness; the people's non-violent policies have been taken as a green light for Government violence. Refusal to resort to force has been interpreted by the Government as an invitation to use armed force against the people without any fear of reprisals. The methods of Umkhonto we Sizwe mark a break with that past.

We are striking out along a new road for the liberation of the people of this country. The Government policy of force, repression and violence will no longer be met with non-violent resistance only! The choice is not ours; it has been made by the Nationalist Government which has rejected every peaceable demand by the people for rights and freedom and answered every demand with force and yet more force! Twice in the past 18 months, virtual martial law has been imposed in order to beat down peaceful, non-violent strike actions of the people in support of their rights. It is now preparing its forces – enlarging and re-arming its armed forces and drawing the white civilian population into commandos and pistol clubs – for full-scale military actions against the people. The Nationalist Government has chosen the course of force and massacre, now, deliberately, as it did at Sharpeville.

Umkhonto we Sizwe will be at the front line of the people's defence. It will be the fighting arm of the people against the Government and its policies of race oppression. It will be the striking force of the people for liberty, for rights and for their final liberation! Let the Government, its supporters who put it into power, and those whose passive toleration of reaction keeps it in power, take note of where the Nationalist Government is leading the country!

We of Umkhonto we Sizwe have always sought – as the liberation movement has sought – to achieve liberation without bloodshed and civil clash. We do so still. We hope – even at this late hour – that our first actions will awaken everyone to a realisation of the disastrous situation to which the Nationalist policy is leading. We hope that we will bring the Government and its supporters to their senses before it is too late, so that both Government and its policies can be changed before matters reach the desperate stage of civil war and military rule.

In these actions, we are working in the best interest of all the people of this country – black, brown and white – whose future happiness and wellbeing cannot be attained without the overthrow of the Nationalist Government, the abolition of white supremacy and the winning of liberty and democracy and full national rights and equality for all the people of this country.

We appeal for the support and encouragement of all South Africans who seek the happiness and freedom of the people of this country.

Afrika Mayibuye

[T Karis and GM Gerhart, *From Protest to Challenge* 13, Hoover Institution Press, 1977, p.716.]

The same day, three cars with the top Witwatersrand police officers pulled up at our house. At home with the children, Mary was confronted by the police who demanded to know where I was. She denied all knowledge of my whereabouts, whereupon they searched the house, fortunately finding nothing to incriminate her or me. The next few days abounded with tension as more and more incidents were reported around the country, and the press filled with news and comment about this new phase of the struggle.

After about five days in hiding, I learned the leadership had reviewed my position. There were several options. I could either leave the country, stay underground or go home. Slovo's view was that if the police had real evidence about my involvement in the explosions they would have disclosed their hand by now. It was thought that, at most, they had only read the report in the paper and possibly obtained some information from a passerby. And so I went back home, full of anxiety but willing to face it out rather than take one of the other more drastic courses. I thought myself very lucky, and for some time it seemed that I would get away with it.

But I was concerned about the amateurishness and bungling of the operation. I went to see Joe Slovo to say that I thought the whole operation had been schoolboyish. My interview with Joe took place in his office in chambers and I was surprised to see that he felt no compunction about discussing these matters in the presence of the telephone on his desk. We understood that the telephone, even when it is part of a switchboard system, is an easy source of listening by the police. Having conveyed my views, I was willing to leave it to him to decide on any other measures. In the meanwhile, we were to lie low while MK reviewed its work and prepared for the next phase.

Over the next 18 months there were 193 attacks, 72 minor and 95 incendiary bomb attacks. A further seven were more ambitious, attempting to destroy railway signal stations and electrical installations. Fifty-eight were in Port Elizabeth, 35 in Cape Town, 31 in Johannesburg and 29 in Durban. There were several attacks on policemen and collaborators, though MK denied responsibility for these, maintaining its position that our targets were only installations and buildings.

THE FINGERPRINT SAGA

As the weeks passed, I was counting my blessings at having survived my debacle of December 16. Our device seemed not to have gone off at all and Rissik Street Post Office remained a constant reminder of our ineptitude and amateurishness. But my complacency was not to last. In April 1962, an Israeli journalist came to Johannesburg seeking an interview with Walter Sisulu. I was asked to set up a meeting at Kathrada's flat, which was conveniently located near the ANC offices in the centre of Johannesburg. Kathy provided tea and biscuits so that we could claim that it was a social occasion and not a 'gathering'.

It was a Saturday morning at about 11.00 a.m. and the four of us were happily ensconced in Kathy's lounge when the Special Branch burst in rudely and arrested Walter, Kathy and me for attending a gathering. We were taken off to Marshall Square Police Station where we were locked up separately for four days. Unpleasant as Marshall Square was, I was not unduly distressed, especially as Mary arranged for me to receive food and clean clothing from outside. But my equanimity was disturbed by repeated visits of the Special Branch who seemed to have a peculiar interest in my fingerprints. On at least four occasions I was taken to an office and each of my fingers repeatedly tested as well as the palms of my hands. I had no idea what this was all about, but had no special reason to be fearful.

However, all became clear three weeks later when the Special Branch arrived at the COD office to arrest me. At first they would say nothing. They searched the office thoroughly, then took me home and searched the house more rigorously than ever before. I was then taken to the Greys, a large office block housing the headquarters of the Special Branch. It was there that I learned how a fingerprint had given me away on the 16 December action at Rissik Street Post Office.

CHAPTER 5

PRISON

There followed the most arduous period of my life, destined to test my character to the full. But it also gave me scope to reflect on the events of the previous years. I came to the conclusion that the 1960 emergency was a nodal point in the evolution of the struggle. Perhaps my judgement is biased by the depth of my involvement in those events, but I am sure that the review of our policies that began then laid the basis for what followed. As I recall my past reflections now, I am increasingly conscious that I am the sole survivor of the underground, which makes it even more important that I not only record these thoughts, as mentioned earlier, but try to be as objective and accurate as I can.

There are three crucial issues about the five-month emergency. First, we made systematic use of underground methods to develop new structures for the movement. Second, the use of violence as an alternative form of struggle was proposed for the first time. Third, the Communist Party emerged in its own name. Each of these represents a major turning point with very significant consequences for the struggle.

On violence, perhaps the main argument was that the movement had been given some very hard knocks by the state in the second half of the 1950s and there was a desperate need to show that we could hit back. Some senior leaders, like Chief Luthuli, had argued that there were no grounds for turning to violence until we had explored all other methods. He said that none of our strikes had been fully supported nationally, showing that we had not yet been able to fully mobilise the masses for peaceful means. Until we had fully explored all peaceful means the turn to violence was not justified. On the other hand, most of us felt that we had reached the limits of non-violence and a change was badly needed. We thought that sabotage would provide the kind of shocks the country needed both to warn the state and to inspire the masses.

Frantz Fanon had made the same point about Algeria, where the people had also reached the conclusion that French suppression had become so overwhelming that the masses were in danger of demoralisation. In Vietnam, too, it was felt that demonstrative strikes were necessary to raise the spirit of struggle among the masses, so they infiltrated small armed groups into the rural areas to inflict blows and then filter away. These groups came from outside and organised a local community. They then used violence against a local tyrant which served as a detonator to raise the morale of the people and encourage them to do the same. But we knew the detonator principle had its own dangers. A large gap may develop between the leading force instigating this kind of action and the masses who may not be ready to respond. We had to be reasonably sure that our actions would not lead to our isolation.

Another problem facing us was that should we ratchet up the struggle, we could not foresee the consequences. We had always understood that every action on our part must take account of the enemy's counter-action. Our best course now was to move to violence in a staged manner, enabling us to gauge the response, but knowing full well that the retaliation would be massive, and we had to avoid the destruction of our movement. It was therefore hoped that by carefully delineating our targets we could minimise the possibility, as far as possible, of the loss of human life. Our object, it should be noted, was not simply to bring pressure on the state but also to create new confidence in the struggle among the masses, which would of course expand and strengthen our capacity to hit the state.

I suppose that most of us would accept that we underestimated that response. While MK succeeded in building a substantial organisation and engaged in a large number of actions, there were also weaknesses in the setting up of structures which could withstand the coming onslaught by the state.

We were also uncertain about how the white population as a whole would react to violence. The statement issued by MK on

16 December 1961 showed, perhaps, a certain naivete on this question. At the back of our minds there was a deep conviction that we had to place the onus for the coming violence on the state and to give the authorities scope for reversing their policies. Govan Mbeki, on the other hand, was quite clear that the die was cast and that the government, and indeed the white population as a whole, would unite against the movement and that there would necessarily follow a strong reaction.

Nevertheless, the point is worth stressing that throughout its history the ANC had always left the door open to a peaceful and negotiated settlement. At the opening of the Defiance Campaign, letters were sent to the prime minister calling for negotiations; during the Treason Trial speeches by the accused and the defence made the same point; and Sisulu's broadcast was in the same vein. The reasonable posture of ANC leaders was always there for those who were prepared to talk. Subsequent events, in the late 1980s, revealed the same spirit.

But for now, the movement began preparing for violence. It was to be expected that some leaders did not enthuse as much as others. Moses Kotane felt very uneasy about what was going on. I seem to recall that he was abroad in the early stages of the development of MK, but I do remember that he came to the COD office on one occasion, almost certainly after the December 16 events, and asked me to come outside the office where he then asked me why we had done such stupid things. He said: 'Don't you know that if you throw stones at people's windows they are likely to come out and break your neck? So don't do it unless you know what you are doing and what the consequences are likely to be.' I was uneasy about Moses's concerns and pleased that he had sufficient confidence in my own judgement to raise them with me. Indeed, by then we had a warm, close relationship.

I believe that Moses's opposition to our actions was due to a feeling that the movement lacked the capacity to carry through the kind of campaign we had begun. But perhaps he did not appreciate that an entirely new momentum had to be imparted to the struggle if the movement was to retain its credibility. In a sense, we were also continuing a long-standing tradition in Congress that drama remain an essential ingredient in political tactics. The Defiance Campaign, the Congress of the People, the Pound-a-Day Campaign, the Western Areas Removal Campaign – all these were projected in a dramatic form in order to arouse and inspire the masses. This was Congress's style. The actions of 16 December held to that tradition although it has to be said that there clearly was inadequate attention to organisational matters and to the creation of a sustainable strategy and tactics which could withstand the responses from the state.

We nevertheless now became caught up in a campaign of undercover work and sabotage, which required that we acquire a whole new set of skills. We were aware that these methods had been used with great success elsewhere in the world and began to inquire how it was done. We also knew that what we had embarked on was not simply military in nature. Some of us had read the work of Menachim Begin who was a leader of the Irgun and Stern gang in Israel and who survived three years underground during the British occupation of what became Israel. His account of his concealment in cupboards and other hiding places while the British security forces searched widely showed us that it was possible to survive in the underground in the cities. We also read books about the French Resistance during the war and accounts of how the Sons of England tried to establish British intelligence and commando activity behind enemy lines during the Second World War.

We scoured the shelves of the public libraries for insights into how secret undercover action and organisation might be developed. It was not easy to develop our own strategy and tactics, largely because we were isolated from international experiences of this kind. We had no possibility of talking to and learning directly from the experiences of the Cubans, Algerians and others and so we learned through texts and through trial and error. No doubt many of our inadequacies stemmed from this isolation and lack of experience.

We lived at a time of the people's victory in so many areas. Cuba was the inspiration of many millions of young people. Che Guevara was a folk hero throughout the world, having stirred the imagination with his bold advocacy of armed struggle as a legitimate and effective means of change throughout the world. We also saw the flourishing of internationalism inspired by radicalism and struggle against authority, which embraced us and drove us on.

It was this favourable international climate which in 1960 encouraged the SA Communist Party to publish the *African Communist*, a quarterly journal edited by Michael Harmel. It was designed to be a forum for discussion across the African continent and beyond that.

We were inspired by Lenin's 'April Thesis', Dimitrov's 'Work on the United Front' and, of course, the excellent study on 'Protracted War' by Mao Tse-Tung. What was particularly inspiring was the way Che Guevara and Mao treated the rural areas as a base for revolution. This was a departure from the classical Marxist/Leninist view that revolution was primarily the business of the urban proletariat, depending in the first instance on trade union struggle and proletarian solidarity.

As I have indicated in Chapter 4 my experience in Pondoland led me to the view that the ANC had also too sharp a focus on the urban areas, and gave insufficient weight to the enormous political potential of the countryside. Furthermore, Mao's emphasis on 'people's democracy' contrasted with the more traditional Marxist conception of a proletarian democracy or the dictatorship of the proletariat. However, we had to face the fact that South Africa's geophysical character was not largely conducive to the kind of terrain suitable for guerrilla warfare. With the exception of Zululand and the Eastern Cape, there were few locations where base areas could be set up. Nevertheless, we began to understand the importance of rural revolt.

Deeply steeped in these texts, I now saw myself as a typical communist revolutionary. I held senior posts in the ANC, SACP and MK. My personal life was now overtaken by my being swamped with work; I was constantly in meetings. Mary had also become fully integrated into the work of the COD as chair of the Johannesburg branch while trying hard not to neglect the boys. They were very boisterous, vigorous and noisy, but they provided a richness to our lives that was immeasurable. It was my removal from their presence that gave me unbearable pain when I was arrested.

ARREST AND PRISON

The most burly of them locked the door behind me. It was a fine touch, calculated to emphasise that I was now cut off from my world. He glanced at me with deep hostility as if to say, 'No one can help you now.' I looked around the room. There were six of them, six hefty Special Branch police, all glaring at me as though I were the most despicable cur on earth.

The major I knew from past encounters at meetings and raids was seated at a desk. 'Sit down,' he said tilting his head toward a chair. I was pleased to do so. He cleared his throat while I wondered what drama was in store for me. 'Mr Turok, we have evidence that you were connected with an attempt to commit arson at Rissik Street Post Office,' he said. 'Do you wish to make a statement?' He sharpened his pencil while my temples were pounding. I was fighting hard to keep the flush out of my face.

'No, I have nothing to say.'

He stared hard at me, made a note on the paper in front of him and leaned back in his chair. 'Your name in full?' I gave it to him. 'Your address?' I gave it to him. The routine had been drilled into me by our lawyers. 'Anything to add?' I shook my head. 'Well, Turok, we've got you this time.'

He stood up, short and tough inside his blue worn suit, opened the door and beckoned to his men to take me out. Rather unsteady on my feet, I left the room and proceeded down the poorly lit passage. Soon I was in the charge office at Marshall Square police station surrounded by four burly plainclothes policemen. This time it was really serious. No bail, nothing like that for sabotage. The formalities over, I was led up a flight of stairs, through a steel-barred gate and into a tiny musty cell. There was a mattress on the floor, a few blankets and that was all. Behind me the door clanged shut and I was alone.

Marshall Square is an old building steeped in political history. It has housed the most renowned rebels in South Africa's stormy past and every political movement has had some of its leaders incarcerated within its dingy walls. There have been trade unionists, saboteurs, mutineers and political protesters of every shade of opinion inside its blackness. I mused that even members of the present Nationalist cabinet had been held there. But now they had forgotten about its black depths, forgetting too, as do so many former political prisoners, that failure to improve their old prisons could prove very painful should they return there themselves. No one is immune. And so Marshall Square has outlived many of its notable inhabitants, remaining a formidable dank house of iron bars. It continues to receive political and other dissidents with profound indifference to their welfare.

A prisoner in Marshall Square gets no exercise since its architects made no provision for this luxury. The windows are painted to make them barely translucent and the walls are black up to seven feet from the floor. The toilets suffer from fatigue and overflow constantly. Judging by the thick crust of dirt in the basins, they have remained uncleaned for many years. The general filth and decay induces a deep depression.

The air is heavy and stale food, cold on arrival, is brought in from the police barracks some distance away. For those obliged to eat from the tin dish it brings no comfort. But I was fortunate. Mary brought me food daily and I knew the movement would act speedily to mobilise legal defence and moral support. But they could not bring me fresh air and the stench hung all around me, aggravated by the overpowering closeness of the hot stuffy cell, bringing on a violent headache. Going to court to be formally charged was a holiday from claustrophobia.

Marshall Square did not keep me long. The officer in charge was fed up with the constant inquiries, the food parcels, my daily newspapers. All this was an affront to his sense of propriety and a violation of his power over me. I was soon transferred to the Fort.

This is an even more illustrious name in South African politics – home for many months to the leaders of the 1915 rebellion, the 1922 strike, treason trialists in 1956 and other rebels throughout the country's stormy political life. It made me quite proud. The large van backed up to the huge solid gates, the door was flung open and I was ordered into the entrance passage. On either side there were wall cavities for the defending riflemen of earlier years. I was led into a narrow passage which opened into a small hall whose dark grey walls and oppressively low ceiling were lit by a tiny bulb. The walls were dark grey and the ceiling oppressively low. In one corner about 20 subdued Africans were squatting in neat rows of four. An African warder armed with a stick and assegai stood over them.

It struck me that this was where I had first seen the hundred or so treason trialists in 1956. We had greeted each other with the thumbs-up salute, triumphantly, as though we were celebrities taking over the prison. My present visit was less sensational. I was alone, outside of the criminal fraternity around me. Reception formalities over, my watch and clothes taken away, my money stored in a bag, I was given a blue card marking my new status as an awaiting-trial prisoner. I was taken to the clean offices of the colonel who was remarkably courteous and personally conducted me to a barred room that proved to be a hospital ward. Five prisoners were waiting for me and we were to spend the next two-and-a-half months together. I was allocated a bed and noticed an open toilet in the corner, a table and some chairs in the middle of the room, all a marked change from my cell in Marshall Square. My fellow prisoners were a mixed lot: a cheque forger, an illegal massage parlour manager, others awaiting trial for theft, burglary and so on. They were friendly enough, especially Van Breda, who was very interested in my case and who had himself been interned during the war with the storm troopers of the Ossewabrandwag and with John Vorster, who was then Minister of Justice and later became prime minister. While Vorster was making his way up the political ladder, Van Breda fell into crime and had already served several sentences for fraud.

I enjoyed talking to him. He was shrewd and knowledgeable, but also dangerous. He was clearly fencing with me, probing deeply despite his apparently easygoing manner. Yet he did not hide his political views or his sympathy for fascism: 'The English told a lot of lies about the war. Buchenwald was a fake, the allies made it up. Hitler was a genius and our John Vorster is following in his path. If Germany had won the war there would have been no Nkrumah, and none of the raping of nuns in the Congo. The kaffirs will never do that here, we'll kill the lot of them.' Yet, crude as he was, our arguments passed the time.

We were allowed out for exercise in a small 10 by 15-yard area adjacent to our cell block surrounded by high walls and a brick building housing segregation prisoners brought from other prisons to face further charges.

We lived very comfortably in our ward. The beds were clean, we all ate the abundant food I received daily from outside and there was plenty to read. My defence was proceeding satisfactorily and I was visited on several occasions by Joe Slovo who was in charge. Joe was extremely solicitous and concerned about my situation. He had briefed the top QC in the country and they had worked out an explanation to account for the fingerprint on the brown paper wrapper on the incendiary device found in the Rissik Street Post Office. The device had failed to go off, partly because it was starved of oxygen in the closed drawer of the magistrate's desk, leaving part of the envelope intact. Joe asked me to write down a possible line of defence for us to consider.

As time passed two incidents disturbed my equanimity. I was sitting on my bed one day when I noticed something gleaming in my shoe. Closer inspection revealed a particle of the chemical from the bomb and quite a number of others. In fact my shoes were a total giveaway and there I was sitting in a cell with five criminals, each of whom would have given a great deal for the chance to put me away to earn some good marks, privileges or even remission from the authorities. At the next visit I asked Mary to send me another pair of shoes to replace mine, but as visits were conducted through a wire-mesh grill in a small room simultaneously with at least four other prisoners and in the presence of warders, I couldn't explain why on earth I should want to change shoes. We had a bit of a shouting match but she agreed and the next day I sent out the offending shoes and was more at ease. But only partly so.

A bitter row had broken out between Van Breda and Jim, the massage-parlour man who was growing steadily more ratty as the case against him was closing in. Since he had already served a long sentence he now faced the prospect of getting a 'blue coat', that is, nine to fifteen years. Jim began to lose his temper at the slightest offence and seemed dangerously violent. On one such occasion he unexpectedly turned to me and said, 'I hate these bastards here, Ben. But you are a gentleman. It's a disgrace that you should be locked up with us with instructions to inform on you.'

My stomach turned. All was now clear. Together with my five fellow inmates, I had received VIP prison treatment for two months for the sole purpose of loosening my tongue sufficiently to give myself and perhaps many others away. And this was why Van Breda had been so persistent in his questions. I now slept with the notes I had been writing for my defence concealed in my pyjamas. I told Joe what had happened and he explained that this is fairly 'normal' and that I should be particularly careful in my conversation, especially as the trial was close. He was confident about the outcome.

Ready to grasp at this straw, I felt fairly optimistic but rather tense nevertheless. I would have to give evidence and this might lead to questioning about the use of violence by the movement, but I was well prepared for this. I was advised, however, not to flaunt my views too brazenly and to stick to the issues at hand.

Preoccupied as I was with my own fate, and with the escalating struggle outside, I was also fascinated by events in the prison. We were now exercising in a larger yard and had been moved into the general section of the prison. Each prisoner was held in a wire cage about six feet square and four feet high, not high enough to stand up in. There was a mattress and blankets and a pot for slopping out. This was done in the early morning when a disgusting stench filled the yard after which there was only a moment to wash one's hands briefly in cold water and without soap before queuing for a breakfast of porridge and bread.

The yard filled with about a hundred prisoners, some charged with murder, rape, violent robbery and a host of offences big and small. It was a weird community with a streak of insanity making it even more so. Standing in a corner of the yard, looking at the human wrecks shuffling around, I thought I had been transplanted to Dickens's Marshalsea. The old and the young alike had an air of destitution about them. Most prisoners shaved only occasionally, usually before a court appearance, and they wore the oldest, dirtiest clothes I had ever seen. The yard walls were grey and grimy; there were rusty drainpipes and smelly open lavatories. All was sloth and torpor. Even the Salvation Army service on Sunday afternoons was conducted with a lethargy and lack of conviction that came from years of indifference on the part of prisoners and visitors alike.

The air of stagnation also infected the warders who sought diversions of one kind or another. They appointed trusties to serve the food and take care of the yard and got much fun out of distinguishing the oddest characters, including some who had escaped from mental institutions and were actually very dangerous. I was eager for this phase to come to an end as prisoners had told me that even if I was convicted, prison proper would be much more palatable than my present circumstances, especially for 'an educated person' who was likely to get a desk job in an office or the library.

My trial date finally arrived, and I was hustled into a large van to be transported to the Supreme Court. The driver sped down the hill from the Fort like one possessed. It was strange seeing all these people in the streets – so clean, so self-possessed, so smug in their command of the streets. Respectability was so comforting to them, I thought. They seemed to be saying, 'We pay our taxes and we are entitled to our place in the sun.' They spared not a glance at our van, and they seemed to feel that we were the enemies of society and must be kept away from their world. I experienced a certain anger: You people who walk so arrogantly down the street, I thought, you have no idea how precious is your freedom and how shabbily society treats those who transgress your rules. Yet I had to concede that only a few months earlier I had shared the same complacency and the same prejudices.

Soon the van drove through a large gate and we were ushered into a basement cell. The other prisoners immediately began smoking and sharing their anxieties about their various cases.

On the wall some joker had written:

Some come here to sit and wonder,
Some come here to shit a blunder,
Some come here for their desire,
Some come here to pull their wire.

Another inscription read:

Live fast, die young, and have a good-looking corpse.

Conversation was all about how they detested the authorities, even the way the authorities treated blacks. One prisoner said: 'If I had my way, I'd give the country back to the natives and apologise for the mess we've made of it.'

THE TRIAL

The court was full when I entered. Mary was seated in a front row and I was surprised to see my parents next to her. Knowing how upset they had been by the whole affair, it was heroic of them to have come. I was both regretful and glad, also rather proud to have drawn so many Congressites to the trial. On the bench sat Justice Kuper who was respected as a lawyer, but he was a known Zionist and might be prejudiced against a Jew for antagonising the authorities by his involvement in ANC affairs.

The prosecution case was straightforward. I had attempted to cause a fire in Rissik Street Post Office by placing an incendiary device in the desk of a judge. So far, no surprises. But then came expert evidence. This was that a new chemical had just been discovered which could identify fingerprints even after the surface was wiped clean – as with a handkerchief. It worked on the basis of a chemical given off by the hand when it was warm.

The defence responded that even if the fingerprint was correctly identified it might have come onto the surface innocently. Joe had developed a line of defence that the fingerprint had inadvertently been placed by me on an envelope taken by a person unknown from the COD office. Since this was the only evidence against me and it was entirely circumstantial I stood a very good chance of getting off. Even the law was on my side. It was rather bizarre, but during the war a member of the Stormjaers who had allegedly stolen a car to commit sabotage apparently left a fingerprint on the bumper. The defence argued that he might have done so innocently – for instance, to tie a shoelace – and there was no reason to associate him with the actual theft. He was acquitted, thus establishing the case law in this area.

I went into the witness box, tongue firmly wedged in my throat, but apparently gave a satisfactory account of how the envelope might have been taken from the COD office and subsequently used as a wrapper for the bomb. It was a time when many members were very militant and some might support violence, I suggested. I was not involved in violence although when faced with another prosecution surprise I had to admit that this was not on principle. The prosecution brought a police witness to say that they had intercepted a telegram from me to Harold Strachan who had just been convicted of sabotage and sentenced to three years which read: 'Solidarity, from Ben COD.' I could not tell the court that I had acted in this rather silly way under pressure from our membership to 'do something' in solidarity with Strachan. I could not then tell the members that I had already done so, namely placed a bomb in the post office.

The trial proceeded well enough and senior counsel was confident. He even asked to be excused from the final day when judgement would be given, but I had a premonition that he would be needed and persuaded him to attend. In the event, the judge delivered a savage attack on me and, after hearing a plea in mitigation, said that the only reason he did not sentence me to a longer term was that Strachan had received three years for a much worse offence. But he would give me no less.

The courtroom was stunned. Mary and my parents had made preparations for a celebratory party for my expected release. In the general hush, I was handcuffed and led away. My father showed extraordinary courage and as he and my mother touched me on leaving court, he said: 'If you are going to do a job, do it properly.' It meant that he had forgiven me and I lived with that comforting comment for a long time. Mary was last in the line and it was a brave but dazed face that saw me off.

I was now a convicted prisoner. On the way back to the Fort I was overwhelmed by the sight of newspaper posters reading, 'TUROK SENTENCED.' At reception I was given prison clothing. Two days later I was taken in handcuffs and leg irons to Pretoria Central Prison, the maximum-security prison where all of South Africa's most dangerous prisoners were held and where hangings took place.

The van entered the large gates and my three companions and I were taken through the most massive iron gates I had yet seen. We were now in the large entrance of Central itself and I could see the 'hall' which is the hub of this sprawling complex with a prominent notice reading SILENCE.

We entered a small office and were told to strip and stand naked outside the door. A warder approached, glared at us and asked in Afrikaans: 'Who is the saboteur?' I answered and he said: 'We'll make you shit here.' Already shivering from the cold – it was midwinter – my knees wouldn't be still. We put on our prison clothes and before long were taken through more huge gates, through the dreaded hall with its SILENCE overwhelming all, to the Observation section where I was locked up in a dark cell. It contained a small table, a stool, a rolled mat and blankets, a pot, a bowl for water and a tin basin. There was a small window which faced onto an inside corridor and a large waist-high vent in the wall so that the cold wind which whistled through the cell from the large gap below the iron door easily found its way around the cell at body height. The floor was concrete. There was nothing to do except sit on the stool, stand up, pace three times in one direction and three in another. That was all. I could then sit again. Lying down was not allowed.

Exercise time came twice a day on good days. I took long slow paces down the passage, my squeaking boots echoing off the walls. The boots had patched uppers and the soles had been hammered on crudely in uneven layers causing them to creak and making my gait uneven as my feet tried to adjust inside the odd surfaces. There were cells on both sides of the three-foot passage. I walked slowly, swinging my legs in a long stride, finding comfort in the rhythmic movement. The eerie silence was broken only by distant commands by warders. Massive gates clanged shut every now and then.

The passage was dark with the only light coming from two single electric bulbs and some windows at the distant end of the passage where lay the slopping-out room. The walls were two-tone, dark and light grey, the floor black, shining from daily polishing by practised trusties for whom this was a privilege. After some 20 minutes, the warder called, 'Kom, kom!' and I was once again locked in behind the heavy door and the iron grille. As he pulled the grille shut, he kept his eyes shielded below the brim of his peaked cap. There is no conversation. SILENCE ruled in

Observation. My cell door was a heavy wooden affair with large handles set in strong steel locks. Each door had a peephole and cover, which seemed to bore into my consciousness. I was under 'observation', I remembered.

I sat cold and numb for hours. Too numb to think but not enough to shut out anxiety. This place was monstrously medieval; I had not imagined that such prisons still existed. After a while, there was a slight click at the peephole. An eye was observing me. There was a gentle murmur of voices and the eye left. But it returned every few hours, irritating me intensely. I sat with my back to the eye but it made no difference. He could observe my bent back, my exhausted nerves.

More hours passed until the silence was broken by a shout: 'Graze up!' People were moving swiftly down the passage, opening the outer cell doors and slamming them again. They passed my cell but then returned to reveal a warder and a trusty who opened my door and thrust a tin bowl of soup under my grille. 'You must stand to attention,' shouted the warder in Afrikaans. I had already learned at the Fort that the appropriate response was 'Ja, meneer' ('Yes, sir'). I remembered Dadoo's advice, based on six prison experiences, that a political prisoner is also a model prisoner. The door opened again and a metal mug of coffee and a hunk of bread were placed on the grille. This time no words passed between us.

I sat down at the table, hungry and eager to experience something other than pacing. The soup stank. My spoon brought out a piece of innards. My stomach turned. The coffee was not much better so I ate the bread, which was delicious, freshly baked in the prison kitchen. 'Dinner' was over by 4.00 p.m. In the distance gates were clanging and warders went off duty. I realised that the section was now closed down for the night so I rolled down my two mats, found a pair of pyjamas, changed into them and lay down. But it was too cold to sleep. I soon got up and started exercising to get warm again. On the wall there were two notices – one a religious tract, the other a reminder that in Observation any noise would lead to punishment of 'three meals' which meant deprivation of food for a whole day and night.

Before dawn a bell woke me and I dressed rapidly. Soon there was the same rush of feet down the passage, doors were flung open and the prisoners were counted. Then came inspection. All the doors were opened again enabling me to see the prisoner in the opposite cell though speech was out of the question. The colonel strode speedily down the passage, taking a squint at me as he passed while I stood firmly at attention, my prison card displayed in my hand.

Then came slopping out, a disgusting practice with urine and excrement splashing all over the place in the bathroom, drawing drinking and washing water and then back to lock-up. A wave of humiliation and anger swept over me. I saw myself scurrying about with a pot full of shit, a basin of water for washing and another for drinking, dressed in a mockery of clothing, anxious not to put a foot wrong in case I displeased the warder who seemed to be holding back some pent-up fury.

Back in the cell I became more aware of my clothing. There was a dark grey hair shirt; another slightly larger one was a vest though it was more scratchy. I put the shirt inside the vest and felt more comfortable. Much too large for me, the trousers were made of tough material. They had seen many a prisoner over the years.

The door opened and a trusty threw in some rags. Grateful for the interruption I cleaned the cell and then made a small ball with which I played a kind of hand squash. And then I sat down or paced the cell for a while and then played squash again. After two days the 'psycho' Steenkamp presented himself, all smiles. He informed me that ordinary prisoners spent three weeks in Observation during which they were 'observed' to see whether they felt remorse and whether they were accepting their lot. They were interviewed several times and then the Board would decide to which section they would be allocated. They were not allowed to converse during exercise time and no reading matter was allowed at first, only the Bible. It was meant to be a time for reflection on the harm they had done to society. Of course in my case other conditions would apply but there was an instruction that I had to be kept apart from all other prisoners. I was in fact more in segregation than in Observation since no one would expect me to express regret or remorse.

Many days passed. I was left out during many exercise periods.

Sometimes I was not let out to slop out and sat through the night with a stinking full pot in my cell. I was allowed to have a cold shower once a week when my shirt and pyjamas were also changed. I slowly adjusted to the food. The most overwhelming feeling was helplessness. The man with the key dominated my existence. He decided whether I had exercise, whether I got my food, whether I could wash. That was the total sum of my rights and over which he had complete control.

In the second week, I suddenly became aware of someone whistling softly in the corridor outside my window. It was The Red Flag, and I could hear a pair of boots creaking as he walked up and down. I put my stool on my table, clambered up and there was a gaunt figure pacing in the corridor, a red handkerchief elegantly hanging from his top pocket. I called out softly. On his return he looked up briefly and winked. The next time my food was brought I managed to ask the trusty who was in the section and he hastily replied that it was another guy just like me.

Harold Wolpe, a comrade who was also my solicitor, came to see me about my appeal. I was taken into the security visitors' room and we sat down. He was shocked by my appearance. I had lost weight and my mouth was covered with cold sores. He was not hopeful and urged me to settle down to serve three years. But settle down is precisely what the warders will not allow you to do. Whether it is to relieve their own boredom or out of sheer vindictiveness, there was to be no routine. The strategy of the warders seemed to be to avoid any pattern, keeping us permanently on edge. Even the supervisory officer of the Observation section, Steenkamp, seemed to get some fun out of opening the door suddenly as though there was some emergency. He also kept me on tenterhooks about the expected duration of my stay in this section. 'It's up to the Board,' he said. And the Board usually saw prisoners after the first three weeks of observation when they had had enough time to repent for their crimes.

My three weeks passed without meeting the Board and it began to look as though I was to be a special case. This was confirmed by one warder who said: 'Instructions are to keep you separate from the other prisoners and this is the only section where this is possible.' This was bad news as there was no work in Observation and no proper exercise either. Observation was a transit camp for new inmates who then graduated to other sections where prisoners were allowed to go to the workshops, kitchen, library and so on. In Observation there was only lock-up and total segregation.

After a few more weeks I was finally taken before the Board whose chairman proceeded to give me a long lecture about my being a well-known troublemaker – in fact, an enemy of the state and a danger to the country. He accused me of working with 'that kaffir Mandela'. He also revealed that during the war he had himself served a sentence in isolation at Koffiefontein concentration camp, without a trial, and merely because he opposed South Africa's participation in the war against Hitler Germany.

Having previously had a futile political conversation with Steenkamp, I declined to discuss politics with the chairman, instead complaining about the lack of exercise and requesting a transfer to another section where I could work. He promised to look into this. But immediately on my returning to my cell, Ferreira, our regular duty warder, warned me about making complaints and that he had the power to deprive me of exercise totally. 'You are just a bloody convict here so watch your step,' he said. I knew what he meant.

But a pleasant surprise followed. A warder brought me two books from the prison library, and I was to have this ration weekly from now on. Tatty as they were, reading was a great relief and the hours passed more easily. I was also transferred to a cell with a proper window facing on the exercise yard. Standing on my table after lock-up in the late afternoon I could now see the sun, the shadows on the walls and the changing sky. The air was fresh here as well. At first I fussed about like an excited homeowner who has just moved into a new home. I moved the table to the best spot, cleaned the walls, polished the floor till it was a mirror and refolded the blankets to make them really neat.

Now and then I took a chance and stood on my table to observe other prisoners walking round the yard during exercise. But the 23-hour lock-up was still a burden. I learned to sit still through the day for hours on end without moving a muscle, shutting off all emotions, feelings and thoughts. It was like a deep freeze, a trance which even the occasional noises in the corridor didn't penetrate.

I complained to the commanding officer on his inspection round about the unfairness of leaving me in Observation when all other prisoners had long passed through, but I received the standard reply that I was a special case who could not be accommodated elsewhere. I came to accept that I could expect neither leniency nor fair play. I thought that in a system where repression was the ruling principle it was bound to assert itself even more freely in prison. Prison was a microcosm of apartheid. The warders had full scope to exercise harshness without limit. The man who held the key to my door held the key to my peace of mind. Even if he denied me all my rights, he was exempt from criticism. There were no reporters, there could be no publicity, no one could help me. It was forbidden to talk about prison conditions at visits so I could tell Mary nothing, only vaguely indicating that things were tough.

As the weeks passed I realised that my claustrophobia was increasing. I was resenting the closing of the door more and more and looking forward to its opening, no matter the reason, with greater eagerness. Relief came one Sunday when a kindly old warder allowed Strachan to exercise in the yard with me, even allowing us to converse. It was an immense release. Words came gushing out. We exchanged information about our cases and then began a long, deep friendship more profound than I had ever had in my life. We laughed often, glorying in each other's company, walking round and round the yard as in Van Gogh's prison painting.

And then new instructions were given that we could now talk to each other during every exercise period which would be in the yard and not in the corridor. But not every warder was informed and each had his own ideas. So we could never be sure that we would be able to chat. Jock's morale was superb. He bore the immense hostility the warders exuded with equanimity. It even seemed to strengthen him and he would ask for no favours of any kind, bearing their injustices with a grim Scot's stubbornness. But his health was not good. He was pale and thin, and the long months of isolation in the two-and-a-half months he had already served, showed. He broke off in the midst of a conversation, trying to collect his thoughts, as though his mind was overloaded with fatigue.

But our new situation cheered him up and there emerged an irrepressible sense of fun. An excellent mimic, he imitated Ferreira's sailor's roll to perfection. He recounted many amusing incidents from jail and outside, and was obviously taking things in his stride. We were sometimes allowed out for cleaning duties and were able to polish the floor of the whole section and rub it down shoulder-to-shoulder, or dance it shiny with smooth rags under our shoes, gyrating and weaving to get the last bit of shine out of that century-old concrete.

FURTHER CHARGE

A rather unwelcome break to isolation came one day in the form of a large Special Branch policeman who informed me that I was to face a further charge for 'undermining the good name of the State President Swart'. Apparently the COD had a few months previously issued a leaflet objecting to the proposed award of the freedom of the city of Johannesburg to Swart on the grounds that as Minister of Justice he had been responsible for volumes of repressive legislation and for advocating the use of the cat-o'-nine-tails for lashes.

On the day of the trial special transport was arranged to collect me from Pretoria Central and we drove the 35 miles to Johannesburg with my face glued to the grille window. Behind us a Special Branch patrol car followed closely. The sight of the rolling grasslands of the Transvaal highveld was overwhelming. My eyes could now focus on infinity instead of only a few yards ahead and this seemed to give great physical and psychological relief. A sweet-smelling breeze was playing over the veld, there were swaying trees dotted around and bright flowers adorned the gardens.

But the Johannesburg Magistrates Court soon loomed and I was taken to the basement cells and then into the well of the court to join the other accused. Mary was in the courtroom and it was wonderful to see her without the barriers of prison. We kissed briefly but were soon separated. Other comrades were in the crowded courtroom and I was wholly indifferent to the proceedings. The outcome was a mere formality as in the existing climate no court could ignore an attack on the state president. I was sentenced to a fine of R175 or six months, the magistrate pointing out that he was providing the option of a fine only because this was the first breach of the new *Constitution Act* setting up the Republic of South Africa after its departure from the Commonwealth.

On the way back to Pretoria the van stopped at a roadside tearoom. The Special Branch police let me out of the van and even allowed me to sit with them at a table to drink tea. I noticed a toilet nearby and asked permission to use it. They read my intention immediately and said: 'OK, but if you run for it we'll shoot you full of holes.' I changed my mind.

The conviction altered my prison status as someone with a 'further charge' on my record. Steenkamp took to paying increased attention to me, opening my door suddenly for no apparent reason, creeping up on my cell silently to stare at me through the peephole and eyeing me closely during exercise time. My hearing became highly tuned to his movements in the corridor. He didn't seem to appreciate that I could hear the swish-swish of his trousers no matter how silent his footsteps, so I was ready for him on most occasions. It was an extreme irritation to have him lurking around though there was some interest in analysing his movements.

Steenkamp was a product of middle-class Afrikanerdom. He had a university degree and a veneer of culture. Unlike most of the other warders, his English was good and he aspired to a rather more sophisticated use of language than they did. His job was to assess the reaction of incoming prisoners to their lot and present a report to the Prison Board on the degree of remorse exhibited by prisoners and their potential for rehabilitation. In practice he regarded all prisoners as being fundamentally anti-social elements who required harsh treatment to teach them a lesson. He coped with his job by escaping into a kind of light-heartedness mixed with vindictiveness and sadism.

The exercise yard was periodically used for flogging and I was able to observe this 'observer' by standing on my stool placed on my table. He was invariably present on such occasions, laughing boisterously as some poor victim was strapped to the 'horse' by leather holders around arms and legs with bottom bared, while one of the more burly warders laid into him with a half-inch-thick cane. The victim was made to bleed by tugging on the cane as it fell on the skin, tearing it open. Most screamed with pain. When it was over a medical orderly placed a linen cloth over the buttocks to soak up the blood and the prisoner was allowed to stumble away, again to the great mirth of Steenkamp and the other onlookers.

The callousness of the warders never failed to stir me. I perceived that it was part of the make-up of white South Africans in their role as 'masters'. The rotten values they exhibited were not exclusive to them as warders but part of the culture from which they sprang. Their choice of language, the poverty of their vocabulary, the constant physical macho contacts between them all reflected a violence in interpersonal relations that went beyond the prison environment. I was intrigued by the frequent use of 'gat' meaning 'arsehole'. If you were told to sit down, it was 'sit on your gat' and so on. I asked one warder whether there was not an alternative word such as 'bottom' as we have in the English. He didn't know, asked his colleagues and even took the problem home. No, there was no alternative, he told me, whereas I knew full well that the polite Afrikaans word is 'agterste' or 'behind'. But telling was not allowed.

Steenkamp came to talk to me about my Jewish background. I told him that I am an atheist, a fugitive from the Jewish community. I think of myself as the personification of 'Free Man' while he is rooted in his backward culture, chauvinistic Afrikaner nationalism, his vicious white racism. I noticed that Steenkamp was getting more nervy and nasty. There was an edge to his manner when he talked to me at exercise time. Unknown to me, the political situation outside had become more tense. Sabotage was on the increase, and there were daily stories in the press about detentions, torture and strife in the townships. A big story was the return of Nelson Mandela from his extensive tour of Africa seeking arms and funds for the struggle. He went into hiding but was arrested and a spasm went through the country.

One day I am summoned from my cell to go to the colonel's office. I fear the worst as I am taken through the huge gates in the hall, passing the SILENCE notice. The floor shines like a black mirror and my boots squeak. We go through another giant gate and down some steps into a corridor with cheerful bright-green walls. There are large windows letting in the sun, though the perspective is only yet another high wall with an armed guard patrol on top of it.

I stand stiffly at attention before the colonel with the tight, mean lips. 'What do you know about Mandela?' he asks. I answer in vague terms about his being a leader of the ANC. He is not satisfied. 'What do you know about his case?' he insists. I plead ignorance about any case. 'Well, he has been caught and is facing a charge,' he says. I have no knowledge about that and ask why I should be questioned on this. 'He has subpoenaed you to give evidence for the defence,' he says. Head Office wants a statement from you on what you know about Mandela before you can be allowed to go to court.' My head is in a whirl. What a disaster for Nelson. I agree to give a statement and am willing to give evidence. The colonel writes down what I have to say and I sign it. It is all very thin and I know that it will not do. Steenkamp comes to see me in my cell to tell me that Mandela's file is full of references to me but I will not be allowed to give evidence for him.

A few weeks later Steenkamp returns to tell me that Nelson has been sentenced and is now in a cell in my prison. He is wearing the garb of an African prisoner – coarse sweatshirt, white shorts – and is barefoot. He sleeps on a coir mat on the cement floor and has no stool or table in his cell. The image of the ever smartly-turned-out figure in these conditions is unthinkable.

Steenkamp visits yet again. This time he has a smirk on his face. His news is catastrophic. Mary and three others have been charged for putting up an ANC poster, found guilty and sentenced. She is to serve six months. And what of the children? I have to await a visit from her prior to her going to prison to hear what arrangements she had made. She struggled to get her mother to take Neil and comrades would stay at our house to look after Fred and Ivan. Mary bears it all with great courage, even with an easy manner, at least during the visit. Her tough resilience is evident and she seems to be more worried about me than herself. There will be no further visits for six months but we will be allowed a letter a month as a special privilege.

I am moved to a different cell but in the same section. No one explains why. At about 11.00 a.m. there is the daily inspection with the colonel and his aides rushing past as we stand to attention behind our grilles. Normally, he doesn't give me a glance. But now, for three days running, he slows down at my cell and scrutinises me like some strange animal. I am uneasy at this unwonted attention.

A cleaner opens my door one day and whispers that there is a great deal of consultation among the warders about me. Justice Kuper, who had sentenced me, has just been shot dead through an open window at his home. The jail is seething with excitement and the rumour is that I was behind it.

Next day I am taken to the colonel again. Did I know that my judge had been murdered? I express shock. No! How could I know? Well, what did I have to say about it since I was clearly involved in arranging the murder? I am astonished. How could this be done from isolation in the country's most formidable maximum-security prison, I ask? But the colonel doesn't believe me. I am dismissed with contempt.

A cleaner brings me lunch and whispers that the murder suspect of Judge Kuper is now in the section and I am being watched very closely in case I try to communicate with him. My isolation is increased and I am on the alert for any machination to link me with the new prisoner. But some weeks go by and the excitement dies away and I am left to the old rhythm.

PRETORIA LOCAL PRISON

The golden rule in any authoritarian system is the denial of information to subordinates. Since prison is the most authoritarian of all systems, keeping inmates in the dark is the essence of control. This applies particularly to knowledge about changes in prisoners' circumstances or conditions. No one must have any warning of impending changes and any change must be carried out in a way that will create a maximum sense of uncertainty and insecurity. Prisoners who have been kept in a particular cell for many months, some even being allowed to keep a hamster, or make some shelving for photographs or whatever, are given no notice to quit. The instrument of surprise is the warder's trump card. He knows that when he suddenly bustles you out of a cell that has been home for a long time, heading for an unknown destination, it will raise your anxiety level and make your heart beat violently. This is his entertainment in one of the most boring jobs in the world.

And so it was for Jock and me. With no previous warning the door was flung open and we were told to pack everything, including the books we had now accumulated, and prepare for a move. In a matter of five minutes we were sitting in a large prison van, escorted by armed warders, being driven to a new home. We were tremendously excited. At last we were rid of Central and bound for a place where we could be held without solitary confinement and given work! But our new home turned out to be only a few hundred yards away, within the same prison complex, and what we recognised as Pretoria Local Prison which was used for black prisoners.

Local Prison was bursting with Africans. Crowds of African women stood outside the main gates waiting to visit their menfolk. Inside, some prisoners were carrying large bags of mealie meal, others were cleaning the cobbled yard, some groups were being hassled by black warders armed with knobkerries. The bustle was so different from the silence of Central. The whole prison seemed to be shuddering with gates being slammed, men shouting, gangs chanting in unison. All was punctuated with the frequent crack of warders' batons and staves hitting bare bodies. Gangs of prisoners were herded like cattle, always moving at a trot, helped on their way by a kick here, a thwack there and sometimes by a brutal blow from a fist. Some sang quietly, others talked loudly, seemingly cheerful and full of vitality. Some prisoners, no doubt trusties, actually looked well fed with shiny brown skins. The entrance courtyard was flooded with bright sunlight to complete the picture of animation.

Jock and I seized our bags of personal effects from the van and two warders told us to mount a staircase in the corner of the yard. We went up to the first floor and were shown to a section of seven cells sealed off by an iron door. We were to occupy cells at either end, no doubt to make communication difficult.

My cell was seven feet by twelve feet, larger than that at Central. There was a high window with broken windowpanes behind thick iron bars. There was a table, stool, a little bedside table, a roll of mats and blankets and a slopping-out pail. A stale smell hung in the air partly due to the smelly, semen-infested blankets. I walked up and down to get the feel of the extra space, tested whether the table would hold my weight for looking out of the window, sat on the stool, walked up and down again. It was certainly an improvement on Central. When Jock and I were allowed out for exercise in the large yard below, we were elated, convinced that we would now get work and better conditions generally. Surely the problem of keeping us isolated from the other prisoners at Central would not weigh so heavily here.

Our hopes were partly realised but only because our starting point was so low. 'Dupe', our section warder, was indeed fair about the full half-hour's exercise. Also, we were allowed to remain in the corridor of the section for much of the morning, cleaning and polishing, a luxury after Central's lock-up. After inspection it was lock-up again for the rest of the day.

The yard was large and sunny. There was a shower and toilet in the centre where we slopped out. We soon discovered that it was also used by the white awaiting-trial prisoners on the ground floor who occasionally left pieces of newspaper in the shower block. Sometimes we fished used newspaper out of the toilet itself, washed the excrement off under the tap and put it into our pots to be read in the privacy of the cell upstairs. It was thus that we learned of the state of the struggle outside.

Exercise now became a really social occasion with a full half-hour to talk to Jock who turned out to be a highly cultured man, a serious Shakespearean scholar and a gifted and knowledgeable literary critic. As a lecturer in art history he was also able to give me extended seminars in this area and our confinement together proved to be the beginning of my cultural renaissance. But most valuable of all was Jock's extraordinary political integrity and unshakable morale. He turned out to be the best possible companion in that world of total isolation.

We had both registered for undergraduate studies by correspondence with the University of South Africa. I was majoring in philosophy and literature while Jock was doing history and literature. While study in Central had been a source of great harassment since the warders used every opportunity and excuse to deprive us of books or letters, here things eased up and study became a serious matter.

I soon realised that my engineering studies had impoverished me intellectually. A stranger to literary nuances, unable to engage with poetry or even write a decent essay, I saw that what emerged from my pen was much more like a technical report. And so Jock coached me as we walked round and round the yard. My understanding of the Jewish theatre in which my mother had played so prominent a part deepened, and I came to appreciate the books my father loved even though he was a man without much formal education. When he bought an ancient complete set of Dickens's works, heavily bound in thick board with elaborate designs, it was not so much to read them as to be in the same room with this storehouse of culture.

Now I could go over this literary legacy with Jock and analyse the works of Defoe, Swift, George Eliot and Jane Austen, among others. And yet, isolated and confined as we were, we could not escape the moods of depression that came upon us unexpectedly. At times the walls exerted a kind of inward pressure, towering menacingly above me as I lay on my mat on the floor of my cell. I experienced fits of suffocating nausea and claustrophobia which clouded around me, inhibiting sleep. 'It's catching me today, Jock,' I would say to him and he understood very well.

My windows now overlooked the southern suburbs of Pretoria and I could see the distant brown Magaliesberg range standing out against the wispy pale-blue background. It made me think of my mountaineering days, of the first time I had climbed Table Mountain and stood at the summit, overawed by the vast stretch of the sea below, merging into the hazy blue horizon where sea and sky were indistinguishable. To recall that mountain now and yet be confined to a cold grey box of concrete was a severe punishment. On Saturday afternoons I gave myself a special treat. By placing my stool on top of the table and clambering up this shaky structure I could see a small section of the main road running past the prison. I could watch the cars roaring up and down the hill, or bicycles crawling along, and even make out the distant shapes of women pedestrians. Jock had a better view and, arousing my envy, gave me intimate portraits of the women passing by.

But it was the activity immediately below us that most held our attention. The section below was part of the prison hospital and consisted of two dormitories, a dispensary and an office. Life began at 6.00 a.m. when the warders came on duty. They unlocked the doors and the African patients dribbled out looking like shell-shocked soldiers struggling out of a bombarded trench. They were like Conrad's 'bundle of acute angles' – thin, emaciated, clad in shorts and thin short-sleeved shirts, with no shoes or socks, carrying their pathetic white linen jackets now turned a dirty grey.

New admissions were hustled in to yells of 'Chaisa! Chaisa!' (Hit! Hit!) from the guards, while their blows rained down indiscriminately on heads, shoulders and backs. The prisoners were trying hard to give the appearance of running, but the group was actually shuffling forward, pressed close together. More shouting and more blows as they were lined up, ordered to strip and stand naked in the frost, waiting for the doctor, clothes in a little pile at their feet. Pretoria often freezes at night and we suffered bitterly in our cells on the first floor with the cold wind hissing through the glassless windows, escaping through the gap at the bottom of the cell door. In the open yard below it must have been like ice. Even with frost on the ground, the prisoners had to stand barefoot, stark naked, waiting and shivering for half an hour or more for the doctor.

The hospital orderly was a short, thickset, ugly man with a deformity of the face apparently due to cancer of the jawbone. Acutely conscious of his deformity, he constantly put his hand to his face to hide his jaw. He grew a beard, which only made him more grotesque. We called him Florence Nightingale since his main mission in life seemed to be to make up for the inequalities created by nature. He seemed to believe that the prisoners were privileged to be sound in body and set out to redress matters. Assaulting prisoners was a way of life for Florence. He had powerful shoulders; throwing his full weight into one smack to the head would send his victim flying across the yard. Or he would make his orderlies set out buckets in the yard and order prisoners to sit on them to defecate while he set about them with a truncheon. He then examined their stools for contraband tobacco usually wrapped in silver paper. When he found nothing he made the prisoners bend over and, using a rubber glove, he poked into the anus with his fingers, pulling and pushing to locate any foreign body until blood was running down their legs. He made jelly of his victims who crouched down in a bundle of terror, waiting for the blows to fall. When he found any object he made the prisoner open it up and then smashed the man with his fist, sending the prisoner flying.

Looking down from above in the early morning, the scene made one angry and miserable. Here was an intensity of violence that must be without precedence – violence in manner, violence in speech, violence with the fist, the baton, the cane, with the cat-o'-nine-tails and, most horrifying of all, violence of the hangman's noose. For those prisoners who were ill there was no hope at all; the death rate must have been very high. Even with my long trousers, socks and boots, the winters were very severe. For the sick prisoners it had to be terrible. This was the hard underbelly of apartheid South Africa. Mortified and appalled, I was glad to be exposed to this side of its reality. Witnessing it made my sentence meaningful and strangely worthwhile.

We were then joined by Jack Tarshish who had been sentenced to ten years for planning sabotage. He was a sick man, suffering from a form of epilepsy, who ought not to have been sent to an ordinary prison and his struggle to survive and low morale were painful for all of us. We tried to get him to settle down but his illness bore down on him, making it difficult for him to sustain a stable routine. I had known Jack in Cape Town where he had a reputation as a political maverick. But in prison his political views were of little consequence. What mattered was his inability to adjust to the harsh prison environment and help us maintain our collective morale. His preoccupation with his own condition and frequent, ill-considered demands to the warders sometimes imposed a severe burden on us.

Time drifted along and then we became aware of a change of tempo in the prison. The warders were once again jumpy and exhibited great hostility towards us, especially the commanding officer, Colonel Aucamp, who passed his moods on to the warders.

THE RIVONIA ARRESTS

It was the shoes that provided the clue, also the badly folded blankets. Sitting in my cell it suddenly dawned on me: there must be a new batch of awaiting-trial prisoners. Their shoes were unusual – too smart and too new for normal inmates – so the new prisoners must be political. When I heard the opening of their cell doors on the floor below us, I knew it was their exercise time. I told Harold of my suspicion and he set about making contact with the prisoner below him by tapping on the wall. It took a long time because once the man below responded with a tap, Harold had to teach him the alphabet code: one tap is A, two taps is B, three taps is C and so on down the alphabet until it clicked. Thereafter we got the news. There had been a raid on the Rivonia farm headquarters, the top leaders had been arrested and with them many others. They were now being held under the 90-day detention regulations to await interrogation.

Soon they were able to leave us a newspaper since we used the same exercise yard and we read the whole story in its awesome dimensions. They had arrested Walter Sisulu, Govan Mbeki and Rusty Bernstein, now in the cells beneath us, all top leaders of Umkhonto we Sizwe. It was a terrible blow, yet I felt exultant to be in such company. That evening the prison was transformed. From one of the other sections African prisoners were singing freedom songs such as *Sizokunyatela ma Africa* (Africa will crush you). The beautiful harmonies, the defiant spirit were more moving than anything I had ever experienced. Prison was now an arena of the struggle, its frontline so to speak, and we could expect to hear a great deal more about the coming trials and struggles.

Unknown to us, Nelson Mandela was also brought into our prison to join the Rivonia men and the singing and shouting of slogans grew even more powerful. But after a few days the warders clamped down and all was silent again. Despite strict instructions to the warders that we were to be kept well away from the detainees, we managed to see them at a distance now and then as we walked to the exercise yard. The supply of newspapers also continued and we became quite well informed about the situation.

But then they took Harold away for interrogation. He was held for a month totally alone in a nearby section. When he returned it was to tell us that a colonel in the Special Branch had spent many hours questioning him but that he had kept silent throughout. They told him what they knew about his work in developing bombs and offered him the option of making a statement or charging him under the *Sabotage Act* with the possibility of a death sentence. They also threatened to detain his wife Maggie. They had not used torture, but the strain of isolation could be seen clearly. He was even paler than usual and had lost valuable weight. They came back a few weeks later and offered him an exit permit and money in return for a statement. He refused. We now knew the seriousness of our predicament and awaited further measures. Unexpectedly, I was taken down to the lawyers' visiting room where Bram Fischer and Joel Joffe were waiting for me. It was wonderful to see them and we embraced warmly. But their news was that I had been listed as a co-conspirator in the Rivonia Trial and should be prepared for pressure from the authorities. They would come to see us again as the trial developed.

The atmosphere in prison worsened as evidence was given. The country had not realised the seriousness of the MK campaign, nor the intentions outlined in the document *Operation Mayibuye*. The warders became threatening, cut our exercise time and used all their tricks to harass us. None of it had any impact on our morale since we knew they were only reacting to the movement's political initiatives.

The trial was drawing to a close. The warders were so excited that they passed on titbits of news to us. Their main interest was in whether the accused would be sentenced to death. On the evening before sentencing, the prison was tense with anticipation. By morning large numbers of comrades stood outside the court and there was a possibility that the death sentence would lead to a nationwide uprising. Then came relief.

All were given life sentences and Bernstein was discharged. Several hours later Dennis Goldberg was brought into our section, a life sentence before him. I was told to take him his food that evening and managed a fleeting hello. He looked firm and strong though the strain must have been horrible. The hangman's noose had been so close.

Next day we were told to clean the passage as usual but there was an extra guard and we were prohibited from talking while we worked. Then came exercise in the yard and we were at last able to brief Dennis on our circumstances. He was appalled. But with all the publicity and the contact with the lawyers, he hoped that conditions would change and he was determined to fight for that. Imbued with the fighting spirit that was the hallmark of the accused in the Rivonia Trial, Dennis believed we were too subdued in the matter of our treatment. He set about writing a letter to Prime Minister Vorster, reminding him that he too had been a political prisoner during the Second World War and that special treatment was due to political prisoners. The reaction was unexpectedly fierce. At the next inspection Colonel Aucamp tore into Dennis, saying he was impudent and that there was no way the letter would be forwarded. Dennis's opportunity came a few weeks later when his father arrived in the company of a lieutenant from prison headquarters to enquire about conditions. Placing his entire future in jeopardy, Dennis described our situation in full, making sure that all he said was taken down by the lieutenant. It was a very brave thing to do. However, I later discovered that none of the information was actually conveyed to the commissioner of prisons. Indeed, nothing changed for the better.

Dennis's arrival was a major event for the rest of us. First, we could hear new stories and we could relate to a vibrant personality. Most important of all, however, he briefed us on the situation outside, in particular the story of Rivonia. Dennis reported that he was asked to join the MK group in Johannesburg and go underground in order to set up a factory making explosives of various kinds, including land mines and hand grenades. He was located on a farm where he set to work. Everything went smoothly until the High Command met at the Rivonia farm to consider the document *Operation Mayibuye* which set out the strategy for the build-up to guerrilla war.

The police had found out about the meeting from someone under interrogation, surrounded the meeting and arrested everyone present. The document was found at the venue in multiple copies. Given its importance, it is reproduced in full in Annexure: Chapter 5.

Walking round the yard listening to Dennis each day during exercise time we were perplexed at the nature of the proposals contained in *Operation Mayibuye* which seemed incredibly ambitious and unrealistic. Imagine bringing thousands of trained guerrillas into the country when it was now an armed camp on full alert. Dennis was himself highly sceptical but being an innovative engineer he had relished the challenge. From then on, discussing Operation Mayibuye was a priority for each of the new admissions into our section.

Next came Dave Kitson and John Mathews. Dave was a talented and experienced engineer who had spent many years in Britain where he became a well-known trade unionist and communist. He had returned to South Africa to assist at the very time when armed struggle was on the agenda with all its attendant risks. The Rivonia arrests followed and Dave was recruited to join Wilton Mkwayi in the new High Command. But the police net had closed in and they were seized. Dave was very critical of Operation Mayibuye and indeed of the whole style of operations. He was scathing about those who had been in the planning stage and then left the country. But he brought a new sense of humour into our section and much light relief. Despite his 20-year sentence, Dave was a fund of stories and information. His courage was outstanding. He had brought a small radio into prison, strapped by Elastoplast between his legs, and five pounds in cash which could have earned him 21 days' segregation on rice water plus lashes. Dave settled down well for a man with such a long sentence though, like everyone else, he had his bad days of depression.

John was a pleasant man of working-class origins whose lack of education was a major handicap as he could not enter into the oblivion brought by study. He did not register for university study and had to be content with lower-level reading which he nevertheless appreciated. He was facing a sentence of 15 years and he did so with remarkable stoicism. He brought me a bit of curious information in that he had taken part in the production of the bombs used in my Rissik Street incident and apologised for the cock-up. He put it down to amateurishness, poor facilities and excessive haste.

And then a new batch arrived, the Armed Resistance Movement

people, an organisation started by members of the Liberal Party and some other radicals. They had actually commenced sabotage operations before MK and this was probably one of the reasons for MK haste. They had pulled off some spectacular actions, especially in the Cape where the railways were put out by attacks on the signalling system. But some of their members had broken under interrogation, including one of the leading figures, and they had been rounded up fairly easily.

The most senior figure was Baruch Hirson, a physicist who was also a Trotskyite. He had also been a somewhat dissident member of the Congress of Democrats and it was ironic that we were now placed in the same cell. I found him to be in poor health with gout and ulcers plaguing him constantly. But he turned out to be a very nice human being and an extremely cultured one and we got on splendidly. Alan Brooks was a former Rhodesian who was on the verge of joining up with the ANC when he was caught. John Laredo was a somewhat unusual person for our community in that he came from a thoroughly Afrikaner and Nationalist Party family. An anthropologist, he seemed to have come into ARM through a deeply held democratic conviction and a sense of justice which enabled him to break with his environment, though only with the greatest difficulty. John was interrogated at great length and, one suspects, with that additional ferocity reserved for Afrikaner 'traitors' and he had attempted suicide by trying to throw himself through a window in the Special Branch headquarters. But they had seized him just as he was on the windowsill and so he survived to join us with a seven-year sentence. He was a delightful, gentle man to have in the yard, though we had to be careful not to tread on his sensitivities in our abuse of the warders who were all Afrikaners too.

Hugh Lewin was a journalist with a strong Anglican background. Not openly religious (indeed he was prone to use some pretty tough language about everything including the church), he was a fine, fair-minded person with whom any problems could be easily resolved. Inevitably there were political problems to be sorted out between those of us who had an ANC and communist background and those from the Liberal Party. But common sense prevailed and the constituencies soon dissolved in the face of the common need to survive.

Dave Evans, also a journalist, was immensely entertaining but also courageous, always willing to take a tough stance on any prison issue. Tony Trew was a quiet post-graduate philosophy student who seemed to be able to sink into his own thoughts, while Raymond Eisenstein of mixed Polish-French origins was the most laid-back of all. Nothing disturbed him and although the warders found his bemused attitude somewhat less respectful than they would have liked, there was absolutely nothing they could do to him which might upset him in the slightest.

And then came the Communist Party group. They were arrested for illegal party activities and interrogated at length including standing treatment, sleep deprivation and the like. Ivan Schermbrucker had been finance manager of *New Age*, the movement's weekly, and he came through the experience rather well though he had made a statement like the rest. He had great inner resilience and proved to be a wonderful comrade in prison. He was severe in his political judgements, however, condemning the whole Operation Mayibuye enterprise unreservedly, and critical too of the exile movement's lack of concern for those left behind, especially the lack of financial provision for the families of detainees and prisoners. Eli Weinberg, another long-standing communist, was less critical, indeed rather reluctant to comment adversely on anything outside prison, and resolved to sit out his five-year sentence with the least possible discontent. He turned to learning African languages with great enthusiasm, putting aside prison concerns from consideration. Norman Levy who had been a close associate in the Congress of Democrats was a disconsolate figure. Furiously critical of the leadership outside, he blamed all and sundry, particularly those who had left the country, in his view without proper justification. Lewis Baker, a lawyer, shared a cell with me for some time. He was also rather sombre, but he was able to break out of depression and was a thoroughly kind comrade. Costa Gazides, a doctor, only received a one-year sentence which he bore lightly. Paul Trewhela made up the rest of the group.

No sooner had we all settled down when yet another batch arrived, this time COD members who had not been integrated into MK, and undertook their own sabotage and came to grief.

Marius Schoon had tried to be accepted despite his Stellenbosch University background and a rather easy lifestyle. He and Raymond Thoms, a rather over-intense COD member, teamed up with someone who turned out to be an informer in the unit to attack a police station in Hillbrow. They were intercepted and sentenced to 12 years. It was with much embarrassment that I had to hear Schoon tell me, while walking round the yard, that he had to go to prison before we could trust him fully. Schoon served his time and joined MK in exile where he suffered the murder of his wife and child by the Special Branch. Thoms was a brilliant classics scholar but extremely neurotic. Before long he was in constant conflict with the warders, creating unwanted tension in the section which always worked to our collective disadvantage. The warders soon manipulated him and he turned against us, giving away all our yard secrets including the membership of our committee and of our escape group. He also led the warders to the radio and our cash. The presence of an informer made life very difficult for years.

The authorities quietly pursued a policy of undermining our unity and morale which had thus far stood up very well. Almost everyone in the section was a university graduate, five being university lecturers. Composed of engineers, teachers, writers and students, we formed a highly intellectual bunch way beyond what the prison service had seen before. Most of us had been through interrogation and some had been badly beaten up. Some were made to stand for days on end, sometimes holding a chair above their heads. Others were repeatedly hit on one spot for hours or threatened with being thrown out of a window. All eventually made some statement or other, often a compound of lies. Where the police had plenty of time, they compared statements with those obtained from other prisoners and the discrepancies were taken up at further interrogations. In other cases the sheer pressure of work meant that fabrications were allowed to stand unchecked. The objective was always to break down the prisoner's will and destroy his self-respect. Once they started talking there was no stopping. The only consolation came with the knowledge that whatever they revealed did not actually lead to the arrest of anyone outside.

Partly through the pressure of having vulnerable relatives outside, the possibility of making deals to secure releases was mooted by the police. This was only offered to certain of the ARM people with the requirement that they renounce violence as a political method. Two did so and were released early. While the arrival of all these additional inmates changed our conditions for the better – we were now three in a cell, were allowed out for section cleaning duties and for serving food – it was now clear that the political situation outside had greatly deteriorated. The leadership had made some catastrophic mistakes with devastating consequences amounting to the virtual destruction of the movement as I had known it. Not wanting to pass judgement while in prison, I nevertheless thought that we had turned to the use of violence without the necessary preparation, sustainable underground apparatuses, necessary skills and logistical support. But while I wanted to spare myself the pain of facing these truths directly, I was undoubtedly influenced by the critical views expressed by the new arrivals. I later conveyed these views to comrades I met abroad with unfortunate results.

HAROLD'S FURTHER CHARGE

The remaining months of my sentence were now diminishing steadily. I had a new way of counting time that sped on the date of my release. Whereas in the first year and a half I counted the months remaining to halfway, I now counted the years and months already completed, which made it seem I had already accomplished most of the sentence. In a way I became rather lighthearted, though there was always some warder who delighted in telling me that I would never be released. Then, Mary visited me on one of my three-monthly visits and told me that she had been asked to inform me of the possibility that I might be deported or given a further charge, like Strachan. This news left a hole in my stomach, even though I had been anticipating something like this since his experience. Confirmation of something in the wind came when two warders entered the yard during exercise and set about giving me a thorough fingerprinting, the kind used in further charges.

Compared to the excitement of the end of my sentence, however, these were small matters. But weighing heavily upon me was the irrepressible thought that I was leaving all these comrades behind. We had become a close community and it was excruciating to think of people like Dennis and Dave facing such long sentences without the slightest prospect of early release. But there was no resentment whatsoever in their hearts. They shared my anxieties about my prospects but they also found joy in the possible end of my ordeal, anticipating that my release would set a precedent for other releases. But Dennis and Dave were also concerned about being forgotten and I was approached rather formally about my intentions on my release. I affirmed that on no account would I leave the country of my own volition. However I was also anxious to assure them that I would do all I could to campaign for better conditions for them.

My final day, 26 July 1965, arrived. I was overwhelmed with sadness about leaving. I recall that last look down the dismal corridor with Evans and Dennis cleaning the light switches as I was taken out of the section for the last time. It was probably my sense of deep regret that filled my soul with resentment and anger. So when I was shown into the colonel's office and saw the two Special Branch men in a corner it didn't worry me. They could do what they liked; nothing mattered.

Colonel Aucamp was all smiles. He handed me my money and odds and ends taken from me three years before, asked me to sign for them, and then said: 'Well, Turok, I hope that we treated you all right and that you will be OK outside.' In a flash of temper I said: 'Colonel, you treated me like a dog. I was in isolation most of the time, I slept on the floor, I was deprived of my rights. I want to see the Commissioner of Prisons to complain and to demand that my fellow prisoners get proper treatment.'

The colonel went pale with anger. But he checked himself and said: 'You have the right to do so and I shall make the arrangements. Now these gentlemen want to see you.' I turned to them and was greatly relieved that they had a lengthy document in their hands which was only a banning order. I read speedily through it, signed as required, and was then shown to the prison's main entrance, not knowing what or who I would find there. My parents and John Benjamin, filled with emotion, were standing outside in the sun. Mary had not been allowed to come because of her banning order. We got into John's car and sped off towards Johannesburg.

CHAPTER SIX

ESCAPE

Uppermost in my mind during those first weeks at home was the commitment I had given to the comrades in the yard that I would not leave the country as so many others had done. It may be difficult to recapture the importance of this issue. When I left prison the number of comrades who had gone abroad for training was small. Subsequently, after the Soweto uprising, very large contingents of young Africans realised the inadequacy of popular mass protest against the violence of the armed state and sought to enter the ranks of MK in order to continue the struggle by other means. This was accepted by most as legitimate and indeed raised the morale of people at home. But in the time of my imprisonment, leaving the country had the opposite effect. It was viewed as a kind of running away, leaving behind decreasingly effective structures to the point where the movement became a shadow of its former self.

July 1965 was a very low point in the struggle. Most of the structures had collapsed; the great majority of leaders were either in prison or in exile. The sense of responsibility to stay even as a symbol was therefore very great. My parents thought otherwise, having come especially from Johannesburg to see me released from prison in Pretoria and to join the family reunion in Johannesburg. They once again began to pressure me to leave the country. At first, I laughed off their promptings – I could do little else when confronted by people who had been through the ordeal with me. But on one occasion when my mother began to hector me, I responded by saying that I would rather hang myself from the tree in the garden than leave the country and abandon my comrades in prison. She then realised that the matter was closed.

Coming home was traumatic enough without these pressures.

Much as I wanted to be close to Mary, to hold and touch her, for the first few nights I could not sleep on the bed since it was too soft. I slept on the floor with Mary in the bed above me until I slowly adjusted to the new situation. The contrast between home and jail was overwhelming. I could not believe the comfort that surrounded me – the taste of good food, the flowers in the garden and all the other pleasures. It was as though I had been deprived of life itself for so long. Being with the boys again was an amazing experience. Now, 6, 8 and 10 respectively, Neil, Ivan and Fred had grown a great deal and become a little gang. Exuberant, boisterous and energetic, they crawled all over me, wanted to be with me all the time and plagued me with questions. They wanted to know about the warders, where I slept, what I did all day and what kind of food I was given. I told them about the horrible treatment meted out to Africans and they were suitably shocked. We played ball in the garden and on the swings in the park next door. They gave me so much joy and yet I became worn out so easily.

Although still disorientated, I nevertheless had two duties to perform. The first was to phone the firm of doctors in Pretoria who had visited our group in prison through all the years and I had enormous satisfaction in speaking directly to one of them about the treatment and gross neglect of my comrades. About Hirson in particular, who suffered from gout and ulcers, and Norman Levy who had what seemed to be a serious ailment. I complained about the prison authorities' callous attitude, gross neglect and failure to provide the basic medicine necessary to survive the harsh conditions in prison. I informed them that I would report them to the Medical Council though I did not know how to go about finding them as they were not listed in the telephone directory. It was only some years later that an organised body of prisoners' relatives was able to make a formal complaint to the Medical Council along these lines.

My second task was to see the Deputy Commissioner of Prisons in Pretoria. Colonel Aucamp telephoned me to tell me that I had been given an appointment to see Brigadier Coetzee, Deputy Commissioner of Prisons in Pretoria. I obtained permission from the Johannesburg magistrate to leave the area and drove to Pretoria, where I was shown into Coetzee's office. It was a strange confrontation. Only a few days after having been locked up as an anonymous prisoner in one of his many jails, now I was suddenly sitting in his office dressed in a suit and tie, facing him across his desk on equal terms. He asked my business and I explained that I and all the other prisoners had been treated in a manner completely at variance with prison regulations, that we had been deprived of many of our rights and that we had been harassed continuously. He expressed surprise and even concern, and listened to what I had to say. But I suddenly realised that he was not taking notes and asked him about it. Would he be willing to take the matter further? He gave only a cursory response. I knew in my heart that he had risen from the ranks of men who were ordinary rank-and-file wardens in Pretoria prison and that anyone who had undergone such a socialisation had long lost any human feeling, sense of fairness or commitment to regulations. I spent an hour and a half unburdening myself, during which time my only satisfaction was to see him squirm. I knew there was nothing more I could do for my comrades in prison as long as I was under house arrest and confined to Johannesburg.

THE CASE OF HAROLD STRACHAN

Meanwhile, the *Rand Daily Mail* had interviewed Strachan about conditions in prison and published three powerful accounts. The police reacted immediately, searched the offices of the *Rand Daily Mail* and Strachan's house and, unfortunately, obtained a transcript of the interview. Strachan was charged with breaking the confidentiality of prison regulations and brought to trial. I was asked to go to Durban to give evidence, which I did, to find Harold in good shape, hopeful that the case would be thrown out. But the magistrate was enormously biased and Harold went back to prison for another year's stretch which, he subsequently told me, was much worse than the first sentence. He nevertheless had the satisfaction of seeing that his case and the published accounts so shocked public opinion that they had an almost immediately beneficial effect on prison conditions. In a relatively short time, the prisoners were given work, and new facilities were created including such comforts as beds and toilets. It was a source of constant surprise to me that even while repression was at its height, the prison authorities were still sensitive to public opinion.

I now had to find a way of making a life for myself under the conditions of partial house arrest. I was also advised that if I were not seen to be trying to earn a living, the conditions of my house arrest would be made more stringent. The conditions of the order were that I should be at home during the weekend and public holidays and between 6.00 p.m. and 6.00 a.m. I was free to leave the premises during weekdays and I used this freedom to rent an office in the centre of Johannesburg and set myself up once again in my profession as a surveyor. I cleaned the old theodolite, acquired some new equipment, bought some furniture and enrolled in the Institute of Land Surveyors where my membership had lapsed. I visited various solicitors and architects in Johannesburg seeking work without success. Everywhere the word was that I was too hot to handle. Even the firm where Nelson Mandela and Oliver Tambo had practised told me it would be dangerous to give me work. Over a period of several months I had only two jobs, both given to me by my nephew who was an architect. The attempts to establish a new life were blocked at every turn.

The state stood supreme as a granite structure capable of destroying all its opponents. The exception was Bram Fischer who, with extraordinary heroism, had gone underground and was trying to rebuild structures even in the face of these appalling conditions. He was in disguise, living on the move as we had done during the emergency, evading the police with great difficulty, yet issuing press statements from time to time. The whole security force was geared to finding him and smashing the small group assisting him. That Bram, of all people, had chosen to go underground was a surprise to everyone. This pillar of Afrikaner society, this modest man who breathed the air of respectability of the Supreme Court and the Johannesburg Bar, who was the chief lawyer for the Anglo American Corporation and other major companies of the establishment, had turned to a life of clandestine operations against all odds. Our members were arrested and tortured in the prisons across the country. Brave men broke down and gave devastating information about their own comrades and cells, which the police followed up to smash whole sectors of the movement so that little survived.

A few weeks after my release, a visitor came to my house or, more accurately, a comrade spoke to me at the gate in the street since under the terms of my banning order she was not allowed to enter the premises. She said that she had a message from Bram for me, asking whether I was willing to rejoin the underground network and work with him. I was taken aback since I had more or less become reconciled to the kind of isolation in which Mary had lived for several years now. I had also been warned by a journalist I trusted that the police had developed a new capability, using a reflecting microphone to pick up speech at a distance. I also knew that the Special Branch frequently parked their car up the street to observe who visited our house and presumably to listen to conversations. I replied that, while I was quite willing to be involved, it would be wise to observe the elementary principles of security and not engage in this kind of conversation in full public view of the police. We agreed that future contacts should be more discreet and this would be conveyed to Bram.

But this experience gave me some insight into the difficulties facing Bram and I feared the worst. The comrades supporting him were not of a calibre who could sustain a clandestine or twilight existence, nor would they be able to stand up to questioning. And so it came as no surprise that before long Bram was located by the police and sentenced to life imprisonment. After a few years he contracted cancer and was released to die in a matter of weeks on his brother's farm.

Mary had found the previous three years extremely tough. Apart from the six months she had served for putting up a poster of the ANC calling for an eye for an eye and a tooth for a tooth, she found life under suburb arrest, where she was confined to one square mile around the house, a trying ordeal. She could not take the children to school since it was outside the area. She lived alone with the children in the house, which was the last in the street close to the wooded fields of a golf club. When the police were not harassing her, she was frightened by the frequent presence of men who hovered around the premises. Although she installed a burglar alarm, there were occasions when someone tried to break into the house. She lived in isolation, traumatised by her condition, but determined to stick it out until I was released.

By this time, many of our comrades from the party were either serving sentences or in detention. One, who had been particularly close to Mary, had made several attempts at suicide by cutting his wrists and arteries in the neck while awaiting further interrogation. And so it was not too much of a surprise when we received information, from someone close to the police, that Mary was on the brink of being arrested once more, with a likely sentence of five years under the *Suppression of Communism Act*. All the police were waiting for was confirmation about her party membership from this comrade who was on the verge of collapse.

The information we received was nevertheless alarming. We could not talk about it in the house since we assumed that our house was bugged. So we took to walking around the small swimming pool Mary had built in the garden while I was in prison to give the boys an outlet for their overwhelming energy. Should we ignore the warning and face the prospect of a long imprisonment for Mary with the boys being deprived of their mother yet again? I would have to be mother and father, a task I did not feel up to, and yet we had made a commitment not to leave the country. We walked round the pool again and again, turning over the possibilities. Could we go underground, could we evade the inevitable arrest, should we stick it out? In the end, we decided it would be unfair to the children and politically a rather meaningless gesture to stay put.

Bram was still underground, so – in what was probably the most difficult conversation I had in all those years – I broached the question with our contact of leaving. I was told that my proposal would be conveyed to Bram. A few weeks later a reply came: it would be preferable for us not to leave the country, but if we felt that we could no longer remain, our departure would be understood subject to three conditions. The first was that I should leave the country illegally without seeking an exit permit. The second was that I should agree to undergo plastic surgery abroad and the third that I should then return underground. I accepted them and began to examine the prospects of escape.

We first considered the possibility of both of us leaving the country through Botswana, the route taken by many before us. But we had the problem of the children. Mary approached her mother who lived in Natal, but she flatly refused to look after the children in the event of our escape. My own parents and brothers were in Cape Town and there was no way I could approach them, nor did I think they would agree. We were left with the option that I should skip the country leaving Mary behind with the children. The assumption was that the police would not want the adverse publicity arising from her arrest while she had sole custody of the children.

And so I began the seemingly impossible task of planning my escape. My contact could not provide any assistance, nor were there any structures of the movement to which I could turn. I was getting rather desperate when a friend agreed to go to the Ordnance Office in Johannesburg and get the map I required of the border between the Transvaal and Botswana. I would have to walk over the border since all cars were stopped and searched at the frontier. I thought a solution had emerged when I met by chance a sympathiser of the movement, who offered to take me out of the country in the boot of her car. I accepted readily, prepared myself and said my goodbyes to Mary, but on my arrival at the venue, the sympathiser said she had changed her mind as the risk was too great.

And so I began an elaborate alternative plan. I hired a car under an assumed name, then bought two grey outfits which resembled police uniforms. I acquired two compasses, a torch, water bottle and other equipment for a fairly long trek through the bush. I then waited for full moon and on a predetermined day, left the house, picked up the car and, with an enormous sense of release, drove out of Johannesburg heading north. I drove through Pretoria, fearful of being recognised, but also elated by the thought that I was breaking all the rules, escaping from the confinement I had lived in for so many months.

Out of Pretoria along surprisingly open highways, I headed through the northwest Transvaal in the direction of Botswana. The roads were beautifully marked out with white paint, every camber and centre line was beautifully distinguishable and it dawned on me that these were no ordinary roads but military highways providing access to South African frontiers with black

Africa. The roads would enable helicopters and military aircraft to land in many places and troop convoys could move with great speed. I realised how much South Africa had been militarised during my stay in prison.

The plan was to time my arrival at a point 15 miles inside the border for precisely 8.00 p.m. when it would be night. I would then remove a wheel from the car, jack it up, pretend that I had had a breakdown and then head off across farmland for the border. However, on arriving at the point, as I was about to take out the jack, I heard a bicycle approaching. I froze but the cyclist was aware of my presence although it was pitch dark. He got off his bike and wheeled it slowly past me. I assumed that he was a police border guard going off duty at one of the posts 15 miles away. I waited with baited breath, pulse racing, fearful that my project was about to end, but he continued wheeling his bicycle for some distance and then rode off into the night.

It was an absolutely black night and so I grabbed my pack, took a compass bearing by torchlight and strode off into the night. It was only then that I knew I had made a terrible mistake. There was no moon and I could not see even my hand in front of me. I realised that the moon would rise later, leaving me to walk for several hours in total darkness through farmland with all its dangers. However, the sense of relief did not leave me and I strode off rapidly across a plowed field. I had gone some 100 yards or so when I heard the loud baying of a pack of dogs. I stopped and they came closer. Once again, I thought that this was the end. I stood stock still, barely breathing as the dogs came ever nearer. I sat down. What was the use of going on? And yet, after a while the dogs seemed to be stationary. Perhaps they were behind some fence nearby, barking only to protect their master's farm and not in pursuit of me after all.

I carefully took another compass reading, shielding the torchlight, and marched on. It was then that the enormity of my escape overwhelmed me. There was now no going back and a deep feeling of regret filled my soul. I was leaving my comrades, I was leaving Strachan and I was leaving Mary and the children. Who could say when we would be together again? What would await me miles ahead and then across the frontier in Botswana and beyond? I pressed on and found myself in the midst of thick thornbush country.

My regrets were overtaken by a new kind of terror. The place was overgrown by a kind of thornbush, the Wag-'n-Bietjie Bos, which had dozens of small strong hooks which seize and hold anything that comes in contact with it and is capable of scratching the flesh and tearing clothing. There was also a kind of cactus thorn – long and spiky and extremely painful. Once I was out of the ploughed field these two bushes awaited me and since the night was absolutely black I had to walk with my hands outstretched to save me crashing into them. Once I maneuvered my way through the bushes I picked up speed, only to encounter another hazard. These farms are separated by strong barbed-wire fences. I walked into many of these and every time the barbs ripped into my skin.

But I pressed on, examining the compass by a carefully shielded torchlight, cursing my failure to anticipate the time of the new moon's emergence. Then I realised that I could take a compass bearing on the stars and walk towards those stars without needing to refer to the compass so frequently. This worked very well and, subject only to confirmation every hour or two that I was on a correct bearing, I was able to make reasonable progress. Pressing on through the night, hands outstretched to fend off hooks and barbed wire, I was aware of the passing of time, but had no idea of the distance covered.

Several dogs barked in the distance. Sometimes it seemed that I was walking close to farmhouses. The sky was slowly getting lighter and, with it, visibility improved. On several occasions, I could see the faint outlines of farmhouses and skirted around them. I estimated an advance of barely two miles an hour, considerably less than I had planned. And then I saw a pale strip before me and realised it was the road I had to cross and which headed for a ford of the Limpopo River 15 miles away. There were no cars in sight and I crossed quickly.

The sky continued to lighten and I was expectant, hoping that the moon would rise speedily and light my way but, instead, the moonlight created great confusion with the bushes now casting long shadows so that I could not distinguish a tree from a shadow.

By this time I was stumbling, crashing into bushes, and it was an hour more before I could make proper headway. Now the ground sloped before me and it seemed as if it had been washed away by floods. This could only mean that I was getting nearer to the river which marks the border between South Africa and Botswana. The vegetation became thicker and the river ever closer. The stillness of the night was suddenly broken by shrieks of strange birds. Soon a cacophony of sounds seemingly shouted out an alarm to the human inhabitants nearby.

I suddenly came upon the riverbed, dry as a desert, cutting its way deep into the fine ground sand which yearned for its waters. By now I was too tired to exult. The birds were hovering overhead, emitting raucous shrieks, and dogs barked in the distance. I strode across the river, climbed over the eight-foot-high fence and knew I was in Botswana. A further walk of only some 15 miles remained in order to get away from any possible pursuers, keeping out of sight of the white farmers spread along the borders of South Africa who were known to have intercepted other escapees and returned them to the South African police.

It was just midnight, four hours since leaving the car. I walked on for an hour and then decided to rest. But the sand was full of nasty large ants which attacked me as soon as I sat down so I selected a large fallen tree on which I lay down for a brief rest. Soon it was time to move off again and I followed a well-worn path which had been used to move cattle. The bush was strangely quiet with only a rustle here and there as some little insect moved nearby. It was eerie yet comforting to be so far from human habitation, although I suspected that danger lurked on some of the large farms I traversed. It was a long night and my fatigue grew steadily. But there was no alternative to pressing on steadily. At five in the morning, with daylight now clearly around me, I reached a road which was deserted but had promise.

I followed the road until I saw an African policeman on his bicycle coming towards me. When he caught sight of me he almost fell off his bicycle. When I approached he said, 'Good God, sir, what happened to you? Did you have an accident with your car?' It then came to me that I was a most unusual sight for this young fellow. He had never before seen a white man walking along a road in this remote area, let alone one whose clothing was badly torn and who was covered with blood.

I hastily explained that I was a political refugee seeking asylum in Botswana. He was incredulous so I asked him to write down my name in his book, along with the road, time and date of our encounter, in case I came across the South African police or in case there was a kidnapping attempt. I then walked on for several miles until I came upon a police station. The sergeant was very helpful and phoned his headquarters at Mahalapye to alert them of my arrival.

An hour later I was put on a bus crowded with African peasants with their chickens and bundles, delighted to be in Black Africa at last. When the bus arrived at Mahalapye two white Special Branch officers were waiting for me. They took me into an office for questioning. To my immense annoyance they were only interested in one thing: How and where had I crossed the border? I politely told them that I would not answer any questions about my escape and merely wanted to record my request for political asylum. They responded that they could not allow an unauthorised person to enter the country without proper papers. I had no passport or, indeed, any other piece of paper on me apart from 100 pounds in South African currency.

The questioning lasted several hours. They returned again and again to the question of how I had entered the country, suggesting that I had come in somebody's car. It never occurred to them that I might have walked such a long way, even though my physical condition provided clear evidence of a rather unconventional entry. At last they relented and allowed me to phone Mary. By this time it was early evening and Mary was waiting anxiously at home. When I told her where I was and that I was safe, we exulted. Now, all that remained was that she should find a way of joining me in exile.

TRAPPED IN BOTSWANA

The Special Branch told me that there were many indications that the South African police and their agents were operating freely in the country. There were also many South African refugees in camps in the town and so they were anxious that I should depart speedily and go north to Francistown. I was instructed to register under an assumed name at a hotel in Francistown and wait for further instructions. I caught a freight train to Francistown and duly arrived at the hotel where I took a bath, changed into my spare clothing and had a decent meal.

During the next four days, I saw the Special Branch on several occasions, always feeling threatened by their presence. However, a British voluntary worker, Peter MacKay, then visited me. He was running a rescue service for political refugees who needed to get out of Botswana. He was an unusual fellow for this sort of work. Clearly an ex-British army officer, he was brisk and efficient, and said little about himself or the operation. I was somewhat suspicious at first, but he assured me that he had been doing this for some time and, in any case, I had no choice but to put my trust in him.

On my fourth night, Peter arrived in an over-sized Land Rover and I joined a group of about eight African refugees who were similarly fleeing the region. We drove all night through the immense forests that are populated with some of the largest elephants in Africa, with much other wild game in evidence. Much of the route coincided with a forest trail and we bumped along with lights lowered in case the Rhodesian security forces, which were patrolling nearby, confronted us. At one point we even crossed into Rhodesia since the rough road took a detour.

Early in the morning we arrived at a small encampment of five grass huts at Kazungula, which was to be my home for the next four weeks. At the camp there were about 20 refugees, most of them from South West Africa and some from Zimbabwe. I was the only South African. They belonged to all the liberation movements in the region – Swapo, Zanu, Zapu – and there was even a Mozambican. We spent our time sitting by the side of the Limpopo River which marks the boundary between Botswana and Zambia with the South African occupied Caprivi Strip located in the middle of the river only a few miles away.

I was able to phone Mary from Francistown but learned that once I had phoned her, the Special Branch had picked up the story on the telephone tap and were at the house within minutes. They harassed her, demanding to know how I had escaped and what her role had been. She pleaded ignorance about the whole affair but they would not leave her alone. The children had not known in advance and they were very excited about the news. When the press got the story, it was blazoned across the front pages of the *Sunday Times*. My parents were delighted to hear of my escape, but were then shattered when another newspaper printed a front-page story with blaring headlines: 'TUROK TRAPPED IN THE BUSH'. It said that I was stuck in the north of Botswana, unable to get farther north and trapped in a refugee camp with freedom fighters from all over the region.

I spent a total of three-and-a-half weeks in Kazungula. Time dragged because we had no idea how long we would have to stay there. But it was a friendly group and we all got on very well. There was lots of time for swimming in the river and watching the hippos while also keeping an eye open for crocodiles.

From the moment I entered Botswana I had firmly in mind the problem of the return. I acquired some maps of the country and kept an eye open on the terrain and possibilities for infiltration. During the weeks in Kazungula I went into the local village on several occasions, talked to forestry officials and questioned at length some of the Swapo refugees who had crossed on foot the thick forests stretching from northern Namibia to the camp. They had had many difficulties with the bushmen who led a wholly separate existence from the rest of the population, living largely off game, fruit and roots, and who knew the forest intimately. However, being desperately poor, they were easily subject to corruption by police and officials and had been recruited to give away any transient refugees. They would clearly be the main obstacle for any move to infiltrate ANC personnel down south. I tried to assess the problems to be faced by a group of comrades on a long march from Kazungula to the borders of South Africa, keeping concealed and living off the land to some extent. I thought that what we needed was a series of posting stages where cadres could sleep over, draw rations and be briefed on the road ahead. By the end of my stay, I had developed a plan that I was anxious to convey to the ANC. It was then that Tennyson Makiwane arrived from Lusaka in a Land Rover to fetch me. I knew him well from the time when he was a cub reporter for *The Guardian* in

Johannesburg, and as a co-accused in the Treason Trial. He was a bright young man of great promise and it was wonderful to see him. Some years later he joined a dissident group in the ANC, then returned to South Africa, became a police agent and was assassinated by an ANC cadre. But for me, at that moment, he was my liberator. With much sadness I said goodbye to my close friends in the camp. Tennyson and I drove on to the river ferry and then north to Lusaka, the capital of Zambia.

En route I started to explain the maps and information, but Tennyson asked me to save the report for other people in Lusaka. On arrival I was taken to the house of Simon Zukas, my old comrade from the Students Socialist Party at the University of Cape Town. In the interim Simon had had a stormy career. On returning to his home in Lusaka, which was then the main city of Northern Rhodesia, he had thrown himself into the anti-federation struggle. As the struggle came to a head, he was detained by the colonial administration and deported to Britain in 1952. When independence was finally conceded in 1964, Simon came back as a hero of the struggle.

The immigration officers in Zambia were white relics from the pre-independence days. They refused me permission to stay and gave me 48 hours to leave. Tennyson advised that I obey, so I boarded a plane for Nairobi, arriving in the early evening armed with two letters from Tennyson. One was for Joseph Murumbi, Kenya's first vice president, the other for Tom Mboya, Minister of Labour, and a charismatic leader whose name was renowned throughout Africa and one of its brightest stars.

I waited for the other passengers to go through the formalities so that I would be last. The immigration officer, who was also white, asked for my passport and papers. Instead, I offered him my two letters explaining that I was seeking refuge. He refused to accept them and said that South African refugees were not welcome in Kenya and that I would be put back on the first plane for Johannesburg. Imagine my dismay! Furious, I told him that on no account would I allow him to do so and that I would fight physically all the way. A flaming row ensued until he relented and gave me a 24-hour stay permit, instructing me to report to Immigration the next day.

Suddenly it dawned on me that I was really free. Once I had put my foot inside Kenya my troubles would be over. Entering the airport lobby I was struck by the wonder of a new life awaiting me. There were whites and blacks everywhere, talking animatedly. They were shaking hands, in one or two cases even embracing, and keeping eye contact in a way that did not happen in South Africa. It seemed that race relations could be normal and that Kenya would be a haven from the hatred to which I had become so accustomed.

I phoned Ezekiel Mphahlele, a distinguished South African writer who, overjoyed to hear from me, was soon on his way to fetch me. He installed me in the Nairobi Club where I could sort out my destiny. The next day I went to Immigration and explained that I wanted to await Mary's arrival since she was due to leave South Africa with the children on an exit permit. We expected no difficulty since she held dual South African and British citizenship, so I was given another seven days.

Nairobi was a beautiful city. I visited the offices of the *Daily Nation* where Tony and Eve Hall worked as journalists. They introduced me to George Githi, the editor, who was extremely friendly and published an interview with me on the front page of the paper. Ezekiel and his wife Rebecca were also very helpful and I spent much time with them. I was determined to stay in Kenya at all costs. My letter to Mr Murumbi led to an interview, and he said he would do what he could to enable me to stay in the country even though this was against government policy.

I soon heard from Mary that all was well, except that the application for an exit permit was taking much longer than expected. Since she was confined to the one square mile around the house, she was unable to go to the Magistrate's Office in central Johannesburg to pick up the necessary form to apply for an exit permit. The officials were adamant that they could not post the form – the Special Branch was clearly very angry. And so my father had to fly from Cape Town to Pretoria, obtain a form, come down to Johannesburg so that Mary could fill the form in, and then take it back to Pretoria. After some weeks her exit permit arrived with a condition that she thereby relinquished all rights to remain in South Africa.

After four long weeks of living on the 100 pounds I had brought with me, Mary and the children finally arrived in Nairobi. It was a joyful reunion with the boys more exuberant than ever while Mary was clearly exhausted by the harassment she had experienced. We took two rooms on a small back street, in Plums Hotel, a rather run-down place where we could sort out our future. We enrolled the boys in a school and began once again the battle with Immigration. But they wanted us to leave for England as soon as possible even though we were determined to stay. After a few weeks when our visitors' passes elapsed, we were living there on sufferance, without the right to work. Mary got a job as a secretary to a publisher just as all our money ran out. She had been allowed to take out of the country only 250 pounds and most of that went on our first month's hotel bill. Fortunately, Mary's mother sent us 500 pounds and, together with the income her job provided, we could survive.

We soon settled into a routine, house-sitting for people who were on leave in the UK. Having determined that we wanted to stay in Kenya, we contacted Tom Mboya who could not see us but wrote us a very friendly letter. Mary had met Mboya at a conference in Cairo in 1960 called by the Afro-Asian Solidarity Movement and had actually spent an evening with him, but that was not enough to get us what we wanted, namely to stay and work in Kenya. So we sent out other feelers. Njoroge Mungai, then Minister of Defence (and a former graduate of Fort Hare University in South Africa) actually came to our hotel to investigate our plight. But that too did not produce any results. I made numerous visits to the office of Daniel Arap Moi, then Minister of Home Affairs, and tried to persuade him to allow us to stay but, although personally friendly, he was evasive and nothing materialised.

We were fascinated by Nairobi although the whites were colonial in their attitudes and racists to an extraordinary degree. They always assumed that we, being South Africans, would appreciate their prejudices. Nevertheless, we felt we could live happily in Kenya. We made many African friends and the boys settled into the mixed school very easily. It was surprising, even to us, how little colour mattered to them. They were fascinated by the black children and enjoyed playing with them. The school was a good one and the boys felt at home almost immediately. We tried as best we could to understand African politics and viewpoints. I talked endlessly with hawkers, people in the street, in pubs and wherever we could meet ordinary Kenyans who seemed very politically conscious. We even joined a tennis club where we met the head of the Kenya Central Bank and various businessmen. We gained some insight into the struggle of the Mau Mau and the wider struggle for independence that had so traumatised the country.

Living in a large house with a lovely garden, we enjoyed the fruits of the white suburbs, the abundant avocado pear trees and the frequent parties. And yet we resented strongly the class and race barriers that were so visible everywhere. In the streets there were three categories. In the cars there were whites, in the buses Africans, whilst most of those who walked in the streets were African women, often carrying amazingly large bundles of firewood and other household goods. We were shocked by the enormous burden placed upon African women and learned with dismay about the physical damage done to their bodies by a lifetime of buckling under huge bundles of firewood.

One day, we received a phone call to say that Yusuf Dadoo was passing through Nairobi and would visit us. This was virtually our first contact with the movement since our arrival in Kenya. We were uneasy about his visit and I suspect that we did not handle it well. We were probably unfair to Yusuf who had, after all, been sent into exile by the movement in order to work with Oliver Tambo in the external mission. In any event, he invited us out to dinner on which occasion I felt it necessary to convey to him what I had, in fact, been asked to say by people in prison and those struggling to maintain the structures around Bram. I told him that there was universal criticism of Operation Mayibuye and that comrades were immensely critical of the fact that certain leaders had left the country when they ought to have stayed to rally the movement. Comrades at home were highly appreciative of Bram in his refusal to remain in London as he was encouraged to do by the exile committee. He thought it was right for him to return and attempt to raise, once again, the banner of struggle from underground.

I told him that my prison comrades felt that efforts should be organised outside to help the prisoners on Robben Island to escape. I told him the conditions under which I had been allowed to leave and that Bram expected those in exile to return to rebuild the underground. I also informed him about the material and maps I had collected on my way out. Yusuf was amiable as ever, but we got the impression that he was either unwilling or unable to take on board the messages we brought out and that it was all rather unpalatable. We had the impression from him and others we met subsequently that the leaders in exile had come to believe that their own situation was actually no better than those who were in prison or underground at home. Yusuf was anxious to placate me and he offered me a trip to a conference in Cairo, but I was not really interested since I was preoccupied with survival in Nairobi. The evening was a dismal failure.

Others visited us too. Ruth First passed through and Ray Simons, who was as warm and comradely as ever, though rather preoccupied with obtaining taps and other gear for the house she and Jack were building in Lusaka. They, too, had decided to stay in Africa, one of the few white couples to do so.

The months went by with no change in our circumstances. I lobbied as hard as I could with Administration and Home Affairs, without success. Everyone was polite but adamant that there was no place for us in Kenya and that we should leave for Britain. I managed to bluff my way into a job with the Survey of Kenya since they were desperately short of qualified staff and they gave me a senior post. Since the system had been set up by South African surveyors, I felt at home, but it lasted only a week. The Director of Surveys called me in to inform me that the permanent secretary, Home Affairs, had heard of my being taken on and instructed him to dismiss me. The one-month's pay in lieu of notice was nevertheless helpful. I took on a job selling *Encyclopaedia Britannica* door-to-door, but it only lasted a month.

George Githi, editor of the *Daily Nation*, invited us to a party at his house where I spent the evening telling stories to a tall, burly, but very friendly Kenyan about how white settlers in Nairobi confided in us about the 'ignorant Africans' who had taken charge of the country after independence. He encouraged me in my story-telling and we had a very convivial evening. However, when George drove us home at 1.00 in the morning, he asked me whether I knew who I had been talking to and told me that he was the deputy commissioner of the Special Branch. Mary and I spent the rest of the night sitting up in bed going over all the stories and assessing the implications of what we had given away. We thought that we had probably said enough to damn us forever in the eyes of the Kenyan government which was bending over backwards to accommodate and conciliate the whites even in the face of racism and self-serving activities.

After several more weeks of struggling to get permission to work I phoned this man from the Special Branch and asked him whether we would ever get permission to stay in Kenya. He was as friendly as before, but said that it was quite beyond his power to assist us and nor could he ever discuss the case with me. I then said: 'I am going to ask you a question. If you do not reply then I shall know where I stand. Is it your advice that we leave the country?' He did not reply, so I knew that we had reached the end of the road. I was also informed by a friend that the South African Special Branch had sent a file about me to the Kenyan authorities and indeed to all the police throughout the region and that this was enough to block my applications everywhere.

As a last resort I wrote to President Nyerere explaining our condition and asking for leave to come to Tanzania. Very soon we received a favourable reply from the Ministry of Home Affairs inviting me to apply for a job in the survey division. I went down to Dar es Salaam, was interviewed and told that they had not seen a person with my qualifications for many, many years. I was offered a job immediately and returned to Nairobi to fetch the family for the next stage of our East African safari.

CHAPTER SEVEN

CRISIS IN THE ANC

I have dwelt at some length in the previous chapters on issues of race and how they affected us in the movement. Even now, looking back on all that happened, and all that is of such concern to us in the new South Africa, I still marvel at the very special way that race is handled among comrades, but also in the larger society. I think that what distinguishes most South Africans, but especially those in the progressive movement, is that we try not to hide from racial differences, or conceal our different language preferences, and strive to maintain calm, mutual relationships which can be deeply meaningful and totally sincere. Of course, sometimes there are rough edges and even misunderstandings that can be directly ascribed to different racial backgrounds, but they can be overcome because we accept our common bond as South Africans.

I reiterate all this because my arrival in what we curiously call black Africa, as though South Africa is not black, was so meaningful. In those days little was known about the rest of Africa because of our isolation. Africa was thought of as the continent of African nationalism led by people like Kwame Nkrumah and Jomo Kenyatta who were either portrayed as wicked racists or as superheroes who had defeated British Imperialism. Later, Africa came to be seen as a basket case where everything had gone wrong because Africans were incompetent to maintain what the whites had built.

But what I found in Africa was quite different and unexpected. Suddenly, I was thrust into an environment of non-racial behaviour where the colour of your skin was noted but not remarked upon – it was indeed not remarkable. People were just too busy being vibrant, exuberant and warm in their social relations to pause and behave differently towards a white man. Of course there were plenty of exceptions, especially among the more bourgeois types, but for the 'people in the street' there seemed to be no concern about colour. I found this immensely liberating, far more so than I had ever experienced at home. I relished this new sense of freedom from being a 'white' person in a black country, or even being a 'white' person in 'white' company as one inevitably was at home. I was suddenly anonymous, just normal, and I recalled how on other occasions I had been irritated at being acknowledged as being 'Jewish' or 'rich' or 'white' or whatever. I have noticed the same feeling in others who at times tire of being labelled. We just want to be ordinary *Homo sapiens*.

I was also struck by the universality of poverty juxtaposed with affluence. It is of course a mark of colonial society that destitution – being shoeless, being clothed in torn shirt and pants, living in a shack – is the lot of most people, while a small group lives in luxurious suburbs. But while at home there are large affluent suburbs where whites may live 'white' lives, in Africa the predominant feel is that of Africans.

I made a point of speaking to many such people in the street, in bars, or hawkers who came to ply their wares at our house. I found the Kenyans, especially the Kikuyu, very politically aware. After all, they had been through a major civil war and had forced the British to retreat, but I also found a good deal of common sense, politeness and decency, for which the South African media machine had not prepared me. The little black children were particularly delightful.

And so I came to fall in love with Africa and that has never left me. When I came home in 1990 and read the reports of white South African journalists who had visited Nigeria or Ghana or elsewhere, and how disgusted they were with the lack of amenities or with corruption or whatever, I was filled with indignation. They simply did not understand, they could not understand, and they were biased by years of racial prejudice. Africa is full of vitality and energy. If only its economies were given a little scope by a hostile global order, Africa would thrive.

These feelings were a vindication of my own sacrifices and commitment to our own movement and the cause of non-racialism.

My children thrived in African schools, they were greatly enriched by the company of black school children, and we were content to make the continent our home forever.

I grappled with the social and economic problems facing these countries. How was it that the obvious sources of wealth around me failed to trickle down to the poor? How was it that public services were in disarray? How was it that officials and the rich of either colour were so indifferent to the poor? How was it that government and parliament was a charade? And so I turned to the literature of political theory, of underdevelopment and political economy seeking explanations for these systemic wrongs. I also read everything I could on neocolonialism, since it was apparent that a new class had emerged in African countries which had usurped the role of the colonial masters and misdirected the whole struggle for liberation and independence.

This is why, when I came to work and teach in Africa, I immersed myself in the problems of Africa, which to some extent displaced my concerns with our own liberation struggle. I have never regretted this and my bookshelves abound with books and papers on African development which, I insist, are wholly relevant to our own situation. Would that our comrades in the ANC had allowed themselves to absorb some of these lessons when they were in exile instead of living in little South African enclaves shutting out the Africa around them.

Even in 1990 when I came home and started a branch of the Institute For African Alternatives (IFAA) in Johannesburg, and urged that the ANC reach out to Africa as an essential home for all of us, my proposals were turned down on the grounds that Europe was our major trading partner and the obvious source of investment and new technology. 'Why do you want us to join a basket case?' I was asked. It has taken a good few years for comrades to learn otherwise.

And so when Thabo Mbeki declared, 'I am an African' and when he launched the campaign for the African Renaissance, I was intrigued and more than willing to exult in this new imagery.

SANCTUARY IN TANZANIA

To return to my story and our decision to go to Tanzania. Early one morning in October 1966 Mary and I and the three boys, accompanied by several suitcases, set off on the long drive from Nairobi to Dar es Salaam. Any feeling of insecurity or disappointment was dissolved by the effervescence and high spiritedness of the children. They loved Africa and were excited by all the adventures they had enjoyed during the past nine months, which was a wonderful contrast to the years of suffocation in Johannesburg. And so it was with a light heart and high expectations that we drove through the dusty countryside to the border post with Tanzania. At least I would have work, Mary could also work openly and we would have official papers to protect us.

We arrived at an isolated post in the bush where a sleepy immigration officer, this time black and friendly, offered me a form to fill in. The boys were looking on, fascinated by this new adventure. The form indicated I had to specify my race and gave three options: European, African, Other. Since I had no visa or passport, I showed the officer my letter from the Tanzanian Home Affairs Office and explained that I was a South African refugee. I began to fill in the form, but when I came to the question about race, I asked which block I should tick. He said 'European', but I jokingly said 'I am not European, I have never been to Europe. I am a South African – can I fill in "African"?' But he refused and said I would not be allowed in unless I completed that answer. We haggled for a while with the boys egging me on. The official explained that the information on race was needed for census purposes. So I offered as a compromise the category 'white African'. He appreciated the point and from then on the boys all adopted that term whenever they were challenged at school or elsewhere and vigorously defended the title 'white African'.

We arrived in Dar es Salaam and drove directly to the headquarters of the Survey Division where I was informed that I had been appointed regional surveyor and town planner for Dar es Salaam and the whole coastal region. I was to be given a government house and placed in charge of the regional headquarters that employed several expatriates, about a dozen Tanzanian technicians and a hundred African semi-skilled workers of various grades. The headquarters of the Survey Division was in a delightful old colonial building right on the harbour. In keeping with the architecture and the general atmosphere, the senior staff were British expatriates who had been in the country for decades. They were typical colonials and it was evident that independence had made little difference to their lifestyle and the way they ran the department. All the juniors were African and the gap between professional staff and the rest was large.

We established ourselves in the large house allocated to us, which was surrounded by dense bush. We soon acquired a domestic servant, Hassani, who was amiable enough, but given to frequent complaining about fevers and illnesses, which slowed down his already lethargic approach to his job. But the boys liked him and we were happy enough.

Dar es Salaam was steamy hot. The humidity often rose to 100 per cent and the flat roof of the house got so hot in the midday sun that all one could do was to lie prone, waiting for the cooler evening. Even then, the hot slab of concrete was menacing and overpowering. Fortunately the work hours of government officials were from 7.30 a.m. to 2.30 p.m. and so one could spend the afternoon doing nothing, as was the custom. I found that the previous incumbent of my office, Jackson, actually took a lunch break, even though we were supposed to work through. Indeed, his approach to the job was so laid back that the productivity of the office was way below its potential. When I took over we reorganised the work and in a few months the office was humming – producing far more than any of the offices in the country and of better quality.

The children enrolled in the mixed-race Bunge School where they settled in happily. African children are generally rather boisterous and outgoing and our boys were no less so than they. With the outdoor life available to them and the excitement of so many new experiences, they flourished as never before. Mary got a research job with Professor Chris Wood at the medical school and so it now looked as if we were settled for some time to come.

We immediately made contact with the ANC office which was located at the other end of town in a rather dirty part of the main street and in a gloomy building which had not been painted for many years. As we entered a dark outer office, we introduced ourselves to the desk officer. Behind him were several little offices all rather dimly lit by electric lights and occupied by several comrades seated at over-laden desks with paper everywhere. A few of the comrades knew about us and welcomed us very warmly. There were embraces and 'Welcome, comrade' and we were privileged to be shown into the inner sanctum of the chief representative, Mzwai Piliso. Piliso was a dour sort of man, very heavily built, not given to much conversation. He had apparently first joined the movement in exile, which was a great disadvantage since he lacked the confidence of those who had spent years in the movement at home. The outsiders were often obliged to assert themselves rather more in order to acquire legitimacy. We had a fairly brief chat and Piliso behaved properly enough, but the disarray in the office cast a pall on our first serious contact with the formal structures of the movement in exile. This was an important milestone for us: we were now firmly ensconced in jobs, a house and had a formal organisational identity – no small matter for a refugee.

We made friends with Josiah Jele who was then a junior official in the ANC. He was a nice man – friendly, gentle, but very disgruntled about his role in the office which was tedious and meaningless. There were contacts with the government, liaisons with the embassies, routine contacts with the administration on behalf of arrivals and departures since there was a constant ebb and flow of members between Dar es Salaam and other centres in the region. We were later to hear that there were also MK camps in the interior and these had to be serviced with supplies. There were also several smaller camps where cadres stayed either because they were ill or for other reasons. The office also produced a monthly news digest consisting of extracts from the South African and other press together with an editorial and this required a considerable amount of administrative work. Jele talked freely to us about the problems of the region. The organisation was not in good shape, there was a great deal of frustration and he himself was immensely bored and wanted to study.

We were the only white members of the ANC living in Dar es

Salaam which was partly because it was against government policy to receive white refugees in the whole region. The Simons were an important exception in Lusaka and we were fortunate to have made it to Dar es Salaam. Most white members had gone to the UK where a substantial colony had established itself. By now we understood the reasons for the prohibitions against white comrades from South Africa. Already in the days of Kwame Nkrumah the PAC had persuaded Africa's leaders that the ANC's multi-racialism was a mechanism for domination by white communists. They had advanced this as one reason, if not the main one, for their breakaway from the mother body, and in Africa where there was no equivalent group to South Africa's white progressives, this explanation was accepted. And so throughout the continent, white South African meant communist, and they wanted none of it.

I was still obsessed with the mandate I had been given by Bram Fischer to return to South Africa and plagued by a sense of guilt. I was also anxious to pass on the information I had gathered about possibilities of returning on my trip to Botswana. After a few weeks I was able to meet Oliver Tambo for a debriefing. We sat on the beach near Dar es Salaam harbour and I unburdened myself about my maps and all the rest for about three hours. He was patient and attentive but his response was that they had tried unsuccessfully to infiltrate cadres through Botswana. The distance was too long and the obstacles too great. He seemed somewhat dispirited and I was unsure about accepting his view that return was not feasible.

I also met Moses Kotane who to my dismay was very cool and barely greeted me. He was then based in Morogoro, as were the other senior figures, and he was treasurer of the ANC and commissar in chief of MK. I subsequently learned that Moses unaccountably held me partly responsible for the debacle of the turn to violence and for the disaster of Rivonia, which was ironic given my actual role. Since he did not raise the matter with me directly, however, I could not explain my own position and doubts. Moses was a somewhat changed person. He was much more reserved, had aged considerably and seemed to keep his own counsel.

Another member of the key triumvirate was JB Marks. JB was a big man and big-hearted as well. He was jovial, well meaning and kind, and I was grateful to him for his warmth and openness. He seemed to be playing a sort of fatherly role in the movement, striving to maintain good relations between comrades and sustain morale. In contrast, Moses, the strong man of the movement, was very much the disciplinarian, strict with money and insistent upon proper procedures and order. His style was also rather different from that of Oliver who exuded goodwill to all, was forgiving of misdeeds and excesses and was, above all, concerned with keeping the organisation together.

On one social occasion when the ANC was celebrating one of its annual days, one of the officials, who was very drunk, actually seized Oliver by the jacket and threatened him. Other comrades dragged him away but no disciplinary action was taken. It seemed to be Oliver's wish that misconduct should not be judged too harshly and that personal and even political differences should be put aside in the interest of unity.

PLANNING FOR TANZANIAN SOCIALISM

With the ANC apparently dormant and no role yet for me, I threw myself into my work as regional surveyor and planner. There was a great deal to be done. I had my own office on the outskirts of Dar es Salaam, a staff of about 100 and a large workload. Our task was to send survey teams throughout the region, which was about 100 miles in radius, who surveyed the areas and prepared maps for planning and registration purposes. I enjoyed the organisational and planning aspects a great deal and steadily improved our efficiency. I very soon developed a great commitment to Tanzania and its people whose kindness seduced us completely. President Nyerere was an enlightened leader who was trying to take the country in a democratic direction and I wanted to be part of that exercise.

I found the ordinary Tanzanians honest, friendly in the extreme and helpful in a way rarely found in other countries. They charmed both the children and ourselves. In the streets of Dar es Salaam we took great pleasure in buying sliced mangos sprinkled with piri piri powder for only a penny. Fruit was very cheap and abundant. On a Sunday evening, our family would go to a little Arab hotel in the back streets of Dar es Salaam where we could get a large metal tray with as much food as one wanted consisting of small cakes, chutneys, curry, sauces and sweetmeats. This was our great party night and the boys simply loved it. We began to travel outside Dar es Salaam in our Peugeot 503 station wagon. There were beautiful mountains on the outskirts of Morogaro where we spent some weekends bathing in the mountain pools and sleeping in a shack that was available for tourists. Most of our social life revolved around friends at the university some nine miles out of town.

It was an exciting time politically in Tanzania, with Nyerere playing the role of enlightened leader in the whole sub-continent and beyond. The university had attracted some of the best Africanist scholars on the continent and there was a group of radicals who were extremely active intellectually. There were endless seminars, conferences and meetings of all kinds. John Saul and Giovanni Arrighi were among our best friends and both were leading figures in the radical intellectual life at the university. My office hours were from 7.30 a.m. to 2.30 p.m. without a break since the heat of the afternoon made it difficult to work. I would go home, have some lunch and then a siesta, which meant that by 4.00 p.m. I was free to do anything else. I decided to take a postgraduate degree at the university but found that there was no Philosophy Department, which would have been my preference following on the philosophy I had done in my second degree while in jail. So I registered instead for an MA in political philosophy under the supervision of Rene Brown in the Political Science Department. I spent most of my afternoons reading theories of socialism and the writings about Ujamaa, usually by Nyerere, and trying to develop a Marxist critique of his positions. My friends at the university were often very helpful. At other times I would take the boys down to the beach nearby and we swam and fooled about.

The politics of Tanzania was transformed when Nyerere launched the Arusha Declaration in 1967, making Ujamaa Tanzania's official ideology and policy. It was a very radical declaration, making the case for a new kind of socialism based on traditional concepts of co-operation and self-reliance, but which also included the nationalisation of the banks, industry and commerce. The whole country went into a paroxysm of debate, not least at our university. Socialist groups came into existence and some of the Tanzanian youth went rather further than Nyerere intended. The leader of the Tanzanian Youth League was detained after he entered a Dutch bank and removed a portrait of the king. Others who took too literally Nyerere's call for a revolution were also detained and Nyerere delivered a warning at the university that Marxism/Leninism was incompatible with Ujamaa. At the same time Nyerere sought to galvanise the country around the declaration. A week of mobilisation was called and, as the senior officer in my department, I ensured that all our trucks were standing by to take the whole staff to town to participate in a march in support.

The march turned out to be rather more enthusiastically supported than I had bargained for. I found myself in the midst of some 30 000 demonstrators shuffling at a trot through the streets of the city shouting 'Chinja' which means 'cut' or 'attack', and the crowd was clearly in a militant mood. Mine was the only white face as far as I could see and there were moments when I thought that I had been rather too bold. But we arrived safely enough in front of the party headquarters where Nyerere addressed us from the balcony. It was the first time I had heard him speak and he was fascinating. Nyerere is not generally thought of as a populist or a demagogue, but he was certainly able to rouse the crowd, and he did not hesitate to generate considerable heat. But he was careful to wind down towards the end. This was obviously deliberate and reflected his ambivalence about involving the masses in political action.

Throughout the period of the Arusha mobilisation, conflicting signals came from Nyerere and the government. On the one hand, we were given to understand that a revolution had been unleashed which would change the whole character of Tanzanian society. On the other hand, there was caution and moderation. This was also true about the way Tanzania treated the liberation movements. On the one hand the ANC, PAC, Swapo, Zapu, Frelimo, MPLA and so on had offices in Dar es Salaam and enjoyed the protection of the Tanzanian government. At the same time the government was obviously anxious about the presence of so many revolutionaries and militants and often very critical of them. Sometimes we were referred to as 'revolutionaries' and at others as 'Wakimbizi' (refugees, or more literally, runaways) and subjected to derogatory comments in the official press and even by Tanu leaders. Nevertheless the overriding atmosphere in the country was exciting and stirring. At the academic level it was one of the most productive in the history of the university, with the left developing new theories about the possibilities of transition in Africa. There was also a great deal of political support for the liberation movements at the university.

On one occasion a two-day symposium was planned in which all of the liberation movements would be given an opportunity to explain their policies. On the first evening, the ANC, Frelimo, MPLA and Zapu would speak and on the second evening the alternative cluster – PAC, Zanu and others of that grouping – would be given the floor. There was much interest in the symposium and a full house was guaranteed. Mary and I made our way to the university in good time for the first meeting. On our arrival I was met by the president of the Students' Revolutionary Association, Yoweri Museveni, later to become president of Uganda. He informed me that the ANC and other organisations had withdrawn from the meeting because of an attack on the liberation movements in the *Daily Nation* that morning which portrayed the movements as cowardly and content to enjoy the fruits of exile. He asked me whether I would speak instead, but I declined on the grounds that I had no official status in the ANC. However, Museveni explained that the platform would be non-political and would consist of a spokesperson from the OAU Liberation Committee, a member of Tanu (the Tanzanian official party) and someone from the Comoros Liberation Movement. I then agreed to speak and joined the group on the platform. To my dismay the Liberation Committee representative spoke for only ten minutes in a low key on the history of that committee. The Tanu speaker did not show up. Another speaker was unable to contribute since he spoke only French and the remaining speaker delivered a brief address in Swahili. So I was left as the main speaker facing a very excited audience of some 300 students and staff who had expected a high-powered meeting about the liberation struggle.

I did my best to present the situation in South Africa and the problems of liberation and was reasonably well received but, in the middle of my talk, I noticed that two people had entered the hall who I recognised to be Stokely Carmichael from the US and David Sibeko, the chief representative of the PAC. Stokely was then the main spokesperson of the Black Power movement in the United States with a reputation throughout the world. When I sat down, Stokely rose and delivered a vicious personal attack on me. He said: 'I refuse to be told about South Africa by a white man. Your father has blood on his hands and he is a murderer. How dare you talk to us about the black people?' He continued in this vein, bringing the whole audience to a frenzy with cries of 'Black Power', raising the clenched fist in salute. I was aghast and for a moment thought that the crowd would descend upon me and beat me up. But I kept my cool and rose to reply, saying that while I agreed with many of his sentiments, he had chosen the wrong target for his attack. I said that I had spent many years in the liberation movement in South Africa and had just emerged from three years in prison, most of it in solitary confinement. He therefore had absolutely no right to impugn my motives or seek to discredit my role in the struggle.

As I sat down there was some applause and I knew that although I had not won the round I had at least drawn the sting of the attack. Many speakers from the floor rose to support Black Power and it was a mark of the intensity of the atmosphere that none of my radical friends rose to my defence. It was left to Walter Rodney, a black historian from Guyana, to present a balanced view. He explained that racism was endemic in capitalism and that it should not be taken out of context. This meant that in the struggle against capitalism white allies might have a role and that Black Power should not exclude such participants. I was immensely grateful to Walter for his contribution, which had calmed down the audience consisting of radical students who greatly admired him as a revolutionary and the meeting ended on a positive note. The next day, one of the newspapers carried a story about the meeting and described my 'heroic' defence of the role of whites in Africa and so it was that many of the white expatriates in my ministry and elsewhere expressed great appreciation. I tried to enlighten them that the report was a total misrepresentation of what I had said but the point was lost with no great damage done.

The next day Museveni and his whole committee came to my office and apologised for the position in which I had been placed at the meeting and expressed regret for the hostility I had been subjected to. We became good friends and I reminded him of this occasion when we met at the government headquarters in Kampala many years later.

There was little other than work and politics to hold our interest in Dar es Salaam. There were no cinemas, hardly any theatre and the only music was a small band of volunteers, including our second son Ivan, who struggled with his violin at the occasional musical evening. The main social activities were the frequent embassy parties. Because of Nyerere's important role in Africa and partly because of the presence of the liberation movements, almost every country in the world had an embassy in Dar es Salaam and competed against the others for the number of parties they could hold. Once you got your name on the list you were invited to almost all of them and it was possible to spend several evenings every week in heavy drinking and socialising at these parties. The embassies worked hard at influencing officials in the liberation movements and there was some personal corruption. It was extremely difficult to maintain a sense of integrity in the face of this pressure, particularly for those who had no jobs, income or even social life outside of the orbit of their own movement.

An exception to the diplomatic norm was the mission of the People's Republic of South Vietnam, which happened to have a house next door to us. They befriended our children and we found them to be people of great modesty and integrity. We spent many hours talking to them and learning about their struggle. They were very interested in the problems of the ANC, particularly those relating to an exiled movement trying to rekindle the struggle at home. They insisted that the only way to generate an armed struggle was to start inside the country with whatever resources one could find, primarily the weapons taken from the enemy itself. This was the way it had been done in Vietnam and all thought of external intervention was unrealistic and unhelpful. I conveyed some of these ideas to our ANC comrades.

We also became very close to Eduardo Mondlane, president of Frelimo and his wife Janet. They were both careful about what they told us about the machinations in Frelimo which was going through some tough internal struggles while yet doing very well in terms of advancing the guerrilla war inside the country. Eduardo was a charming person, educated at Oberlin College in the US and, we thought, sometimes uncomfortably close to Americans in Dar. But he seemed to know what he was about and it was not our place to comment. Periodically there was a scare about his security and one evening he came to our house to say that he felt his life was in danger. We tried to persuade him to stay with us for a while, but he decided against this as it would send the wrong signal to his cadres. His fears were fully justified for in 1969 he was blown up by a letter bomb which had been placed under his chair in his study at home, resulting in a horrific blast which tore him to pieces and shattered the room. There was much speculation about who was responsible but we concluded that it was the Portuguese secret service. In 1975 he was credited as the father of Mozambique's independence.

We also saw much of Marcelino Dos Santos and his wife Pam who was a South African and had been a member of the COD at home. They lived in a small flat in Dar and it was our privilege to invite them for dinner and, in turn, visit them. Through these contacts we gained much insight into the difficulties of waging guerrilla warfare from a foreign country even though in their case it was a neighbour sharing a border. And so our world consisted of constant talk about warfare and liberation politics mingled with the problems of Ujamaa. In retrospect it seems that we were insufficiently aware of quite how historic those events were. But then the whole Third World seemed to be engaged in tough struggle, some of it violent, and the world itself was in great turmoil.

Meanwhile, our boys flourished. Ivan and Neil were extremely fortunate in having a pair of teachers, Scottish twins, who were both excellent at their work and totally dedicated. It was the period of 'new maths' and the boys benefited enormously from these women teachers who gave them such an intensive training that when we subsequently arrived in Britain they were streets ahead of their contemporaries. It may be that their subsequent success in the academic field was based on that preparation. Fred was less interested in schooling but he loved the open-air life of Dar es Salaam and had many friends. He began to walk around barefoot, acquired a sheathed bayonet that he wore dangling from his belt, and adopted Swahili as his main language. He even got himself a job at State House in the school holidays, serving as cleaner of the president's stables and could often be seen with the men exercising the horses on the beachfront. The only snag was that he seemed to be slowly losing the education he had previously acquired and was becoming too much of a street urchin and not enough of a schoolboy. He participated in a national youth day parade in a stadium, marching at the head of the procession, bayonet and all.

RURAL VILLAGES AT RUFIJI

It was some time in 1968 that the Rufiji River came down in flood, driving some 120 000 peasants out of the seven-mile-wide river delta which was one of the best cotton-growing areas in Tanzania. On this occasion the floods rose much higher than usual, destroying everything in their path, including thousands of huts built on stilts which were normally able to withstand the river. President Nyerere immediately set up a relief commission under Vice President Rashidi Kawawa consisting of all the regional heads of department in the Ministries of Water, Irrigation, Engineering, Community and so on. I was invited to the first meeting of the commission, which was told that the president wanted to take advantage of the new situation and establish permanent Ujamaa villages which would be flood-resistant on the banks of the river. We were to draw up plans to set this in motion and we were to act urgently since the distress of the local people was considerable. The president announced to the inhabitants that he would once again supply grain to feed them but that this would be the last time that he would approach foreign governments, in this case the US, for food aid and that henceforth the villages would have to become self-reliant in food.

A series of meetings followed in Rufiji, which was some 100 miles from Dar es Salaam, to persuade the villagers that they should leave their traditional places in the riverbed and start cultivating and living in communal villages on the riverbanks. Nyerere himself came down for a three-day tour of the region, and I was asked to accompany him and explain the planning aspect. It was a fascinating experience to travel with Nyerere's entourage and to see him speak to the villagers deep in the bush. He used two microphones, one to address the gathering of about 100 villagers and the second to circulate among the audience for questions and comments. Nyerere had enormous charm and was capable of communicating with the simplest of rural people and winning their support. They raised many questions about the project, including the most basic one, which was: If they left their traditional planting areas in the riverbed for the new unknown areas on the riverbank, would the government guarantee their food if difficulties arose? Nyerere's response was first to proclaim the importance of Ujamaa as a philosophy of working together which had to be recaptured from African tradition and put to work in the new circumstances. Secondly, that self-reliance had to become the main principle if the country was to be self-sufficient in food and independent of foreign aid. However, he agreed that initially the state would make available emergency food, seeds and fertiliser in order to launch farming in the new areas. The state would also provide organisational and technical back-up and perhaps even some army personnel to assist in building the new villages.

My role as the planner on the commission was to conduct a very rapid survey of the area and to design and lay out some 25 villages of some 250 plots each. I discussed the project with my heads at the ministry and found them totally sceptical. They argued that it would be impossible to complete such a survey in less than a year or two and that we had neither the staff nor equipment for the job. I went back to the field and developed a scheme that was simple but effective. Using existing aerial photographs and the standard cadastral maps, I consulted the regional commissioner about the location of the new villages. We carried out a tour of the whole region, selecting the most desirable locations in consultation with the local peasants. In a matter of weeks we had chosen the sites for the new villages and I was instructed to draft a model plan. But first I had to persuade the regional commissioner, Songambele, that Nyerere would have to set down certain criteria for these villages before I could proceed. I required to know how many families were expected to live in a typical Ujamaa village, how large a plot each household would be given, what facilities would ultimately be built in the village and the scale of individual and communal farming envisaged. Mr Songambele had been a taxi driver before independence and had very little education so our conversations were conducted in Swahili, of which I had now acquired a working knowledge, but it was very difficult to discuss things like planning, and principles of social organisation and production with him. Nevertheless, the guidelines I sought were soon obtained and I moved almost my whole staff down to Rufiji to begin operations.

Each of my technicians had a theodolite which was used to set out the basic framework of the villages, all of which were based on the same plan, but blocks could be moved about in accordance with the terrain. Once the main lines of the village were laid down and marked out by iron pegs, the villagers were brought in to subdivide the blocks with lengths of rope whereupon they could themselves clear the lines of each individual plot. A process of selecting plots among the villagers followed. Squads of army volunteers were then brought in to help cut poles for building houses and the whole area was seething with activity. Engineers arrived to dig boreholes and lay out irrigation channels. In a matter of a few months the riverbanks were transformed as the villages grew. Rufiji became famous as the first large Ujamaa project in the country and people constantly asked about the project. I had great hopes that the villages would succeed. There were enormous problems, not least the resistance on the part of some villagers to leave their traditional fields and gamble with new farming areas.

At some of our meetings the regional heads of police and army attended, both arguing for the use of force. It was said that some of the resistance was led by witchdoctors and elders who said that it was sacrilegious to leave the graves of their ancestors. But the message came down from on high that force should not be used and that the villagers should be persuaded to move of their own accord. Many did so and there was optimism throughout the region about the possibility of a new life.

But there were problems too. I thought that Tanu and the government were not consulting the people enough, not providing enough information about the project as a whole and there was insufficient personnel for mobilisation purposes. Things seemed to work top-down with the area commissioner playing the main role. The civil service began to exercise too much influence so that the party cadres and grass-roots people were subjected to orders and commandism. A new secretary was appointed to our commission who proved to be a very bad choice. He was a civil servant who had previously owned two houses, one of which he rented out to an embassy for a fee which exceeded his salary. However, under the Arusha Declaration, this was not allowed and he lost his income. He was embittered and hostile to all suggestions of Ujamaa. Under his leadership the administrative aspects of the project became predominant and the mobilisation aspect downgraded. In the end, much was achieved though some years later I learned that some of the villages fell into disuse while others grew beyond the scale of the Ujamaa concept: they had become small towns. Other parts of the country began similar experiments in Ujamaa building with uneven success. Even though I had to work extremely hard, for me it was an exciting time.

PROBLEMS IN THE ANC

Absorbed as I was in my duties at the ministry my thoughts reverted constantly to the movement, reinforced by the contacts with comrades in Dar es Salaam. We were still not being integrated in the work of the organisation and came to the conclusion that we were distrusted. I wrote to Oliver Tambo expressing this disquiet and asked for tasks within the organisation. On the other hand, many of our old friends came to visit us, and our house became a kind of haven for those who wanted to get away from the tensions pervading the movement. I was invited to write the editorials for *Spotlight*, a movement broadsheet, and was asked to do some fund-raising at the university. But I was troubled by the apparent malaise in the movement and wondered whether our own non-involvement was due to an unwillingness to reveal to us just how deep the malaise was.

Seeking a political rather than an institutional explanation I came to the conclusion that one of the problems was the looseness of ANC structures and the lack of political coherence. I was also surprised by the total absence of the Communist Party, which had served as a kind of glue at home. Many of our visitors who had been in the party at home spoke to me about this and there seemed to be an assumption that my primary concern would be the party. There had, for a long time, been a subtle division of labour in the movement, with our black comrades giving a higher priority to the ANC and a small group of whites giving their priority to the party.

On one of his visits to our house I discussed the question of the party with Moses. His coolness had gone and some of our former camaraderie had returned. Indeed, I was extremely fond of him and he reciprocated in his own brisk manner. I broached the question of the lack of a party presence in the region. In his usual quizzical style, he asked what role I thought the party might play in the conditions operating in Tanzania. I replied that there was a serious lack of an inner disciplined core in the ANC, which could act as both an ideological and political vanguard since this was the method which had worked so well at home. He asked me to write to him along these lines, which I did. When his reply came, it was an astonishing rebuff. In a brief letter he said he thought there was no role for the party in the present circumstances and that any attempt to recreate the party would lead to the expulsion of the ANC from the region by governments which were hostile to communism. I was dumbstruck. Here was the secretary-general of the party saying that it should not exist in the region while it could continue to operate in remote London. I felt that this letter could be very damaging if it fell into the wrong hands, so I burned it. I nevertheless knew very well that conditions in Tanzania were unfavourable for the ANC since important elements within government, including the head of the OAU's Liberation Committee, favoured the PAC.

I soon learned that there had been many problems about the party and about Marxism in the camps. It seemed that the Sino-Soviet dispute had generated a great deal of heat, with study classes being formed around the Soviet position and the Maoist position.

Conflicts flared and the peace and unity of the camps were threatened. The ANC leadership thereupon banned all Marxist literature in the camps and the national liberation aspect of the ANC was brought to the fore.

Mary and I developed a close friendship with O.O. Adesola, the Nigerian official seconded to the Liberation Committee. He was not very political but was sincere in his support for the liberation struggle and for the ANC. He informed us of the machinations of the Tanzanians and others of the committee and how both funds and arms destined for the progressive groups of liberation movements were often diverted to others.

On the basis of intelligence placed before the committee, he also told us that there were serious problems in ANC camps and other structures, confirming the impressions we had gained. Long years in exile were taking their toll. As one comrade expressed it later: 'There's a great deal of position-mongering and self-assertiveness here. One wouldn't bother about it if all the careerism and individualism promoted our cause, but it holds no promise for the revolution. Instead there is anarchy, with no control over the chaps. Anyone sleeps out as he pleases, chaps are now dictating the terms and holding the leadership to ransom.'

One of the people who visited us was Joe Slovo, who was based in London. I did not hesitate to inform him of the misgivings of people at home. Of course he did not like to hear this but I felt duty bound to convey it to him. His main task seemed to be representing the interests of the party. His was a difficult role, especially given the serious reservations of Moses and others about the party. But Joe was determined and persistent. On one visit he showed us a letter from the Central Committee of the party proposing regular meetings between the party and the ANC. Joe persuaded Moses to sign the letter on behalf of the party and I believe that formal meetings took place from time to time. Although Joe was welcome to stay with us on these trips, I had some reservations about his role as a peripatetic revolutionary. I was also unhappy about his slack security. On one occasion he was searched at the airport in Dar es Salaam and a long list of contacts taken from him. I discussed the question of the role of the party with JB Marks. He too believed that it was too dangerous for the party to have a presence in Tanzania. I offered to serve as a representative for the *African Communist*, the journal of the party, in order to ensure that at least this material would be available to our people. JB said he would discuss it with others, but nothing came of it.

I again complained about my non-involvement in ANC work. Duma Nokwe came to see me to inform me that I had been appointed an intelligence officer of MK. My task was to assist in preparing cadres going home, to collect what information might be useful and pass it on. I was very pleased about this and took it seriously. I knew that cadres were sent home from time to time. Two of these comrades, Matthews and Zanemvula, were brought to me for briefing and stayed with us for several months. They were going by sea and would be dropped in Cape Town, and my task was to prepare them for that. As a Capetonian, I had to explain the geography of the city, the social character of the population and alert them to hazards they might face. They were a splendid couple and I was full of admiration for the way they approached their coming task. I did feel, however, that their briefing had not been thorough enough and feared for their future. I later learned that they had survived for a few months and even worked their way north to the Transvaal, but were subsequently arrested.

One of my tasks was to study the movement of ships in the region and to report on what opportunities might arise for infiltrating people home. Minor as these duties were, I nevertheless welcomed them greatly.

ARMED STRUGGLE

Frustration was growing dangerously in the camps in the late 1960s largely because of the difficulties of getting cadres to the borders of South Africa, and some of the MK camps were in ferment. Many of the young cadres had been there for years after they had received military training in several countries such as the Soviet Union, China, Algeria, Cuba and elsewhere. But none had seen any action and most were languishing patiently in the camps. It was apparent that the leadership had not solved the problem of going home. Political cadres were also frustrated and there was a sense of futility among them. Many of the middle-level cadres told us about their dissatisfaction. We also heard that some members of the national executive of the ANC felt that a far bolder approach was needed. The most outspoken of these, Flag Boshielo, actually took matters into his own hands. He and one other slipped out of the camp one night and seized a rowing boat to cross the Zambezi, but they were waylaid by South African security on the other side and never heard of again. They may have been killed on the spot or taken into the country, tortured and disposed of.

These problems were exacerbated by the lack of organised underground structures inside the country. The trained cadres in the camps were close to rebellion when it was decided to send contingents into Rhodesia who were expected to fight their way through to South Africa itself. There followed the campaign known as the Eastern Front and Wankie. I learned about these activities from friends who were involved and knew about the poor preparation – commandos had not been properly trained in reading maps and using compasses – and felt sure that no amount of heroism would lead to the objectives set for these groups. In the event, the contingents sent in were far too large, apparently in one case consisting of 100 men. When locked in battle with Rhodesian forces, they suffered heavy casualties. None reached South Africa, some returned to Zambia, many were killed. The failures of these attempts led to further demoralisation in the camps and in the movement as a whole. The urge to go home nevertheless grew and there was widespread discontent.

An open call came for the creation of a new leadership, which would be younger and bolder in planning the return home. I was shown a document drawn up by Chris Hani that made serious allegations about the way the struggle had become stalled and about deficiencies in the leadership. I knew that his allegations were correct and that something drastic had to be done. Hani had himself led a revolt in one of the camps for which he would have paid very heavily were it not for the intervention of some of the wiser leaders.

It was in this climate that the leadership announced the convening of the Morogoro Conference. This was to be the first major consultative meeting in exile and was to review everything about the policies and actions of the movement. A secretariat was appointed with Joe Matthews as secretary. Everyone who wished to was asked to prepare a submission to the convening committee setting out their views and criticisms freely. I sat down and drafted a lengthy document and received a full reply. [They are both reproduced in Annexure: Chapter 7.]

However, my contract with the Ministry of Lands had come to an end and I had to decide whether to stay on in Tanzania or not. The ministry was anxious that I stay and Songambele insisted that I give up all thought of leaving Tanzania, inviting me to become a citizen. I knew, however, that citizenship would take at least seven years and that even then the prospects of actually acquiring Tanzanian nationality were slim. The children were all approaching the age when their education was crucial. The schools were all moving steadily towards the adoption of Swahili as the main language of instruction and they faced the prospect of acquiring their higher education in that language, a prospect not to be relished since, although Swahili is a rich and lovely language, it was far too undeveloped for higher education. Subsequent experience has shown that our reservations were justified in that the adoption of Swahili as the medium of instruction in high schools and even at the university led to a serious erosion of standards.

There was also a problem with my terms of employment. I was paid at the local rates and in local currency, but if the boys were to go to university we would be required to pay private rates which were much higher, and the boys would not be eligible for the kind of scholarships given to Tanzanian children. To cap it all, I was still a refugee without citizenship and without a passport and my refugee status hurt. When Mary and I were offered a free holiday in the Soviet Union I had to report to the permanent secretary in the vice president's office, only to be told that 'refugees don't need holidays abroad, we have very nice game parks here'. I replied that I had been denied overseas travel by the South African government for many years and now the same was happening in Tanzania despite my holding down a senior job which included very sensitive security work. But he was unbending. I left in a fury. I went to the home of the Minister of Home Affairs to appeal to him since he knew of my work in Rufiji, and finally received a piece of paper enabling us to travel to the Soviet Union.

And so we reached a point of decision and, with extreme reluctance, decided that the boys' interest, particularly in education, required that we go to Britain where they would get a sound education and citizenship as well. It was a depressing but necessary decision. I conveyed this information to the ANC on 28 January 1969:

January 1969
CONFIDENTIAL. NOT FOR PUBLICATION.

The President and Members of the National Executive Committee, African National Congress

Dear Comrades,

I am writing this letter to you in order to explain our decision to leave Tanzania, where we have been working for the past two years. I well understand how undesirable it is to introduce personal affairs into political life but I feel that the step we are now taking, which is a difficult one for us, needs some explanation. I offer such an explanation in the hope that our experience will bring to your attention a weakness in our movement and thereby go some way towards correcting it.

I would like to recall that both Mary and I have been deeply involved in the liberation movement for a long time. We were active in youth work even before there was a Congress Alliance. I also want to record that both of us went to prison, Mary for six months, myself for three years, for the Congress Movement. Only when conditions in South Africa became such that living there seemed both hazardous and politically futile did we leave, in the hope that we could better continue in the struggle outside.

Believing that the brunt of this struggle lay in East Africa, I decided not to try for an exit permit from the South African Government but to jump the border in the hope that this would make me more acceptable to East African Governments. This proved to be the case and we were finally admitted to Tanzania against many odds. But our expectations as far as the movement was concerned were ill founded. During the first nine months of our stay in Dar es Salaam we were in fact treated with so much reserve that we got the impression that we were suspected on security grounds. Direct offers of total involvement were made to both Comrade Tennyson Makiwane in Kazungula and Comrade Tambo in Dar es Salaam but nothing resulted from them. In fact, no matter with whom we raised the issue, and there were many, we were unable even to get an explanation for our anomalous position and all our efforts to join in the work of the organisation met with polite but negative reactions. Even the attempts we made to keep up with the activities and policies of the ANC so that we could better defend them among the people we met went in vain.

We waited for a long time for the situation to improve, not wanting to believe that our close comrades of before could have changed their attitudes to us so much. But it gradually became clear to us that the reason for the estrangement was our whiteness and nothing else. The question arises as to whether the individual leaders of the ANC with whom we worked in such harmony at home have changed their political outlook or whether they have been influenced in their attitudes by other considerations. Broadly speaking, there is little evidence that there has been a significant alteration in political commitment to non-racialism as a long time objective; we therefore ascribe our experience mainly to the yielding to pressure from the chauvinism now found in East Africa, pressure that we have ourselves seen in operation frequently enough.

Yet there has also been some change in mood in the ANC. Nothing else would explain the breach in close comradeship that is evident between ANC members and others in the world of exile. It is this phenomenon that has brought us to write such a letter. We see that our movement, which has gone through so much persecution in unity, is being thrust back more than a decade by artificial considerations of race. Against this violation of our past one must speak out, embarrassing though it may be.

So that there should be no misunderstanding of my motivations I should like to express my views on some of the political needs of the day. When we left South Africa in 1966 we were acutely conscious of a tremendous acceleration in hatred of white minority rule and of the 'white man in the street' on the part of the African people. Clearly, any political movement which does not take this mood into account, is closing its eyes to the major contradiction in our society and thereby losing its influence on the masses. In concrete terms it means that our liberation movement must not only be led by Africans, but it must be SEEN to be led by Africans, and that the primary interest of the liberation movement must be seen as the freeing from bondage of the majority of our people, the African people. This emphasis must always be present in our work if we are to play the role of liberators. To some extent it was unfortunately absent in the past. Yet a nationalism which turns into chauvinism will inevitably be eaten up by its own bitterness. Men who seek to advance human history must be men of vision or they inevitably fail. When national leaders speak with vigour and revolutionary ardour for their own people they dare not fail to take all humanity into account. This is what is meant by the combination of a policy of nationalism with internationalism. It implies that discrimination against countries or peoples or individuals on the grounds of colour alone is a policy of bankruptcy from any long-term historical view.

To conclude, we would like to urge that the cancer of colour be not allowed to play the part it is now playing within our movement. Tactical arrangements can always be understood and accepted if they are carried out in good faith: but discriminatory practices on any other basis are to be condemned out of hand. The South African liberation movement has a heavy duty to our people at home, to the continent as a whole and, we dare say, to the world at large. For no other country contains within it quite the same conflicts and potentialities. What we do now will play an important part in determining whether we meet up with the challenge in the future.

Perhaps without sufficient justification, we nevertheless feel that in leaving Tanzania we are leaving the battle front. Indeed I know some of our comrades in Mkhonto look at our departure in this light. Yet to remain in Tanzania is becoming a sacrifice not justified by the minimal contribution we are making. Instead, we hope that our energies and dedication will be more fully utilised in London where we are now going.

Yours in the struggle for a free South Africa.

Ben Turok

DEPARTURE

To my chagrin, the date for the Morogoro Conference was set for one week after my arrival in London. It was a massive disappointment since I was bound to miss it. I had already arranged for the whole family to travel aboard an East German ship from Dar es Salaam to London and we had begun to pack our household goods in large wooden crates. It was then that Moses Mabhida, a long-standing trade unionist and leader of the party at home, came to see us to say farewell. His message to the comrades in

London was that it was essential that the party be rebuilt and that without the party the ANC would remain weak and ineffective. I was surprised by the firmness of his commitment since he had taken no initiative himself to do so, but I undertook to convey his message to London and did so soon after our arrival.

I also made contact with Oliver Tambo and suggested that I use the opportunity of travelling by sea round the coast of South Africa to examine the terrain carefully and he was keen that I do so. Arrangements were made for me to use the ship's equipment to inspect the coastline of Pondoland and the Transkei, relating what I saw to the charts available in the Master's cabin. Oliver also gave me his personal code so that I could convey my findings to him from Britain. I was told to report to Joe Slovo in London, since he was in charge of this aspect of the movement's work in the UK, easing my misery about leaving.

Within a few weeks our family was embarking on a modest cargo ship with cabins for six passengers leaving Dar es Salaam for London. The journey would take some three weeks during which we had to entertain ourselves and pass the time – quite a formidable prospect with three exuberant boys grown strong and lusty in the healthy environment of Tanzania.

CHAPTER EIGHT

CHANGING FORTUNES

There were further personal difficulties before we reached the glorious victory of 1990. Going over that ground is painful since it revives old hurts and reports on mistakes that were made by the movement generally. That we ultimately triumphed must be ascribed not only to the justice of our cause, but also to the fundamental wisdom of the movement and its leadership. It is not without good reason that world opinion swung behind the ANC and helped it to come to power against such a formidable foe.

The decades of 1970s and 1980s were difficult for many of us both at home and in exile, though I am only able to deal with the latter. I often thought about the moment in 1960, while I was underground in Johannesburg, when Moses Kotane and Michael Harmel declined to go into exile on the grounds that it would remove them from the scene of action. They based their judgement partly on the experience of other movements where transferring the leadership abroad had had damaging consequences. I have no doubt that their decision in 1960 was correct. This was borne out since in a matter of months we were able to return to our homes and continue our work, whereas if we had left the country illegally we would have returned to a prison sentence.

But it is also the case that the movement sent Oliver Tambo and Yusuf Dadoo abroad in order to commence an international campaign in support of the struggle. Others subsequently joined them – some on instructions and others on their own account. In a few years it became a flood and new structures of the ANC had to be set up in exile.

In time some of our best cadres spent many years in frontline ANC camps. Exile was difficult for all of us but despite some problems I was located in normal conditions, living with my family, well clothed, well fed, well cared for. Others experienced great loneliness and longing in exile. The harsh environment generated both camaraderie and selfishness. Unfortunately, it was more of the latter that dogged our people in London.

Exile wastes the spirit. The resources of encouragement are scarce and not shared equally among the comrades. Those with senior positions harbour them carefully, for they are more important to the spirit than any material wealth. But pity the musket bearers who have little with which to comfort themselves. Most people in London had sufficient food, clothing and shelter. A welfare system ensured that those who were unable to get jobs nevertheless enjoyed reasonably comfortable conditions of existence. In Africa the ANC welfare system was less well endowed and many experienced real hardship.

To be in exile is to live on remote hope. Every mite of news from home is passed around, chewed on like tough steak, embellished: 'Did you hear that Paul received a letter from Kathy?' 'It's quite amazing he remembers the names of so and so's children.' 'Did you hear that so and so's been released from detention?' And so time is passed, mulling over again and again at dinner parties the experiences of detention in the 1960 emergency, the difficulties of getting out of the country, how this one walked through the night and that one was smuggled in the boot of the car.

Much of exile is spent in reflecting on the past. Not reflecting so much as brooding, like a toothless old man sitting in a rocking chair, ruminating over his youth. There is some pleasure in recalling the past escapades, a former virility, minor triumphs. Yet one is reminded now and then that what seemed to be large events are now puny in long perspective. So many people have been tortured, so many have died, so many have been through the hell of struggle, so that the peaks of pain suffered by the exile in former times are but hiccups in the scale of suffering.

All this needs to be understood, not by South Africans, for we have graduated past that phase, but by others on different continents, where exile may be an option. It may be a world of safety, but it is an environment of great pain.

EXILE IN THE UK

Mary and I had been warned by several people – Hilda Bernstein, Wolfie Kodesh and others – that the exile community in the UK was in a bad way. Morale was low, there was conflict between individuals and factions, and we were advised to keep clear of these controversies. For the first few weeks we were able to do so, being preoccupied with settling down.

On our arrival by sea in Bristol, immigration was fairly easy about my entry since Mary was British by birth, and I was given a clear permit even allowing me to work. The Buntings had booked us into a hotel but we soon found a temporary London flat in Muswell Hill, having been advised by the Buntings that a lot of our comrades lived in North London and that we would find good schools for the boys. Ivan and Neil went to William Ellis where they flourished in the strict academic environment. Both did extremely well with Neil maintaining his remarkable record of getting an 'A' for every exam irrespective of subject. Ivan was not far behind.

Meanwhile Fred got a place in a comprehensive school where discipline was extremely lax and teaching weak. He had serious adjustment problems and left school early. Later, when he went to a technical college, he was taken up by an excellent sociology lecturer and Fred gained a reasonable level of education enabling him to go on to college.

Absorbed as we were with family concerns we were not, however, removed from the movement. Our first major contact was with Brian Bunting to whom I expressed the view, ironical in the light of subsequent events, that the ANC was failing to get its act together down south and that the disciplined coherence of the Communist Party was lacking. He agreed that without a party the ANC was too amorphous to wage a serious struggle. Mary and I were then integrated into the London party structure and became members of separate party groups. She joined a group with Brian and Sonia Bunting while I was placed in a group with Joe Slovo, Rusty and Hilda Bernstein, and others. The groups met monthly to discuss the problems of the movement as a whole, which included the ANC, SACTU and the Anti-Apartheid Movement, indeed the whole spectrum of struggle, 'at home', 'down south' and in the UK.

We also reported to the ANC office at Rathbone Place where Reg September presided as chief representative while MP Naicker was director of publicity. Nearby at 39 Goodge Street the *African Communist* had its office, run by Sonia Bunting, and across the road there was another rather less known office inhabited by the London members of the new Revolutionary Council established by the Morogoro Conference, namely Dadoo and Slovo.

I also reported to Slovo my findings on the boat journey and he asked me to commit them to paper. In my report I recommended my continued research on the topography of South Africa and its coastline. I also suggested the purchase of British nautical charts for the area and permission to go to the GDR in order to consult with experts. Joe seemed to be very interested, but when I told him that Oliver had given me his personal code for further communication he showed no desire for this to be followed up. I raised the subject of the further research with him on many subsequent occasions but to no avail.

I was about to complete my Masters and hoped to get a teaching job. But MP cornered me and persuaded me against my better judgement to take on a job as editor of *Sechaba*. He trained me in layout, design and a host of other functions and I relished the challenge. I wrote introductions to interviews with leaders and friends in the movement as well as news items and editorials that actually took up issues and sought desperately for interesting political material. The problem was that the movement was somewhat demoralised after the defeats of Wankie and the Eastern Front, and not even the positive outcome of the Morogoro Conference made much difference.

Sechaba had an editorial board consisting of MP Naicker, Brian Bunting, Rusty Bernstein and a few others. All the planning was left to me with the others mainly contributing ideas about articles and doing some writing. It was a lonely job at times and even though the movement was largely in the doldrums, it had to be presented as being engaged in armed struggle in the same way as Frelimo, MPLA and PAIGC.

The ANC office was a busy place. There were frequent publicity drives, statements to be issued, the news digest *Spotlight* to be produced, and many other activities. The Anti-Apartheid Movement was then a small organisation but it had extensive contacts across the spectrum of British politics and we were constantly being called upon to provide support of all kinds. In addition, there were many debates on policy relating both to the ANC and to the broader solidarity movement.

The ANC UK Branch was a fairly small organisation of perhaps a hundred members, with the majority being white, a substantial number of coloured and Indian members, and a sprinkling of Africans. There seemed to have been a process of clustering in exile, depending on the willingness of countries to admit us. Africa was closed to all but African comrades. Despite all the activity it became increasingly apparent that the movement was in some disarray. Men like Robert Resha, Joe Matlou, Thambi Mhlambiso and Lionel Ngakane clearly felt that non-Africans were too dominant in the region and that the traditional African image of the ANC was thereby jeopardised. They also resented the presence of so many known communists in the leading posts of the ANC and the presence of the *African Communist* and the party apparatus.

The Africanists were initially led by Robert Resha, who had openly sustained an Africanist posture throughout his political life. But Resha's staunch loyalty to the ANC made him break with the nationalists when they went into open revolt. It is difficult to define this posture, but one might suggest that it embraces a notion that African interests should be given primacy in the struggle, that the movement itself project an African image, particularly in the personnel leading the movement, that the ideology of the movement should reflect its African culture and personality, and that it should not embrace Marxist notions such as the primacy of class interests including those of the working class. Finally that its international policy should give priority to relations with the African continent over those of any others including the socialist countries.

In practice the nationalists directed their opposition against the party. Although membership in the party was still secret, Slovo, Dadoo, Bunting and others were quite open about their activities. The fact that the three London members of the Revolutionary Council were communists and not African also aroused great resentment, especially as they were in charge of the internal work based on London. I disagreed with the critics on the substance of their arguments but I did feel that the leadership was insensitive in the style of work. Matters came to head in a serious rumpus which led to the expulsion of the more dissident members, known as the 'Group of Eight', from the ANC – the most serious rupture the ANC was to suffer in exile.

This was a big shock to the movement as the group included some very well-known names going back to the struggles in the fifties. It was also the occasion for some rather critical commentary about the ANC and its weaknesses, which were set out in a publication, but the movement withstood the criticisms and survived largely unscathed. It was apparent to all that the ANC had solidity based on its long and illustrious history which could not be shaken. Undoubtedly the calibre of Oliver Tambo and some other leaders also sustained it. Most important of all, however, was the conviction now well established internationally that the ANC policies were fundamentally correct and that the visions expressed in the Freedom Charter were wholly appropriate for a future South Africa while those of its critics were not.

The Communist Party issued a document called *The Enemy Hidden Under the Same Colour*, responding to the allegations of the group that the Morogoro Conference was called under pressure from the party, that the conference was dominated by non-Africans, that the new executive of the ANC was constituted under pressure of communists and non-Africans, that non-Africans were integrated into the ANC wrongly, that non-Africans wanted to revive the Congress Alliance in exile, and that the party's relations with the ANC remained a continuing problem. The party document vigorously rebutted all these allegations, arguing that the group was betraying the political and organisational principles of the movement, and was motivated by anti-communist and racist positions. It condemned the demand that non-Africans in the struggle should 'humble themselves' as racist, and argued that they wanted to dilute and eliminate the revolutionary content of South Africa's liberation struggle. The expelled group tried to form a new organisation, but failed and collapsed.

Unfortunately, the disarray in London had not been taken up

in time by the headquarters in Lusaka which had its own difficulties. And so we soon came to be known as 'The London Problem' and leaders passing through tried to keep their distance, which made my job as editor of *Sechaba* even more difficult. I was often driven to cornering a reticent member of the NEC in a restaurant in order to get some ideas for my next editorial.

LIFE IN THE PARTY

Apart from my duties in the ANC office and the meetings of the ANC Branch, I was also expected to attend the monthly meetings of my party unit. Several such units of about ten members each in London met secretly on a monthly basis. At each meeting there would be a report from the London District Committee, news from South Africa based on a digest of the press, and a discussion of current issues in the ANC followed by a general discussion of wider interest.

In my group there were some very interesting personalities like Joe Slovo, Rusty and Hilda Bernstein, but most of the members were long-standing rank-and-filers who had been in the party at home. A few were newcomers, having joined in exile, and what caused me concern was the ease with which they slipped into an uncritical dogmatism and how intolerant they became. They accepted everything they were told without question and when they doubted it was in the private recesses of their minds, rather like someone who fears the consequences of revealing feelings of a forbidden love. I imagine that when I first joined the party I was equally devout, but the world had changed since then and our movement particularly needed critical, clear-headed thinking.

As I saw it, the problem was that our objective situation was fraught with problems, most of which related to our structures in the frontline states, which I had experienced at first hand. However, our London leadership – no doubt for the best of motives – wished to conceal these difficulties from the membership.

Yet, at first, I felt quite comfortable in this quite cordial atmosphere where one could expect a nice cup of tea and cake on a cold London night in the house of one or other comrade. Meetings were moved around to avoid setting up a pattern which the

British or South African Special Branch might spot too easily and it was thought important that non-party ANC members should not know who attended these meetings since party membership was secret.

The most important person in the group was Slovo since he was a full-time official and travelled to Africa and Eastern Europe frequently. But Rusty often carried weight because of his lucid thinking and neat analytical skills, as well as a certain detachment. It was clear that he was not defending a personal position, nor did he seem to be covering up for past failures, although in time I came to feel that he did have some responsibility for the wrong policies we pursued and that he ought to have come out against some of the obvious mistakes being made.

Hilda was made in a different mould. She saw through many of the pretences, especially about Eastern Europe, but also about our own work, and often flared up at meetings. In time, we often found ourselves in the same camp. There were two related issues which agitated me. The first was the pretence that the party had a viable structure in the frontline states and at home; the second was Slovo's personal control over who could participate in 'internal work', that is, work directly related to South Africa.

That my instincts were not wrong was borne out by documentation produced around an augmented meeting of the Central Committee in mid-1970 attended by a 'broader collective' for the first time since 1962. In a pre-conference document we were informed that after the Rivonia arrests and the impact of torture in prisons there was 'almost the complete elimination of all levels of our organisation'. Once some leaders were in exile steps were taken to reorganise abroad, but members of the Central Committee were scattered. Bram Fischer was advised to avoid using vulnerable contacts at home and efforts were made to recruit 'clean' personnel, but progress was 'slow and painstaking'. The 'injection of experienced personnel from abroad remained on the agenda' since effective day-to-day leadership required an internal apparatus. We were told that a plenary session of the party leadership in 1967 'self-critically' noted that no progress had been made towards creating proper contact and resolved to circulate an inner-party bulletin. A further plenary session in 1968 again noted failure in establishing proper contact between members and decided to create party units.

We were also told about the problems in the relations between the ANC and the party. Before the Rivonia debacle the two organisations were 'uniquely close' and the relationship was 'understood by most' even though the alliance between the two was not formalised. After Rivonia the ANC set up a provisional headquarters in Africa and took over exclusive control of all functions of leadership of the struggle with the party accepting that for the time being the ANC would represent the whole alliance. Hence the party became more and more isolated from the higher bodies in MK.

In 1966 the Central Committee created a commission to examine the lack of links with the ANC as well as the situation of members from the minority groups (most of whom were outside Africa). The 1968 plenary meeting resolved to call for a role for the party within a united front. As a result of these pressures the party was represented by its delegates at the Morogoro Conference for the first time. Thereafter the ANC agreed to 'regular, non-public joint meetings on common problems' and that the right of the party to maintain contact with its members was not in question. The party was concerned that some individual leaders were too engaged in ANC work to the detriment of the party. And so, after the Morogoro meeting, the Central Committee resolved that 'without collective decision making and collective political activity the party could not fulfil its leading role, which goes beyond the participation of individuals'.

A political report was issued by the Central Committee before the above meeting which stated that the Morogoro Consultative Conference had come at a moment of grave crisis for the movement, the ANC, the army and the party: 'Discontent with our leadership had mounted to serious proportions, accompanied by demoralisation, factional and regional disputes, and the threat of disintegration of the forces, at any rate those in exile and training, which would have set at naught the effort of so many years of patient and tireless work ... Many of the grievances frankly expressed at Morogoro were directed at the style of leadership that had been allowed to develop. Many ANC leaders had behaved in an intolerably bureaucratic and arrogant manner towards the rank and file. Justified complaints were ignored or dealt with in a militaristic administrative way, as if it were a crime or breach of discipline to criticise. The rank and file were starved of information, of political leadership, of opportunities for discussion on all the questions of policy and strategy that vitally affected them.'

For many the problems in the ANC were connected with weaknesses in the party. In a document of the Central Committee, the *Inner-Party Bulletin – Number 1* issued in July 1970, it was stated that the primary task was 'to reconstitute the party as our main contribution to the furthering of the revolution' and the concept of its leading role as the Marxist-Leninist vanguard of the working class was reaffirmed. A section of the bulletin [see Annexure 1: Chapter 8] described the relationship between the ANC and the party. However, the main organisational task of the party 'remains the reconstruction of our internal machinery by the creation of organised units in a manner which will safeguard them against enemy attack and infiltration'.

The bulletin also dealt with the emergence of factional disputes after the Morogoro Conference (relating to the 'Group of 8') and other broader issues. One of these merits quoting here, namely the incursions into Zimbabwe which were carried out with 'damaging inadequacies, even failure of preparation of supplies, logistics, maps and other equipment'. These deficiencies were ascribed to a too large gap between the military and political components of the movement which could be overcome by the creation of the Revolutionary Council.

These documents were discussed in party units in London and elsewhere and provided much-needed enlightenment about our real situation. At the same time, since Frelimo and the other liberation movements were engaged in bitter guerrilla warfare within their own borders, something we could not yet achieve, the movement was bound to make larger claims in order to appease the appetite of our supporters internationally. I recall a public meeting in Dar es Salaam where Vice President Karume poured scorn on the liberation movement cadres as drunkards and cowards dependent on handouts. In Europe critics were less hostile but everyone wanted to see pictures of guerrillas in action. It was also important to paint a rosy picture for the people at home and those who were isolated in various training camps around the world. And so the ANC, and myself in *Sechaba*, continued to trumpet our great achievements, even when conditions were dire.

STATE OF THE MOVEMENT

Eventually I wearied of the charade and of those who traded mutual confidences as commodities of exchange. The objective difficulties also affected the atmosphere in the ANC office. In August 1973 I was able to discuss these matters with Jack and Ray Simons who were on a visit to London. Ray was somewhat noncommittal, but Jack was expansive and open. He said that the ANC was stagnant in the frontline areas, had undergone a loss of purpose, made little contact with people in South Africa, and was suffering from arrested development because of the older leaders' stifling control. On the day of her departure from London, Ray called to see me after hearing that I had resigned from my post at *Sechaba* and was already working elsewhere. I told her I had no intention of damaging the movement in any way but felt impelled to take an independent view of the situation.

I was also becoming increasingly critical of the position of the party on international issues. Our documents were couched in a stiff officialese, in the tradition of the world communist movement and in line with the dogmas of World Marxist Review. There was a sameness of approach, a linear movement of thought which, deliberately or not, brought a sense of strength for being part of a world movement, but also a fatigue in that everything was cast in a similar mould no matter the specifics of local conditions. Curiously, Slovo's pamphlet on the 'Problems of Socialism' records that it was in this area of policy that change was most difficult. No doubt this was because those responsible for international relations were the most deeply embroiled with the Soviet Union and the structures of World Marxist Review which was a kind of substitute for the Cominform.

At the same time, I was still haunted by guilt about doing so little to advance the struggle. I felt that London could be a base for serious interventions at home despite the problem of distance and that committed people should be more adequately involved. This was confirmed when I was invited to a meeting by Slovo attended by about six people including Ruth First and a few others. Opening the meeting, Slovo said it was for purely consultative purposes rather than to set up a new structure. It might or might not meet again, depending on results. We discussed methods of propaganda work inside the country and several people made suggestions. I thought the meeting had been fruitful, and certainly merited continuation. But it never met again, at least not with me.

Slovo's main preoccupation at the time was with leaflet bombs. The technique was to hoist a bucket containing leaflets to the top of a building or some other high point and then trigger a small explosive device or some other mechanism which would shower leaflets onto a crowded area below. The leaflets urged the people to take action against the regime and increase protests of all kinds. At the meeting Slovo produced a folder containing samples of these leaflets and the publicity they attracted in the press.

But Slovo was not alone in maintaining in a façade of militancy when the real situation was far from rosy. A meeting of all ANC members was called to hear an address by Tennyson Makiwane, then head of the International Department. There was quite a good turnout and expectations were high. He addressed us in the most enthusiastic terms along the theme that we should all prepare to go to the frontline for action and 'the transports are waiting' when there was clearly no such intention.

PERSONAL CRISIS

Having decided to leave full-time work at *Sechaba* and return to study, I registered at the University of London for a Ph.D in philosophy on a part-time basis and continued editing part-time. But I could not settle down to study. Instead I took a part-time teaching job at the Mid Herts College of Further Education, where I taught Third World Studies. Soon thereafter, in 1972, I found alternative employment as a part-time tutor in Social Sciences in the first year of the Open University and then a full-time post as a senior counsellor responsible for several thousand students covering the North London area. The university was bursting with innovation and excitement and I threw myself into the work, loving both the teaching and the administration. I was in charge of some 50 part-time staff for whom a whole new educational methodology was being worked out. It soon became clear that the Open University would be a great success and turn into the most innovative university in the world.

But I also maintained my involvement with the party and the ANC. There were the usual group meetings of the party and meetings of the ANC membership as various structures were set up. There were also many consultations with Anti-Apartheid Movement officials to work through the policies we should adopt in the solidarity movement.

Beneath it all there was an urge to write down my view of the situation and I began work on two articles on strategic problems of the liberation movement. Mary helped research the history of our strategy and tactics in the pages of *The Guardian* and various journals which were housed at Brian Bunting's home. They were published in successive issues of *The Socialist Register* in 1972 and 1973 but made hardly a ripple. Slovo wrote a reply to the first article, but apart from a certain pique, there was no serious retaliation. Then Don Barnett, a Canadian anthropologist whom I had known in Tanzania and who founded the Liberation Support Movement in Canada and the US asked me to edit the articles into a single essay for publication as a booklet called *Strategic Problems in South Africa's Liberation Struggle: a critical analysis by Ben Turok*. I did so, and within a few months of its emergence the storm struck.

The problem was that the LSM had links with many leftist groups throughout the world and supplied them with the booklet which was read avidly as the first critical account of the struggle by an insider. Thereafter, ANC speakers at public meetings throughout Europe found themselves facing questions derived from my essay based on my rather differing view of the situation.

I was confronted by an ANC representative who travelled across Europe and who was questioned about the truth or otherwise of my assertions. I also received a letter from The Africa Groups of Sweden stating that they had been told by Sobizana Mquikana, the ANC representative in Stockholm, that the ANC had 'condemned the book'. Life became difficult and my isolation grew. Yet, I knew that my work was correct and that the essay was being used very widely as reference material by scholars on South Africa. I was encouraged to find that every major publication on South Africa referred to it.

At this time, 1974, my parents informed me that they wished to visit the Soviet Union to see their respective brothers. I raised the matter with the Soviet embassy and they agreed to make an exception in my case and allow my parents to enter the country even though they travelled on South African passports.

My parents and I eventually arrived in Moscow, staying at the Rosia Hotel in the centre of the city on what was my first visit there since the official visit in 1969. We immediately made contact with Morris, an elderly gentleman, who was an old friend of the family who visited us at the hotel. However, he told us that my mother's brothers were unwilling to come to the hotel while he had been unable to trace my father's brothers and feared that they had been killed during the war. A meeting was arranged in the large park not far away and the next day my parents and I sat on a bench near a statue of Lenin. My mother was highly emotional as we waited. Suddenly she was reunited with her brother after a separation of 50 years. After long embraces and many tears he explained that it was impossible to acknowledge her existence since during the war any Jew who had relatives abroad was treated with great suspicion. He had denied her existence and could not now go back on this. We had two further meetings at his flat, which we entered in single file, one at a time, so as not to arouse the interest of neighbours. We met the other brother and his wife and daughter, and were treated to a delicious feast. I was able to converse with the daughter in broken Yiddish and was astonished to learn that although she had been a member of the Communist Youth (her father was a party member) she now rejected communism and was reading up the history of the Jewish people to recover her identity.

A social was also arranged with another branch of the family where we were entertained to dinner and discussion behind closed shutters. We learned of serious anti-Semitism resulting in dismissal and about the awful political situation in the country.

Morris was a violent critic, having nothing but contempt for the regime which he said bore no relation to socialism but was based on nepotism. He himself was not afraid since he had been a senior forestry officer and was now living on his pension. He took us around Moscow, its exhibitions and art galleries, all the time talking about the miserable social life of the people.

It was depressing and in great contrast to my earlier experience in 1968. On my return to London I felt overburdened by it all since I had been an apostle of the Soviet Union along with the rest of the party and the ANC. I went to discuss matters with Alex La Guma who often visited the Soviet Union and was one of its ardent supporters. I hoped that Alex, a sensitive writer, could throw some objective light on my experience. I told him of my impressions and asked his opinion of Soviet society since I had perhaps been given a wholly one-sided view by Jews who felt aggrieved. But he was full of the old certainties. Soviet life might be less luxurious than that in the West, but it was far more moral. As for the Jews, weren't most of them petit bourgeoisie, and therefore unable to settle down to a communist system which deprived them of privileges and pseudo-freedoms? We talked and disagreed.

RESIGNATION

This was the period of the spontaneous eruption of labour militancy in Natal. In 1973 there had been the famous Durban dock workers' strike when workers were forced out of their hostels. This set in motion a wave of unrest throughout the country and was the basis for new unionism. I received several appeals from Harold Strachan for financial assistance for his group which was working secretly to support the creation of unions in Durban. Jock's letters became increasingly desperate and critical of the exile movement which he felt should have been focusing all its efforts on supporting the emerging structures at home rather than running around the world. I raised these matters in the party but got the standard response that our internal units were taking care of it.

Then Harold's wife, Maggie, arrived in London at great personal risk and got in touch with me through a third party. Her story was dramatic. Both she and Harold were in considerable danger of arrest. On one occasion someone had fired through the open front door and they had been fortunate to get away with their lives. But they were continuing with the union support work, were working with people like MD Naidoo, an old communist and Indian Congress activist, and badly needed money.

I arranged a meeting with Joe Slovo to report on this discussion and was pleased to find Rusty with him as he entered my parked car at Camden Town. Mary sat beside me in front. I told them what I had learned from Maggie and appealed to Slovo to do something to get funds to Harold. He was amazingly cool about it, saying something about the structures being in place and that all was being taken care of. I pointed out that Maggie had risked a great deal in coming to London, since she must be a suspect, and that she was unwilling to either come to my house or meet with Slovo himself. As I pressed on he suggested that perhaps Harold was not working within the movement structures but could not be specific about this. He wanted to meet Maggie herself. At this point I totally lost my temper and said that his attitude was reprehensible, that he was merely protecting his own corner. But he was immovable.

A few months passed after which I was visited at the Open University by a young woman from Oxfam Quebec who wanted to do something in solidarity with the South African struggle. I proposed financial assistance to Strachan and we agreed on £2 000 which I sent to him in small amounts. The system I used was cumbersome and not safe. I approached Hugh Lewin, a South African liberal who had been in prison with me, who greatly respected Harold and had numerous international contacts. He arranged to transfer £1 000 through an international organisation, IUEF, based in Geneva, in which Craig Williamson, South Africa's master spy, held a senior post. Hugh was perfectly satisfied with his credentials at the time, he had entertained Williamson at his home in London and he thought that this link was far more secure than anything the movement could achieve. Indeed, I was well aware that the movement's London-South Africa links were insecure. There was also some disregard for security. For instance, I was astonished to receive a note in the post from Barry Feinberg for information about the Oxfam grant of $5 000.

After a time I received a surprise visit at home from Rusty and Barry Feinberg, who said that the party had been informed through a contact in Canada, Peter Bunting, that Oxfam had given me money for internal trade union work and they were very perturbed about this. What was going on? I told them everything except the name of the recipient of the money, which I refused to divulge on the grounds that it would be a violation of the trust placed in me. I said that our security was not as good as it might be and that I did not want to be responsible for his arrest.

The discussion was reasonably cordial, but I knew that I was in for it. They said my refusal was a serious breach of discipline and would lead to severe sanctions. I said that rather than give the name of my contact I would resign from the party.

A month or so later I was visited by Barry Feinberg who had a letter dated 27 February 1976 stating that the Central Committee had expelled me from the party on the grounds that I was assisting opposition groups in the country. It alleged that the money was sent to an apparatus which had no connection with the party, SACTU or ANC. In the absence of a full disclosure it was assumed that my conduct was designed 'either to encourage opposition groupings to our liberation movement, or reflects a total lack of trust and confidence in the leadership'.

'Such an approach is an outrage against the basic principles of communist discipline and, if persisted in, is clearly inconsistent with continuing membership of our Party.

'The CC calls upon BT to make a full and detailed disclosure of the apparatus in question (including the identity of its members) and the history of his own association with it. If he persists in his refusal to make such a disclosure, appropriate action will follow.'

I started to put the letter in my pocket, but Barry lunged forward, trying to seize it and saying it was against the rules for party letters to be kept. But I refused, turned on my heel and went indoors to recover from one of the most traumatic moments of my life. I had a sinking feeling that my world had collapsed.

I then put my resignation in writing:

12/3/76
The London District Representative

Dear Comrade

This letter is to tender my resignation from the party. I am doing this on the grounds that I find myself unable to reveal the name of my contact as requested. To do so would be a breach of confidence and security.

You will appreciate that resignation does not come lightly after 22 years but this is not an issue where sentiment can enter.

The letter from the CC suggests that my conduct is consistent with encouraging opposition groups. I reject this wholly and would not be a party to such activity. I have supplied funds for legitimate work which I understood to be in the overall interests of our movement and would not have co-operated on any other basis.

I am asked to reveal the names of all persons in the apparatus in question. I am unable to do so since I only know one person and am not even aware of what kind of apparatus, if any, he is attached to. I can vouch for this person, however, as a man of the highest principal and commitment to our struggle.

Although the immediate cause of my resignation is set out above, I should say that for some years I have felt a sense of alienation and uselessness in my membership in the party. This was entirely due to the fact that I was excluded from any meaningful work such as that connected with our struggle at home and our return there. I have come to believe that there is indeed an inner party which controls the rest and which has no confidence in others. My participation and that of the others has seemed to me to be purely that of providing a degree of legitimation and financial support for the inner core. This is a worthless role not worthy of long-standing party members committed to the ideals of our cause.

The letter from the CC refers to the requirements of party discipline. I would answer that discipline, to be meaningful and effective, must be based on mutual trust and taking the membership into a measure of confidence on the part of the leadership. This has not happened. Instead blind loyalty is demanded contrary to all the long experience of organisations like ours. A cipher cannot be a good cadre.

I only want to add that I believe that history will yet afford me the opportunity to play my small part in the South African Revolution and I hope that my resignation will not preclude that.

Ben Turok

The Central Committee replied as follows:

6th July, 1976
To the London Committee

Dear Comrade

The Central Committee has now had an opportunity of considering Ben Turok's response to our letter of 27 February 1976 a copy of which is attached.

We note that Ben Turok persists in his refusal to make a full and detailed disclosure of his secret association with and financing of internal contacts and/or groups for Trade Union or other political purposes.

We consider that his conduct in relation to the matters raised in our letter of 27 February constitutes a flagrant breach of communist discipline.

In the circumstances the Central Committee has unanimously decided to expel him as a member of the South African Communist Party. We reject his letter of resignation as an attempt to pre-empt the Central Committee from taking the only course which was left open to it by his disloyal and anti-Party activities.

Yours comradely,

YM Dadoo
Chairman, Central Committee

A few weeks later I saw Jack Woddis, a leader of the British Communist Party, to seek membership there. To my astonishment I was told that they had consulted the South African Party which objected and so I was turned down. I reflected that the terrain of politics is tough and the penalties can be severe. Many leading politicians have experienced severe trauma in their careers. Since my basic views have not changed, since I continue to adhere to Marxism – though with fundamental qualifications now – it has been a constant source of uneasiness. And yet it has also given me a certain spiritual comfort to know that I have for so long dissociated myself from Stalinism which was so patently rotten and which most of our leaders knew to be seriously flawed. I have much satisfaction in that I was no sycophant for two decades and my conscience feels clean of the corruption that membership of the party entailed. It could even be that the iron that entered my soul in prison ensured that never again would I be a silent recipient of bullying or hesitate to speak out when conscience demanded it.

But it was all at great cost. The Communist Party is unforgiving. With my resignation I knew that I was surrendering any prospect of ever again holding any office in the movement as a whole since the party has influence over the whole domain of South African struggle and has a range of techniques for isolating its critics.

Yet the struggle would not leave me alone. I received a letter from Ivan Schermbrucker that money was needed by the long-term prisoners for such things as toiletries and to pay for the weekly film they were now allowed. I enquired from Defence and Aid why they were having these difficulties but got little satisfaction. So I made a minor collection among friends and sent it off to Ivan. Soon I received another letter asking for money for certain welfare disbursements for people who had been released from prison and who were not being adequately being cared for. I again raised the matter with Defence and Aid but was not satisfied. And so I once again went the rounds of friends, including the wealthier ones like Mannie Brown, showing Ivan's letters and asking for donations. The reaction was both swift and vicious. Several people took me to task for interfering in affairs outside my sphere and demanded that I desist. I immediately wrote to Ivan and told him I could do no more. His response was devastating. He accused me of selling out the people at home for the sake of my own peace of mind and at the behest of people who cared nothing for those suffering at home and I could go to hell. Only Ivan could be so violent in his language and so direct in his attack. I was crestfallen.

I also encountered MD in London and asked him whether the money I had sent to Strachan was used for legitimate purposes and he confirmed this. So on 13 January 1978 I wrote to Rusty as follows:

London
13/1/78

Dear Rusty and Barry

I am writing to you as the persons directly involved in interviewing me in connection with my expulsion. I want to propose that this question be reopened in the light of new evidence now available as a result of the arrival in London of MD.

You will recall that it was argued against me that I refused to make a full disclosure and that I had sent money to the 'an apparatus which has no direct connection with the Party, SACTU or ANC ...' I denied the latter as well as the suggestion that my conduct could in any sense be seen as encouraging opposition groups, a suggestion I rejected absolutely though it has to be conceded that I could only know what I was told and at long distance at that.

I have had a discussion with MD and he is willing to confirm that he knew about the supply of funds to a certain person (his identity is of course known to Rusty) and approved of it. Furthermore, he also knew that an embargo against disclosure had been placed upon me though he did not know its precise extent.

In the light of the above I request that the matter be reopened for the hearing of his evidence. I believe he expects to be in London for some weeks. I regret that I myself shall not be around to respond to anything that comes up since I leave for Lusaka on the 31st Jan. However I shall be reachable there should the need arise.

I must urge the greatest caution in the handling of this matter, for obvious reasons.

Ben

I received a reply on 10 October as follows:

10th October, 1978

Dear Ben

I passed your letter regarding MD and the information he can give to the proper authorities who have given me their reply and asked me to communicate it to you. In this, I am acting strictly as postman.

They feel unable to reverse their earlier decision in the light of your letter. They say that the original complaint was NOT that you had appropriated any money for yourself, or that you failed to spend it legitimately. The complaint was, in fact, that you acted unilaterally and without consultation in the spending of it, and refused to give any explanation of the purposes for which it had been used – even when faced with a specific request for information.

Regards and best wishes.

In the movement there was much talk about loyalty and discipline. The party issued a document from the political bureau called *Guidelines* in February 1978 couched in communist-party speak:

> The South African Communist Party is the highest form of class organisation of the South African working class in the struggle for national liberation, socialism and peace in our time. It is guided by the scientific principles of Marxism-Leninism.
>
> Marxism-Leninism teaches that the Party of the working class has the leading role in the struggle for the elimination of exploitation of man by man and the building of a Socialist society which will eventually be transformed into a Communist society. The working class can only carry out this mission if it is organised and guided by its political vanguard – the Communist Party.
>
> The Guidelines must be regarded as Party directions and must be observed. It is the duty of every member and every unit to defend the Party and its policy and to carry out all majority decisions.

The document went on with a whole series of 'musts' and references to 'duty' which seemed unduly oppressive and certainly did not reflect the conditions in the movement. It was a relief not to fall under this kind of pressure.

The years dragged on and I was elected to the ANC London Committee.

I threw myself into my work at the Open University where I was learning a great deal about education in general and distance learning in particular: a new career had opened up. Soon I was developing a new technique of teaching by telephone and pioneered this method in the OU, which innovation was welcomed enthusiastically. I was giving papers at conferences and writing articles in various journals. I also enjoyed the Social Science teaching I did as a tutor, and was even more fulfilled when I joined my first course team at headquarters on D 302 Patterns of Inequality.

I wrote a double unit on South Africa as a special case in inequality. To my great delight it was classed the best unit on the course by the tutor advisory panel.

But the urge to return to Africa remained too, so I took up a senior lectureship post at the University of Zambia funded by the British government whose provisions for such postings are rather generous. In October 1978 I arrived in Lusaka to take up the job of co-ordinator for the Social Science foundation course which catered for some 450 students and which was an obligatory interdisciplinary common course for all students in the school. It was a great chance to serve in a conventional teaching capacity at university level and I enjoyed it a great deal, developing a special technique for first-year students accustomed to this kind of learning. I was also asked to do some teaching on higher-level courses where my more specialised knowledge was useful. I enjoyed the students immensely and learned at first hand the difficulties and problems that exist at this typical of universities in independent Africa and which was so useful when I later set up the Institute For African Alternatives (IFAA).

One of my first actions was to seek an interview with Oliver Tambo with whom I had had many personal discussions in London and who knew about some of my difficulties there, and to ask to be integrated in the movement during my stay in Lusaka. He readily agreed and arranged for a meeting with the head of information of the ANC. The interview took place at the ANC office and we agreed that my task would be to set up a research reference unit with all the material required. I set about the task with a will, obtained lists of journals and papers, costed out filing cabinets and other materials, and found a location in an ANC residence just out of town. We met two or three times and then he began to fail to turn up. Eventually I gave up. However, I maintained my very cordial relations with Tambo who sent me many notes on a variety of topics:

As From: Box 1791
Lusaka
21 October 1976

Dear Ben

Your note of July 3 only reached me this afternoon. I do not believe that either you or the postal services are to blame. Anyway, thanks very much. It (the book) is certainly most useful – and I have not come across anything more comprehensive.

What about the rest of the material that you produced or handled on the South African situation? You make reference to Martin and Harold who write profusely. I'm supposed to be getting the latter's papers but, the rolling stone that I am, I hardly stop long enough at any one place to gather some moss. In the result reading matter sent to me tends to be grabbed by the office staff who naturally have the need, and unfortunately also the time, to read. I was delighted to hear from you, although your notebook took 4 inexplicable weeks to reach me. I was pleased to note that the situation in our country continues to receive your productive attention, to the benefit of us all. Our Movement has been guilty of gross wastage of our own talent, as if it was afraid to reach in a hurry the goals it has set itself – or rather, the goals set for it by our people. Yours is a case in point. But never mind: So many cannot have sacrificed so much, all in vain. Victory is certain – wanton wastage notwithstanding.

Regards to Mary – and to the 'kids'.

Matla
Oliver

AFRICAN NATIONAL CONGRESS
(SOUTH AFRICA)
P.O. BOX 1791, LUSAKA, ZAMBIA
Tel: Our Ref:
Date: 2.4.80   Your Ref:

Dear Ben

Not only did our letters cross, but I was not even in Lusaka when they did so. Last night (the time now is 2.15 am, Tuesday – rather Wednesday) I read both your letters (dd. 15/3/80 & 23/3/80), having returned to Lusaka Sunday evening (30th) to a terrible chain of appointments. And at 9 a.m. today, I'll be at the airport – off again!
From all this you will see that:

(a) We can't meet – & I would have loved to have a chat both on the question of foreign policy & on the very valuable observations you make in your second letter.
(b) I am scraping the bottom of the barrel for energy & time to complete what MUST be done before I leave.

On the question of the election results ZAPU comrades were stunned – and this includes those who were in the country electioneering. Their own prognostication on the results gave cheer to their well wishes. Certainly I found depression among our ranks – the result of erosive confidence in the 'certainty of victory'. I was pleased with the results (a) because Botha's side had been defeated very badly – crushed with a miserable 3 seats out of 80! That was surely victory for our side. The sharing of seats between the 2 wings of the Patriotic Front was less important and more internal to the Zimbabwe situation.

The relations between the ANC & ZANU are fairly good and in some instances it can be said very good. I certainly have no problem with them whatever. But of course this is because I do think about the future sometimes, and the future often requires that you make as many friends as possible. I fear, however, that I have not been able to infect my comrades with this approach to life. My family likes to stay in its own house with its own friends. It does not like going out & shaking hands with 'strangers' – unfortunately! Even so, we have done fairly well on the whole. With the frontline states we are on good terms. No worry.

Matla OR

AFRICAN NATIONAL CONGRESS (SOUTH AFRICA)
PO Box 1791 Lusaka Zambia – Phone 72319
17 March
Year of the Charter

Dear Ben

A thousand thanks for your letter of 4th March and the draft which is very good. I have made a few amendments and additions.
Alfred should have seen you after I had discussed the school with you. Perhaps he will yet do so.
It's disastrous I have not been able to call in. I am beginning to feel whoever decided there should be a mere 24 hours in the day miscalculated very badly. We need 12 more.
Regards to Mary.

Amandla!

Matla
OR

15/4/78
Lusaka

Dear Ben

Thanks for your note. Why don't we get together again? Why not see me at our office say, lunch time Friday (we can munch at sandwiches or something, with coffee/tea – what a superb menu!)
Thanks for the important hint ?????????

Matla
OR

When Mary arrived in Lusaka we set up home in quite a decent house provided by the university. We both attended the weekly ANC unit meeting with people like Jack and Ray Simons, Doc Randeree and Mavivi Manzini, where we discussed the political situation, ANC policy, and the welfare provision for comrades. I had still not given up on getting a real task in the ANC and made an appointment to see Alfred Nzo about this who welcomed me warmly in his office at the back of the headquarters building. I told him my concerns and asked whether there was any obstacle to my involvement that he knew about. He replied that there was the usual gossip about people in exile, but that there had never been any formal complaint about me. The only concrete allegation was that I had written a book, *Strategic Problems in South Africa's Struggle: a critical analysis by Ben Turok*, which had been heavily criticised but he had not read it and couldn't pass judgement. So I offered to give him a copy and delivered one to his house where he lived with two other comrades in rather Spartan conditions.

Nzo duly read my book with an unexpected outcome. He summoned me to a meeting with several members of the working committee who were in town (I recall Josiah Jele, Andrew Masondo plus two or three others) and I was confronted aggressively by Nzo for calumniating the leadership especially with the phrase 'an ageing leadership far from home' which had upset him a great deal. He found the book wholly destructive and wanted a public apology. We debated this for some time and I made some conciliatory statement but was unable to offer a public retraction since the book was not being reprinted.

And so passed the remainder of my two-and-a-half years in Zambia. We made many good friends, I did a lot of research towards my book, *Mixed Economy in Focus: Zambia*, learned a lot about the post-independence problems of Africa, and returned to the Open University where I worked for two years on a course entitled 'Third World Studies'. In 1986 I took early retirement and set up the Institute For African Alternatives (IFAA) which became the focus for a new life. At the same time I continued attending my unit meetings and doing what I could for the movement.

I learned that Strachan was having a very difficult time finding work in Durban, so invited him to spend some time with us in London. It was wonderful to see him and renew our close comradeship. I also asked him about the money I had sent him and as a result of what he told me I once again wrote to Rusty:

24.7.1986

Dear R

I am writing in connection with the transfer of certain monies by me to South Africa in 1975. You had a role in connection with this matter so I am addressing this letter to you for suitable action.

You will understand that I reopen the question with much distaste and only do so because of continuing smears about my conduct over all this period. It was recently brought to my attention that a leading figure in the ANC asserted that I have 'betrayed the movement'. My assumption is that the allegation referred to the matter of funds in 1975 since I can think of no other issue which might evoke such language.

I have looked again at the evidence which I have kept over the years, namely bank account data, letters and notes. The facts are as follows:

I was approached in the early 1970s by Harold Strachan to supply funds for trade union work in Durban. I did nothing for a long while, but then quite fortuitously the opportunity to raise money came when I was visited by an official from Oxfam Quebec who wished to support our struggle. I asked for and received in due course the sum of Canadian $5 000 which I banked in the name of an Education Fund in London. I have all the counterfoils etc. The money was earmarked for trade union work in S.A.

I had no doubts whatsoever of the legitimacy of his political work having learnt of his staunch commitment to our movement during many years in prison with him.

I could not face the possibility that Strachan might go to prison for a third time due to my having divulged this information about illegal activity.

I left the matter there, until MD Naidoo arrived in London and since I had subsequently learned that he had been associated with Strachan, this gave me the opportunity to investigate whether the funds had been used for legitimate purposes. He confirmed this and spoke highly of the work of Strachan.

Coming to the present, I now have for the first time an opportunity to check what actually happened in South Africa due to the visit here of Strachan himself. He says quite categorically that he gave the money to MD Naidoo in good faith as the attached letter sets out.

I want to get the record straight. It is true that I refused to divulge Strachan's name to your enquiry team and my reason had nothing to do with factional activity, it was to protect a man with whom I had been locked up for three years and for whom I had the highest esteem. Furthermore it is now clear that the money was properly passed on for the work of our movement.

I look forward to hearing from you.

Ben Turok

However, I received no reply.

We drifted in this fashion for four years, trying to keep a finger on the pulse of the struggle which was moving to a critical stage. I made one last effort to get involved in the real struggle by talking to Ronnie Kasrils who advised me to write to Joe Modise, commander in chief of MK. My letter read:

Turok
The Lane House
Barnet Road
Arkley, Hert
EN5 3JT, UK
Tel: 01-449-5170
2.5.86

Comrade Joe Modise
Commander in Chief
Umkhonto Wesizwe
African National Congress,
Headquarters,
Lusaka, Zambia

Dear Joe

This letter will not come as a surprise to you since Comrade Kasrils will have seen you by now. However he asked me to put in writing the subject of our discussion and I am doing so, albeit rather briefly. You would not want me to be indiscreet on sensitive matters.

What I want to say is that I consider that the situation inside the country has changed fundamentally and that this requires us to change as well. There is a new challenge facing all members of the movement if we are to live up to the ideals we proclaimed for so long.

Some three months ago I spoke to Comrade Aziz Pahad about how I felt and offered my service for new duties. We discussed this at length and he recorded notes of the interview. However I have still to get a response from him.

More recently, I was in Lusaka where I left a letter for Comrade Slovo at HQ which said that I thought it was time that the embargo on my participation in the struggle was lifted since all hands were now needed to advance that struggle. I have had no response.

Last week I had a lengthy discussion with Comrade Kasrils where I made the same point. His advice was that as a former member of MK (though I never resigned) I should write to you. I am doing so out of an acute feeling that the suffering of our people should not be ignored by those who worked so hard in the past to bring about precisely the conditions now obtaining – an enemy driven into extreme repression by the march of the people for their liberation.

I would like my feeling to be known to you and other comrades. If you too wish to ignore this then at least I will have done what I can to declare myself. The revolution will proceed and victory is indeed in sight regardless.

Yours fraternally

Ben Turok

I received no reply.

But the struggle was advancing favourably without my assistance. When Walter Sisulu was released, Mary and I began to talk about going home. We felt an acute obligation to return and stand by those comrades. We made enquiries from South Africa House and found that we had to fill in forms applying for visas despite our using British passports. We were clearly on a list of people embargoed.

CHAPTER 9

THE 1990 MIRACLE AND ITS AFTERMATH

On Friday 2 February 1990 I was working on an article at home in Arkley, London. At one o'clock I switched on the lunch-hour news and was astonished to see President de Klerk speaking as the main item. It was incredible to hear him announce the unbanning of the ANC and the SACP, the forthcoming release of Mandela and the return of the exiles. My excitement was unbounded.

When Mary returned later that afternoon, we toasted the news and immediately resolved to return to South Africa for a visit. Knowing that the London ANC leadership would frown on such a proposal, we decided to keep it quiet but phoned our lawyer in Pretoria to alert him to possible police action. We also phoned our three sons to inform them – their reaction was that we were being reckless. But Mary and I had been discussing our return for some time and under far more risky circumstances, so the present opportunity seemed tame by comparison. The next day we went to a British Airways travel agent and booked two return flights to Johannesburg.

We left Heathrow the following Monday evening and arrived at Jan Smuts airport on the Tuesday morning. A hollow feeling lined the pit of my stomach when, as we descended from the plane, I immediately saw men in uniform with dogs patrolling the tarmac. As we entered the grey, bleak terminal building we saw other soldiers and policemen dotted about. I was struck by the bare walls, devoid of advertising, and the sparse seating. It looked more primitive than the terminal buildings of any of the airports I had seen in the poorest Third World countries in Africa.

We approached the immigration desk but hung back in order to be the last to present our passports. The officer took my British passport and entered something in his computer. His mouth fell open. 'God,' he said, 'You can't come in here! You are prohibited!

Stand on one side!' I did so and Mary took my place. His face resumed its hangdog expression and he took Mary's passport and entered something in the computer. Then he flushed blood-red and blurted out: 'God, the same problem! You can't come in here!'

'What's the matter?' I asked.

'You are both listed,' he replied. 'We can't let you in.'

I responded: 'Don't you know that President de Klerk has unbanned the ANC and has said that exiles can return home?'

'Ja,' he said, 'but you are still listed. You must return to London.'

'No way,' I said. 'We are here and we insist on our right to come home.'

He became angry and demanded: 'Stand there and wait.'

Another official arrived who put us through the same drill. He called yet another beefy official who was clearly Special Branch and asked us why we had come and what we wanted to do. I replied that I wanted to see my brother Hillel in Cape Town. We were told to wait.

We were left alone for a while, so I went to one of the public phones on a nearby wall and dialled the offices of our attorney, Gordon Hay, in Pretoria. The phone was out of order. I tried another with the same result. An official came to see what we were doing but did not intervene. After he left I tried the third phone. Although I had no South African coins, the system allowed a half-minute conversation before interrupting, and this time my call went through. When a woman announced the name of the firm, I spoke hastily: 'Please tell Gordon Hay that I am at Joburg airport and the authorities are holding us.'

'What did you say?'

I rang again and made no more progress. On my fourth attempt, she caught on, and said she would inform him.

We sat down to wait. Two more officials arrived to ask the same questions, only this time more aggressively. There seemed to be more police with dogs around as well. They persisted with questions about our intentions in coming back. We were adamant that we were entitled to do so. They left to consult others. We saw small groups of officials in a huddle in an office nearby. They left. We sat. The hours went by. We had no South African money and therefore no food or drink.

After four-and-a-half hours, two new, more senior officials approached. One said: 'If we let you in what do you want to do?'

I replied: 'We want to fly to Cape Town to see my brother in Camps Bay.'

'For how long?'

'One week will do.'

'OK. We will give you a visa for one week. Then you will return to London.'

We were delighted. 'Thank you very much!' I said.

Back to the glum passport officer who seemed relieved. He stamped our passports and we were in South Africa! What a scream! We later learned that Hay had intervened with the authorities and assured them that our intentions were innocent.

We walked over to Baggage Reclaim, grabbed our bags and found Domestic Departures for our flight to Cape Town. Here again, police were loitering around and there was only a small scattering of passengers. The ominous police state was glaringly obvious.

The flight to Cape Town was uneventful except that we were very hungry. The hostess served only soft drinks and dry biscuits. I asked whether there was any food but she replied that food was only served on a few flights; otherwise it was biscuits and Coke.

In Cape Town we collected our luggage and took a taxi to Hillel's house. There was an extraordinary reunion after many years of geographical and psychological separation. Without telling us, he had phoned the *Cape Argus* and a reporter called round for the story, which made the front page: 'The first exiles to return home.'

But I was restless. Two days later, I left for Johannesburg and Mary for Durban to see her sister, Jane. I checked into a hotel and immediately went down to ANC headquarters where I met my oldest and closest comrade, Walter Sisulu. We shared an emotional embrace and a wonderful talk when he subsequently took us to the airport.

Joburg looked rather stark. Its streets were full of black people, many hanging about doing nothing. Whites seemed to be rushing about and there was a very obvious police presence. It felt as if I had entered a forbidden zone.

Mary joined me for the last three days and we were able to meet some old friends. One unforgettable experience was seeing the release of Nelson Mandela on television on Sunday 11 February 1990, along with his reunion with Winnie, and hearing his speech on the Grand Parade in Cape Town. It was all so moving that it made all our hardships over the years pale into insignificance. At the end of the week we returned to London, delighted at the successful mission, and shared our experiences with the boys.

The news of our trip soon reached the ANC office in London. Within a week we were summoned to see Mendi Msimang, the chief representative, who was stern and disapproving. He asked whether we had gone to South Africa and if we had obtained permission to do so. We said no to the latter and received a severe reprimand with a promise that the matter would be reported to headquarters in Lusaka. We had expected a rebuke and were not over-concerned. As soon as we got home we began preparations for the next visit home.

The ANC branch met monthly to discuss a range of issues, and the next meeting included a report on the new situation following De Klerk's speech. The general view was that he was not to be trusted and that it might be a trap. Sentiment was that we must all go home together. I thought this view ludicrous. We could not hire an aircraft or ship and, in any case, each family had its own problems with children at school and no job prospects in South Africa. We knew some would never return.

Then began a four-month battle with the South African embassy in London. We applied for a visa to return and they balked, offering a variety of excuses. The long wait gave us pause for reflection. Mary was in no doubt that this was the correct course. I was less certain about the urgency. I had a fascinating job at IFAA, was very productive in my writing and at the meetings I attended in Africa, and had built up a solid reputation in the UK as an Africanist. I was not concerned about there being no prospect of a political role for me in the new South Africa.

So why persist in returning? Was I entrapped by some peculiar obsession? If so, why? Did I want to prove something in the face of my expulsion from the party, my exclusion from MK and my marginalisation in the ANC? If so, was this not a futile exercise?

Many others who had also disagreed substantially with movement policies had simply dropped out and then got on with their lives in exile.

Then, too, perhaps I was overwhelmed by a sense of guilt for having left the country while some comrades were still in prison. Or perhaps it was my unfulfilled promise to Bram Fischer that I would undergo plastic surgery and return. After all, I had met only one of his three conditions, leaving the country illegally. Was I motivated by my critical attitude towards some of the leaders around me? Was I trying to prove how wrong they had been in accepting life in the comfort of exile for so long? Was it a kind of protest at the hypocrisy of people like Tennyson Makiwane with his 'the transports are waiting'? Or was it an acceptance of the challenge from Harold Strachan and Ivan Schermbrucker that we should all come home and challenge the regime to do their worst? Or was it the sheer heroics of someone who had independent tendencies, never reluctant to go ahead when others were more hesitant – acting out a kind of voluntarism? Someone who had contempt for the robots in the movement?

At the end of such reflections, I concluded that my commitment to the ANC was not in doubt and I had to do what I thought right.

And so we nagged the South African embassy until we finally got permission for another short stay and off we went. By then the situation in the country was beginning to settle down. After many hesitations a group of ANC leaders left Lusaka for Johannesburg, expecting the worst. But negotiations with the regime began and the prospect of some agreement was a possibility. Nevertheless, the ANC insisted that MK should remain armed and that mass action should continue, with Chris Hani the most outspoken advocate of militancy and preparedness for the renewal of hostilities.

During the three weeks' stay we looked around for a permanent home and offices for the branch of the Institute For African Alternatives. We visited Shell House, headquarters of the ANC, met numerous old comrades in the corridors and after much pressure managed to get a letter stating that we were bona fide ANC cadres who should be allowed back into the country on our ultimate return.

We also managed to get an appointment to see Cyril Ramaphosa who was then the secretary-general of the National Union of Mineworkers and a member of the internal leadership. He was in a jovial mood, very friendly, and rather frank about the uncertain situation and the prospects before us. We were also able to see Zwelakhe Sisulu, another of the senior internal leaders, who was equally frank and open about the years of struggle and the hopes for a new beginning.

We negotiated to rent a flat and office premises, and once again returned to London where we began preparations for our final removal to South Africa. Back in Johannesburg once again, four months later, I set about establishing IFAA with a small staff of four. We immediately began to hold workshops on the topics we had pursued in London and throughout our African network and found that our work was not popular at Shell House. The interests of the African continent were not a priority with the leadership; the ANC was engaged in regular interaction with the IMF and World Bank and with business interests both at home and abroad. There was intense pressure from external forces to ensure that the ANC showed moderation in political and economic matters and it was under constant threat to do so or face global hostility. However, there were also many militant voices in the movement that wanted to assert the radicalism of exile, notably in the SACP.

There was a strong feeling that the party should not be sidelined in the new conjuncture and the party decided to hold a mass rally to inaugurate its launch in the country as a mass party. Ramaphosa told us how he turned up at the rally, having previously joined the party as an ordinary member, and was persuaded by Slovo to chair the event. He told us that he had no idea what to say, but that mattered little, since his mere presence was enough to give the event a much-needed legitimacy, especially as thousands of mineworkers had been brought to the rally.

I was astonished that the party could be so foolhardy as to break with the tradition of a small but highly effective core, working mainly within the structure of the national liberation movement while at the same time issuing ideological and educational material upholding the vision of a socialist outcome. I believe that many of the subsequent problems of the party derive from that critical error.

Nevertheless, I still felt a deep loyalty to the socialist cause despite my alienation from the party. After a few months I wrote to the party secretary asking for a commission of inquiry into my status. Nothing happened for a few months until I again raised the issue with Jeremy Cronin, who had by then become a highly prominent party spokesman. After a while, he visited me at my offices and, to my extreme consternation, gave me a vigorous lecture on the unreasonableness of my request, saying that the party did not have a disciplinary committee in place and that there were other priorities based on the needs of more deserving comrades who had worked hard in Lusaka. In effect, my plea was dismissed with contempt. I later learned that the matter never reached the Central Committee leadership and that Cronin acted under the influence of Joe Slovo.

Used to being marginalised by the London and Lusaka leadership, I was resigned to plough my own furrow in IFAA. Despite numerous difficulties in obtaining funding and finding suitable staff, we organised many lectures and seminars, largely on the themes of the global economy and African development. We began a busy publishing programme and from my personal point of view it was a highly fertile period for my writing. I once noted that I had written 27 papers in the course of a year. But it was tough going, especially in the absence of positive signals from the ANC. Foreign donors were shifting funding from NGOs to government. Getting people to write serious papers took much effort and we had to generate new editorial capacity to help Mary who was principal editor. I managed to negotiate an agreement with the Extramural Department at Wits University to run development-studies courses in tandem with them and this gave us a sound base for our course work and the development-studies teaching that I enjoyed. At the same time we were breaking new ground all the time and IFAA gradually gained a reputation as a dynamic, if small outfit.

THE CODESA COMPROMISE

Yet around me bigger things were happening as the country stumbled from massive political turbulence to negotiations. In his first speech after his release from prison, Mandela had called for the intensification of struggle on all fronts, including the armed struggle. When the first formal talks began in May 1990 at Groote Schuur, the two sides were far apart; nevertheless, De Klerk lifted the state of emergency in June and there were hopes that the atmosphere would improve.

But then violence from Inkatha in March 1991 in Alexandria and the mini civil war in Natal rekindled tension and the government seemed to be involved. Mandela lost his trust in De Klerk. Despite these stresses the ANC convened its first internal national conference in Durban in July 1991 and Mary and I were invited as veterans. It was a huge gathering, filled with emotion and nostalgia, as so much history and so much suffering was laid before us. And yet there was a spirit of optimism and cold determination never to be forgotten. Mandela was elected as president, replacing the exhausted and ill Oliver Tambo who was given the honorary position of Chair of the ANC.

The conference endorsed the policy of continuing mass action to maintain pressure on the government and even the negotiations were described as 'a theatre of struggle'. On 20 December 1991, at the most unlikely venue (a trade exhibition centre in Johannesburg) the Convention for a Democratic South Africa – Codesa – was opened. Month after month these negotiations held centre-stage and we were all enthralled by the drama. The ANC was pressing for a fundamental transition to democracy, but the regime, headed by De Klerk, wanted to hold onto white power at all costs, repeatedly saying that it would never give way to simple majority rule.

The negotiations reached a deadlock and the ANC responded with a call for renewed mass action. At a rally in Soweto to celebrate 26 June where I was invited to recall the Congress of the People, Essop Pahad urged for 'rolling mass action' against De Klerk and even against the new democratic government and, if need be, against a future socialist government. He was reflecting a new fascination for the 'Leipzig option', the popular overthrow of the communist government of East Germany which seemed, paradoxically, to have become part of the revolutionary ardour of some of our comrades.

There can be little doubt that the ANC outmanoeuvred De Klerk and that more was conceded than was ever dreamt of. The constant manifestation of a huge capacity for mass action was probably decisive as the demonstrations following the assassination of Chris Hani showed. Slowly, in the midst of high drama, and almost at the eleventh hour, an agreement was reached to establish a government of national unity, and the country could move to nationwide elections based on a universal franchise.

In the meanwhile I had become active in my Johannesburg East ANC Branch and became the chair and representative in the provincial structures. I was appointed head of the Provincial Economic Department and soon became a member of the Provincial Executive in Gauteng. During this period I found occasion to interact with Trevor Manuel and Tito Mboweni who were respectively head and deputy-head of the Department of Economic Planning at Shell House. I raised the issue of a policy for involvement with Africa but was told that this was not a priority – our trading partners were in the West and in any case Africa was 'a basket case'. I also advocated strong opposition to any deals with the IMF and World Bank but met with a very cold shoulder. In retrospect, although my position was correct in principle, it was possibly too radical, given the political imperatives of the day.

My difficulty was borne home when Adebayo Adedeji invited Rob Davies, an academic, Stef Coetzee, head of the Africa Institute in Pretoria, and myself to Nigeria to discuss the holding of a conference on South Africa's relations with the rest of the continent. Adedeji was scathing about the ANC's abandonment of the continent, preferring to build relations with the West and its multilateral financial institutions.

It was a wonderful trip, taking in Ibadan and Adedeji's village where he had set up his institute, ACCDESS , which was very similar to IFAA. I had encountered Adedeji several times in Addis Ababa when he was the formidable head of the UN Economic Commission for Africa, but on his home ground he was a courteous and gentle person with a wry sense of humour. He was particularly courteous to Coetzee, whom he knew to be an Afrikaner who had been heavily compromised under apartheid. His previous post was head of economic policy at the Development Bank of South Africa, a government-funded institution which claimed to espouse liberal developmental economics but was deeply enmeshed in the bantustans.

We spent a full day discussing the proposed conference, ending up with the theme 'South Africa and Africa – Within or Apart?' to be held in Windhoek, Namibia. That evening we were invited to dinner at our host's home and encountered a praise singer on the veranda for Adedeji, who is a very senior traditional leader, and we spent a joyous evening with his friends. My own friendship with 'Bayo' was cemented and we continue to enjoy warm and ongoing contact from time to time. As the African Union and Nepad become more prominent, his contribution to the political economy of Africa becomes ever more appreciated, and he has been invited as a keynote speaker at official seminars on several occasions. This is in contrast to his treatment in earlier days when I was unsuccessful in my efforts to persuade Trevor Manuel to invite Adedeji to advise on our policies.

BATTLE FOR THE RECONSTRUCTION AND DEVELOPMENT PROGRAMME (RDP)

During the latter anti-apartheid years the non-governmental organisations (NGOs) within South Africa gained steadily in strength and in policy capacity. Various networks were established around themes such as housing, education, urbanisation and so on, attracting some of the best intellects in the country who initiated progressive developmental policies. Funding came from sympathetic foreign agencies and governments that saw this as an important contribution to the anti-apartheid cause. As the prospect of a democratic system became more certain, these groupings sought to generate new national policies and programmes, increasingly interacting with the ANC.

This process gained impetus as the ANC examined its own policies under the label of the Reconstruction and Development

Programme (RDP). This was seen as a continuation of the policies developed in exile and at home, and which emphasised the link between reconstruction and development, and the democratisation of the state and society. An important contributor to this work was the Macro-economic Research Group (MERG) set up in Johannesburg by a group of radical British-based economists, but who soon became alienated from the ANC and whose work was ultimately ignored. The reason for this was said to be a clash of personalities, but major policy differences were certainly at the root of the disputes.

Nonetheless the RDP policy process proceeded apace, largely through the drive of Cosatu Secretary General Jay Naidoo and ANC Deputy Secretary-General Cheryl Carolus. As the head of the RDP in the ANC provincial structures, I participated in many meetings of cadres from across the country as the range of themes developed by the NGOs and within the ANC were being consolidated. We owe a great debt to Jay Naidoo who brought enormous energy and the institutional backing of Cosatu, by now a powerful trade union movement behind the RDP. Cheryl Carolus smoothed the path within the ANC and ensured that it gave its official blessing to the process. I joined the final editorial group which then consisted of Alec Erwin, then a trade union leader, Jay Naidoo and Jeremy Cronin, among others, with Patrick Bond as the administrator. I recall one meeting where we suddenly realised that the document was thoroughly statist and top-down, and we agreed to rewrite it, democratising the text to include concepts like 'people-centred and people-driven' development.

One critical meeting held at the Johannesburger Hotel in Hillbrow decided the fate of the RDP. Some of us knew that certain leading personalities in the ANC had serious reservations about the document and they had insisted on the insertion of a number of paragraphs on fiscal discipline and the importance of macro-economic considerations. One clause was '... to ensure a macro-economic policy environment that is stable'. Another read: 'Government contributions ... must ... avoid undue inflation and balance-of-payments difficulties'. However, the impetus for the RDP was sufficient to allow it to proceed although it took eight drafts to get agreement.

A national RDP conference was then convened which drew some one thousand delegates from branches and structures across the country and who met at NASREC, the large exhibition centre in Johannesburg. At the final plenary, chaired by Trevor Manuel, an attempt was made to defer adoption on the grounds that the draft needed further work, especially on the role of the provinces. Alec Erwin rose to oppose deferral and I seconded him. This received full support from the grassroots delegates in the hall, and we gained the adoption of the document. Subsequently, the cabinet made some relatively minor changes and the RDP was adopted as the basis for national government policy.

A similar conference followed on 28-31 May 1992, also at NASREC, to determine the whole range of policies for the ANC and which resulted in a document entitled *Ready to Govern*, which remains one of the planks for current policy. After the formal opening, I headed for the economics commission where I found Mandela, Sisulu and others from the top leadership among over a hundred delegates. Tito Mboweni was in the chair amid speculation that this was going to be a critical session for the future government's economic policy. Mboweni presented a document entitled 'The Growth Path for the New South Africa.' Fresh from the battles over the RDP, I was deeply concerned about the absence of any reference to 'development'. I asked for the floor and proposed an amended title, 'The Growth and Development Path for a Democratic South Africa.' Alec Erwin seconded and the motion was passed without opposition. I saw that Tito was very irritated.

We then examined the document paragraph by paragraph until we came to the section that referred to privatisation and nationalisation. Alec Erwin immediately got up and stated that Cosatu objected to privatisation and would oppose its insertion vigorously. After some discussion Mandela rose to say that he had recently attended the World Economic Forum at Davos where he had said: 'Taking some key enterprises into public ownership will itself be a major step towards overcoming the huge inequality in the ownership of our country's wealth.' These remarks were unfavourably received while those of De Klerk and Buthelezi – who had also spoken and advocated a free-enterprise system – received a much better reception. He warned our commission that an overt call for nationalisation would meet with much opposition in the West and the conference should pay heed. I rose and said that as the author of the economic clause in the Freedom Charter I was bound to remind the meeting that there was a commitment by the ANC to the transfer of certain basic industries 'to the ownership of the people as a whole'. I argued that this concept, which was not necessarily the same as nationalisation, was not at all foreign to many countries where the capitalist system was in place. Indeed, the notion of public ownership could be found everywhere though in different forms.

The discussion continued without a solution in sight. Someone then proposed that a small group tackle the formulation outside the commission and report. We agreed to this and the group reported back in due course with a compromise formulation which referred to 'increasing the public sector, for example, nationalisation ... [and] reducing the public sector ... in a mixed economy'. The basic idea was that this would be done on a case-by-case basis and not on ideological grounds. This formulation remains official ANC policy to the present day.

THE PROVINCIAL CABINET

My standing in the ANC structures of the province was now solidly established and I participated regularly in the weekly meetings of the executive. Tokyo Sexwale, who served 13 years on Robben Island with Mandela, chaired the committee. He could exhibit considerable charisma and intelligence and soon became the darling of the media, who played on his ostensible sex appeal, especially to white women. He soon became identified as a possible candidate for deputy president and a significant rival for Thabo Mbeki. Tokyo enjoyed this attention and even pandered to it, which in my view diminished his standing as the leader of the Gauteng ANC.

The secretary of the provincial ANC was the tall, rather laid-back Paul Mashatile – a decent, kindly comrade whose laconic style hid a sharp political brain. Executive meetings were often poorly organised, however, and agendas cobbled together at the last minute. Tokyo was relaxed in the chair, seemingly unwilling to exercise discipline over members or lose favour with anyone. Yet, the probability of taking over the government of the province became ever more certain and I began to urge that appropriate policies be made and concrete organisational measures taken. This met with general approval but little was done to follow through.

I used the facilities of IFAA to arrange a seminar on a systems approach to the transformation of government. The result was a document which examined the basic changes we would need when the ANC took control. Tokyo invited me for breakfast at his Lower Houghton mansion where his wife served us a splendid meal. He had by now developed a rather gracious style of living in keeping with the luxurious suburb in which he lived. (He later left government and became a very wealthy captain of industry.) I proposed that our provincial executive set up a transition task team to examine in considerable detail how we would go about setting up a new government in the province. We would have to create virtually a wholly new administration since the former Transvaal would cease to exist and we intended to set up our government in Johannesburg, not Pretoria. The dislocation would be immense and had to be planned in advance. Tokyo agreed and proposed to place the item on the agenda at the next meeting of the executive.

However, when I made a presentation on the subject I encountered immediate opposition. Jesse Duarte obviously thought I was planning to seize a dominant role in the coming transition and she was supported by Mary Metcalfe. They moved a counter-proposal that one of the existing consultant bodies should hold a workshop where some of the existing papers and sector studies could be consolidated into a transition programme. This met with agreement, but the two volumes of papers that eventually emerged had no consistency and were never even considered. We later paid a heavy price for this omission.

Soon, an enlarged executive meeting was called to elect the personnel who would take office in the provincial cabinet when it came to be constituted after the national and provincial elections. The expectation was that we would win enough votes to get seven out of the ten seats in the provincial cabinet.

The 40-odd participants were supposed to be the most senior

representatives of all the ANC and Alliance structures in Gauteng Province. Instead, some who should have attended failed to make it, and one had the impression that the proceedings were unduly informal. However, after some discussion nominations were called for and to my astonishment I ended up in seventh place. Mathole Motsegha, the vice-chair of the province and a bit of a maverick, came in tenth, which upset him enormously, and he raised numerous points of order to strengthen his claim to office. But he could not change his position and the die was cast. By this time I was high up on the provincial list for the election while Mary was well placed on the national list and was elected to parliament in due course.

We were each allocated a voting district and I was sent to Heidelberg where I worked strenuously with the local ANC prior to the election and during the count. Once the results were announced, we realised that we had indeed won enough votes in the province to get our seven cabinet seats. We now had to determine how the cabinet posts were to be allocated. Tokyo called an urgent meeting of some 12 top provincial leaders to decide on this. Here again, the haphazard style we adopted came home to me. Tokyo and Paul had prepared a set of recommendations which was presented to the meeting. Tokyo was to be premier and again, to my amazement, I was proposed as the Member of the Executive Council (MEC) for Finance, with other posts following. Some discussion followed about the suitability of individuals and Mary Metcalfe said: 'I have a problem about Ben in Finance. He doesn't listen.' No one endorsed this view, but it was enough to change the list, and I offered to head the RDP Commission which was supposed to be a cabinet post.

We won the election convincingly with 62,8 per cent of the national vote and a similar proportion of the Gauteng provincial vote. When we met just prior to the swearing-in ceremony that evening the lawyers informed us that there was no post for the head of the RDP, which was to have the status of a commission in the Office of the Premier. Mary realised what she had done and asked whether I wanted to take up one of the other MEC posts, but I was satisfied with the RDP Commission. I discovered my mistake the next day when we all went to a large building in

Simmonds Street, central Johannesburg, which was set aside for the new provincial cabinet, with each MEC being allocated a suite of offices. None had been allocated to me and I was told that I would be part of the premier's suite. It soon dawned on me that I was to be considered as an adjunct of the premier's office – a kind of adviser with no staff of my own.

However, I was invited to the first cabinet meeting and was informed that I would be an ex-officio cabinet member and able to participate fully in all deliberations. Although I would not have the same salary, car, bodyguards and facilities as an MEC, all this mattered little in the wonderful atmosphere of taking power. We arranged a swearing-in ceremony for our premier, Tokyo Sexwale, which was to be held outside the Johannesburg Civic Centre. A platform was erected where the Transvaal Chief Justice, resplendent in his robes, performed this solemn task. Then followed a march-past of police and army personnel which included armoured vehicles and troop carriers, the very same kind of contingent that had been shooting our people in the townships only months before. I wept at the wonder of it all. All the literature on revolution, all our own rhetoric about the seizure of power, was as nothing compared to what we were witnessing in the streets of Johannesburg. Black and white participants, suitably dressed in our best, were here to celebrate a transfer of political, military and police power such as we had only dreamed of. Here was politics for real!

The first meeting of the cabinet was fascinating. There we were, Tokyo as premier, seven former ANC cadres as MECs, three National Party MECs, myself as head of the RDP Commission, and a young lawyer, Mark Philips, as the premier's legal adviser. Some of the ANC MECs had never been near public office; indeed, some had only worked in the movement and so had no formal employment experience at all.

Tokyo managed to introduce a fairly good-humoured atmosphere, and everyone was introduced and their roles ascertained. The leader of the NP was Olaas van Zyl, an experienced politician, who could be very tough at times but who was also willing to co-operate most of the time. After all, we were constituted as a Government of Provincial Unity, in line with the national agreement. If

De Klerk could stomach being deputy president in Mandela's cabinet, Van Zyl could do the same at our level.

Having ascertained our roles, Van Zyl raised the matter of perks. What offices would we get? What kind of official car? This triggered an hour-long discussion as members speculated on what kind of car was appropriate for our status and which particular model they preferred. Tokyo felt that a Mercedes was too flashy, but a BMW, especially one of the higher range, was good enough. This discussion was to continue at tedious length at several other meetings of the cabinet to my rising irritation.

However, I grabbed the opportunities now before me with both hands. I met with many officials, occupied a suite of offices without authority and recruited a small staff, all on the understanding that I had Tokyo's support even if he no longer had the time to meet with me regularly. In short, I behaved as if I were a head of department, and all this was made easy by virtue of the popularity of the RDP. Amazingly, a document that had aroused huge suspicion in the media and among business when it was ANC policy suddenly became the flavour of the day when it became a White Paper and the centrepiece of government policy. The press found all sorts of positive elements in it and business became enthusiastic about job creation and building physical and human infrastructure.

My work began in earnest and I met with enthusiasm everywhere. A few journalists were suspicious of my role and labelled me 'a Marxist economist'. *Finance Week* even dug up some inside information about my marginalisation in exile. But the tide was running strongly and this was but a minor irritation. My status was also raised by an invitation from Professor John Daniels to become a visiting professor of Political Science at the University of Durban Westville.

I heard that President Nyerere was visiting Johannesburg so I contacted him and Mary and I were invited to his rooms in a local hotel. Over the years, I had participated with Nyerere in a number of seminars after his retirement and had come to know him quite well. Mary and I joined him and his wife in a small hotel lounge for several hours where we talked about the South African transition to democracy and the experiences across the continent. He was a bit put out about being ignored by our government and declined to take any initiative here until Mandela opened the door for him. I gave him a copy of the RDP's policy document and he phoned the next day to say that no other African country had produced such an excellent development plan, but he was doubtful about it being implemented.

I was an ardent exponent of the RDP, seeing it as a culmination of the development advocacy I had been involved in over many years. I was also hugely encouraged by the response from some of 'the old guard' as we called them in the public service. For instance, I was invited to address the senior management of the Transvaal Provincial Administration at some remote venue north of Pretoria. I drove from Johannesburg and found that it was a small conference centre in the middle of the veld.

I entered a small reception office, received a very warm welcome from the director-general, and was shown into a crowded hall of about 150 white faces. I had expected a small meeting attended by a select few and a short, cursory discussion lasting about half an hour, so I was quite unprepared for this large exposure. But I launched into a full exposition of the RDP which, to my surprise, received prolonged applause. I questioned whether anyone had even seen the document and at least a dozen hands went up, brandishing their copies. One elderly man rose and said that he was the head of the provincial health service. He said: 'We have been waiting for something like this for years. We support you wholeheartedly.' Others followed in the same vein and what I had anticipated as a dull, perhaps even hostile meeting, became a rave for the RDP.

I had numerous similar experiences and often addressed three or four meetings a day. By this time I had a good set of offices, a few excellent staff led by Salim Aziz, an official car, driver and bodyguard, and a growing reputation as the saviour of Gauteng.

However, I became concerned that the RDP was being interpreted in a narrow sense as the building of new physical infrastructure in the cities. I felt that this would maintain the marginalisation of the townships, where the vast majority of the people lived, and that the benefits of RDP spending would not trickle down to them significantly. Instead, it was white-established business that would benefit, especially the white-owned construction industry.

We discussed the problem in our commission and decided to

call a meeting, 'Plan the Renewal of the Townships', at Vista University in Soweto. Some intellectuals criticised the idea on the grounds that we were concentrating on the historically neglected townships instead of integrating black and white in the white-dominated areas. But I thought we were on the right track and so we sent out notices to all ANC branches, hoping that at least 150 delegates would attend, and catered accordingly. On the day, 900 turned up and we had a wonderfully enthusiastic meeting which could have turned the whole RDP programme around if we had been allowed to maintain the momentum.

However, my ANC colleagues in the provincial cabinet were becoming very anxious about my activities and questioned them in the ANC cabinet caucus. They wanted to know why was I dealing with education and health issues when there were MECs for these portfolios. Why did I deal with finance and the economy when this was not my immediate brief? I explained, patiently at first and then with some exasperation, that the RDP was a holistic development programme that was cross-cutting and comprehensive. But my explanations were not accepted and I found myself increasingly on the fringes of decision making. My RDP counterparts in other provincial governments were experiencing the same treatment. There was clearly something wrong with the institutionalisation of the RDP even though it was then, and remains even now, the programme of government.

Even within ANC structures I was finding diminishing support generally and in Mary Metcalfe, MEC for Education, outright hostility. Mary and I had been very close in earlier days and I found her new aggression hard to take, especially since she attacked me at almost every meeting. Unfortunately, Tokyo gave me little support, concerned to protect his own position as leader. The crunch came when Jabu Moleketi, the MEC for Finance, refused to give me the R12 million that was apportioned to my office by the national RDP Minister, Jay Naidoo, from the RDP fund.

I had attended useful meetings of all the provincial heads of the RDP with Jay Naidoo in Pretoria to compare notes and plan our campaign. But it became increasingly evident that he was losing favour and was being marginalised in cabinet. On the pretext that the existence of the RDP fund, which amounted to billions of rand, led to double budgeting and cut across departmental lines of control, the RDP national office was closed down and Naidoo was made Minister of Posts and Communications. I then knew that a similar fate would follow for me.

Tokyo's legal adviser prepared a document which argued that my position was legally *ultra vires*. I then obtained a counter opinion by a very distinguished lawyer that disputed this. Tokyo dallied for a while but eventually I was called to an informal meeting of the ANC MECs to discuss my position and Sicelo Shiceka moved (and Jabu Moleketi seconded) that the RDP office be closed down and that I move to the back benches in the provincial legislature.

It was a bitter blow. I had worked heart and soul for the RDP, both prior to and after the election, and I was now humiliated by a small group who were steadily becoming narrowly focused on their own departments. My misery was compounded by the fact that Mary was now in Cape Town, having been elected to the National Assembly, and was away most of the time. I spent day after day in our Kensington home ruing the mistakes I had made and resenting my colleagues. My anger was particularly directed at the Communist Party in Gauteng, where Moleketi was provincial secretary, and which I expected to be the mainstay of the progressive policies we were pursuing in the name of the RDP.

In retrospect, I felt that my style of participation had been too intellectual and had tried to introduce issues that others felt were premature and impractical. Indeed, it may be that throughout my political life in the ANC, I have been driven by ideas rather than practical politics, trying to move the process faster than objective reality allowed. At the same time, it must be acknowledged that the ANC has allowed me ample scope to raise new ideas and I believe that many a seed has been sown which has eventually borne fruit.

MOVE TO NATIONAL PARLIAMENT

I set up an office in the Gauteng Legislature and employed Harlene Jasset, an old friend from exile, as my part-time assistant. Attempting to start work on RDP issues in the legislature, I met with much resistance. It was now understood that the RDP was being sidelined. After only two months, my break came unexpectedly. Elias Mosunkutu, a Gauteng MP, was leaving parliament in Cape Town, resulting in a vacancy. I negotiated a transfer to replace him, so I joined Mary who was by now well settled in parliament in Cape Town. I moved into her flat and we put our Johannesburg house up for sale. It was an immense relief for me and a new life dawned once again.

Parliament is a daunting place for the newcomer. Even the swearing-in ceremony is intimidating and it takes months to find one's way around the building. But I was pleased by the welcome extended to me. Many comrades told me that they had read my *Revolutionary Thought in the Twentieth Century* in the days of the underground and that it had even been copied out by hand on Robben Island and used as the main text for the secret seminars held there. Some of my other publications had also been read.

I joined the Portfolio Committees of Finance and Trade and Industry and soon became deeply immersed. The work was far more complex than that in Gauteng and I felt very privileged to sit in the House with so many distinguished and talented members. Mary was one of the most dedicated members and very hard working. We both took our work home which was effectively a sub-committee of parliament. But we felt a sense of elation and achievement. We were the only husband-and-wife team and we both believed that it was a fitting climax to all the years we had given to the movement. However, there were also moments of exhaustion when home was not a place of relaxation, and in time we came to believe that our lifestyle was too filled with tension and stress from which there seemed to be no release.

Parliament is a unique institution without parallel. It is filled with members from the most varied backgrounds and with a wide range of skills. Some are expert and highly competent speakers while others have little education and not many technical skills. Yet they are required to exercise important judgements on the most vital issues. I threw myself into finance and economics.

One of my first duties was to join the ANC group working on the Bill of Rights headed by Shepherd Mdladlana and part of the preparation of the new national constitution. I immediately saw that there was no reference to socio-economic rights and raised this with Shepherd. He laughed and said this was a contentious issue and was being avoided. I recalled a visit to London by Albie Sachs, and another by Pallo Jordan, relating to a document called 'Constitutional Guidelines' where this issue was raised and met with an unsatisfactory answer. The ANC was clearly nervous about including such provisions in the Bill of Rights.

I had been involved in several conferences in London, at the UN Ecosoc in Geneva and in Jordan on socio-economic rights, was familiar with the UN Convention on Socio-economic Rights and had written some papers on the subject. I made contact with Sandy Liebenberg, a human rights academic, and was advised that Fink Haysom, Mandela's legal adviser, held the key to any changes. I spent an hour with him and was asked to bring some documentation which I then arranged to be couriered from London. I also gave a set to Geoff Budlender, head of the Legal Resources Centre, an NGO in Johannesburg. After a few weeks of further lobbying a new draft of the Bill of Rights emerged. I was delighted that socio-economic rights were well covered, though the limitations clauses were designed to curb any unreasonable demands on government. The essence of the clauses was that everyone is entitled to certain socio-economic rights subject to the availability of state resources. I have to concede now that government's anxiety about these provisions was not without good reason as the Constitutional Court has ruled in favour of certain entitlements in the famous Grootboom Judgement. This could lead to substantial financial expenditures for the state, but I have no regrets about my actions and believe that the correct path was followed.

I was allocated to the Paarl Constituency and opened an office in Mbekweni, a typical African township seven miles from the town centre with few transport links. I struggled to be accepted in the township and even by the ANC leadership who would have preferred a local representative. Instead they were faced by a white intellectual parachuted in unceremoniously. In truth, although I can claim many achievements, not least the establishment of a small clothing factory in an old building in Mbekweni, I had little to show for five years of slogging constituency work.

Even my prize project, the proposed housing estate at Groot

Drakenstein, did not come off, despite support from national government. The resistance from a united group of local landowners and farmers, local government officials and officials from the provincial government has been enough to stall the process. In my frustration I seized an opportunity in the House when I was offered an interpolation and had a ding-dong debate with the Minister of Land Affairs in the presence of Mandela and a team of ministers. I felt triumphant, but it did not lead to victory. For all my strenuous efforts, I was rewarded by the local community with the proposal to name the village 'Ben Turok'. But the scheme remains unrealised.

BATTLE OVER ECONOMIC POLICY

While the ANC continued to maintain the high profile of the RDP, the treasury was actually implementing an austerity programme designed primarily to reduce the cost of servicing the national debt and hence reduce the budget deficit. The argument was that the domestic debt was too high and had to be brought down to sustainable levels. Thus as each budget was brought to our Finance Committee and then to the House, we had to disentangle the rhetoric about spending on jobs and poverty relief from the hard numbers of reduced spending. In most cases we were given nominal rather than real data which disguised the actual spending because one had to strip out inflation. The official line was that 'we must rid ourselves of the culture of entitlement' and called for fiscal discipline and belt-tightening.

At the ANC's 49th National Conference in Bloemfontein on 17 December 1994, the leading economic spokespersons, Trevor Manuel, Tito Mboweni and Alec Erwin, dominated the economics commission and ensured that budget-deficit reduction and macro-economic stabilisation remained the top priority. I made every effort to understand their view and to canvass what an alternative policy would entail. But the literature was hard to come by and it was only some years later that people like Joseph Stiglitz, Jeffrey Sachs, Dani Roderik and Paul Krugman became outspoken critics of the Washington Consensus, the fundamental policy of the International Monetary Fund. Yet, as time passed, the data generated by Statistics South Africa and the trade union movement Cosatu showed that there was a remorseless increase in poverty, closely tied to rising unemployment.

One afternoon in June 1996 some 20 MPs were invited to come to a meeting room in parliament where we found Minister of Finance, Trevor Manuel, waiting to address us. He announced that a new economic document had been prepared called 'Growth, Employment and Redistribution' (GEAR), and he presented an outline. Some questions were allowed but access to the document itself was refused on the grounds that it might be leaked to the press prior to its presentation to the whole of parliament the next day.

GEAR was drafted by a team led by Iraj Abedian, but with Richard Ketley, a seconded official from the World Bank, as the principal author. It immediately evoked a storm from Cosatu, who complained that it was a form of structural adjustment and that it was being imposed on the movement without consultation. They also argued that it flatly contradicted the RDP. Many of us were nonplussed at the manner of its introduction and found great difficulty in reconciling its assumptions with those developed by the movement over the years. GEAR, however, became the mainstay of government's economic policy, leading after several years to a much healthier financial situation, but with social consequences which will be difficult to redress. As I write, the government is stressing micro-economic reforms and substantially increased spending on infrastructure and social services designed to counter job losses and poverty.

Differences on economic policy have driven a serious wedge between the ANC on the one side and Cosatu and SACP on the other, with many non-partisan economists holding serious reservations about the degree of austerity we have adopted, given the social legacy of apartheid. This debate about the balance between stabilisation and social spending is critical for all developing countries and urgently requires resolution everywhere.

In the meanwhile parliament was itself undergoing a shakeout. Many of the most talented individuals were either made ministers or attracted to senior business positions outside. Some became senior public servants. The quality of debate in parliament suffered as their replacements were increasingly drawn from lower-ranking ANC cadres – mostly without higher education and little work experience. Parliamentary debates also suffered from a degree of uncertainty about how seriously parliament was to undertake its oversight role. The parliamentary system is supposed to be based on the free and open debate of all issues, no matter how sensitive. Yet, every member owes his or her presence to the fact of belonging to some party, a consideration that has particular importance in a proportional representation system like ours. ANC MPs were reminded of this from time to time in weekly caucus meetings when we were encouraged to give support to ANC policies in all our parliamentary work. To a degree this was in conflict with our duty to interact critically with the executive, when necessary, as is required in the constitution in terms of the separation of powers. The tensions arising from this conflict can be severe on MPs and there is little formal guidance available on how this should be handled. The ANC has yet to produce a substantial document on how it sees the role of parliament in the transformation of South Africa.

In the 1999 national election I was once again placed on the ANC list and returned to parliament. In the reshuffle I was allocated to the Muizenberg Constituency where I am resident and where I spent much of my youth. I opened a local office, appointed a diligent woman as administrator and set about my duties. Since most of the south peninsula is dominated by a large white minority and controlled by the Democratic Party I could expect much opposition. But I have a strong, sentimental attachment to Muizenberg and see its transformation as a huge challenge, but that is a subject for a later exposition.

Meanwhile my parliamentary work escalated, as well as my involvement in the ANC. I was drawn into difficult discussions in the ANC's Economic Transformation Committee, a sub-committee of the national executive, and was called upon to teach topics like globalisation and the Bretton Woods Institutions at a number of ANC national schools for cadres, which I found quite exhilarating if exhausting. Among the lecturers were Kgalema Motlante, Pallo Jordan, Jeremy Cronin and various other leading comrades and I considered it a privilege and a matter of enormous satisfaction to do this work.

During these sessions I often came across strong criticisms of our economic policies, and even some concern about the government's performance as a whole. It was my task to present a balanced view without holding back on my own reservations. I would point out that the ANC had achieved a miracle in overthrowing a system of white domination, that it had placed in positions of power some of the most outstanding leaders anywhere, including that international icon, Nelson Mandela, that there was now a prospect of tackling white power in the economy and introducing a serious development programme, and that our government was assuming an increasingly high profile in the international arena.

I also reminded them of the most important element of advice from the Soviet Union in the wake of the reverses in many African countries like Ghana, Tanzania and Zambia: Progressive governments should avoid 'over-strain' if they are to avoid the counter-revolutionary backlashes experienced by Allende in Chile and other radical leaders in the Third World. So, given that we had inherited a society which was fraught with powerful contradictions and where a great deal of residual power remained with the white minority, but where a new aspirant African bourgeoisie was rising fast, the ANC had to find a correct balance between its social transformation agenda and the need to maintain stability. I stressed that policy development remained a critical function in the new environment, hence my initiative in starting a journal called *New Agenda – South African Journal of Social and Economic Policy*, a new preoccupation which would see me into retirement.

ANNEXURES

CHAPTER 5

The document *Operation Mayibuye* was put before some of the leaders at the Rivonia headquarters sometime in 1963. While it was certainly discussed informally, there is still disagreement among those who were present about its formal consideration or adoption. What is not in doubt is that aspects were put into operation. The document below is republished from the Karis and Carter documentation history and is included in full as it has been the focus of much controversy ever since its first appearance.

Document 73. 'Operation Mayibuye.' Document found by the police at Rivonia, 11 July 1963

PART 1
The white state has thrown overboard every pretence of rule by democratic process. Armed to the teeth it has presented the people with only one choice and that is its overthrow by force and violence. It can now truly be said that very little, if any, scope exists for the smashing of white supremacy other than by means of mass revolutionary action, the main content of which is armed resistance leading to victory by military means.

The political events which have occurred in the last few years have convinced the overwhelming majority of the people that no mass struggle which is not backed up by armed resistance and military offensive operations, can hope to make a real impact. This can be seen from the general mood of the people and their readiness to undertake even desperate and suicidal violent campaigns of the Leballo type. It can also be gauged by their reluctance to participate in orthodox political struggles in which they expose themselves to massive retaliation without a prospect of hitting back. We are confident that the masses will respond in overwhelming numbers to a lead which holds out a real possibility of successful armed struggle.

Thus two important ingredients of a revolutionary situation are present:

a) A disillusionment with constitutional or semi-constitutional forms of struggle and a conviction that the road to victory is through force;
b) A militancy and a readiness to respond to a lead which holds out a real possibility of successful struggle.

In the light of the existence of these ingredients the prosecution of military struggle depends for its success on two further factors:

A. The strength of the enemy. This must not be looked at statically but in the light of objective factors, which in a period of military struggle may well expose its brittleness and
B. The existence of a clear leadership with material resources at its disposal to spark off and sustain military operations.

The objective military conditions in which the movement finds itself makes the possibility of a general uprising leading to direct military struggle an unlikely one. Rather, as in Cuba, the general uprising must be sparked off by organised and well-prepared guerrilla operations during the course of which the masses of the people will be drawn in and armed.

We have no illusions about the difficulties which face us in launching and successfully prosecuting guerrilla operations leading to military victory. Nor do we assume that such a struggle will be over swiftly. We have to take into account and carefully weighed numerous factors and we mention some of them:

a) We are faced with a powerfully armed modern state with tremendous industrial resources, which can, at least in the initial period, count on the support of three million whites.

At the same time the State is isolated practically from the rest of the world, and if effective work is done, will have to rely in the main on its own resources. The very concentration of industry and power and the interdependence of the various localities operates as both an advantage and a disadvantage for the enemy. It operates as a disadvantage because effective guerrilla operations can within a relatively short period create far greater economic havoc and confusion than in a backward, decentralised country.

b) The people are unarmed and lack personnel who have been trained in all aspects of military operations. A proper organisation of the almost unlimited assistance which we can obtain from friendly Governments will counter-balance its disadvantage. In the long run a guerrilla struggle relies on the enemy for its source of supply. But in order to make this possible an initial effective arming of the first group of guerrilla bands is essential. It is also vital to place in the field persons trained in the art of war who will act as a nucleus of organisers and commanders of guerrilla operations.

c) The absence of friendly borders and long scale impregnable natural bases from which to operate are both disadvantages. But more important than these factors is the support of the people who in certain situations are better protection than mountains and forests. In the rural areas which become the main theatre of guerrilla operations in the initial phase, the overwhelming majority of the people will protect and safeguard the guerrillas and this fact will to some measure negative the disadvantages. In any event we must not underestimate the fact that there is terrain in many parts of South Africa, which although not classically impregnable is suitable for guerrilla type operations. Boer guerrillas with the support of their people operated in the plains of the Transvaal. Although conditions have changed there is still a lesson to be learned from this.

Although we must prepare for a protracted war we must not lose sight of the fact that the political isolation of South Africa from the world community of nations and particularly the active hostility towards it from almost the whole of the African Continent and the Socialist world may result in such massive assistance in various forms, that the state structure will collapse far sooner than we can at the moment envisage. Direct military intervention in South West Africa, an effective economic and military boycott, even armed international action at some more advanced stage of the struggle are real possibilities which will play an important role. In no other territory where guerrilla operations have been undertaken has the international situation been such a vital factor operating against the enemy. We are not unaware that there are powerful external monopoly interests who will attempt to bolster up the white state. With effective work they can be isolated and neutralised. The events of the last few years have shown that the issue of racial discrimination cuts across world ideological conflict albeit that the West proceeds from opportunistic premises.

The following plan envisages a process which will place in the field, at a date fixed now, simultaneously in pre-selected areas, armed and trained guerrilla bands who will find ready to join the local guerrilla bands with arms and equipment at their disposal. It will further coincide with a massive propaganda campaign both inside and outside South Africa and a general call for unprecedented mass struggle throughout the land, both violent and non-violent. In the initial period when for a short while the military adv. [sic] will be ours, the plan envisages a massive onslaught on pre-selected targets which will create maximum havoc and confusion in the enemy camp and which will inject into the masses of the people and other friendly forces a feeling of confidence that here at least is an army of liberation equipped and capable of leading them to victory. In this period the cornerstone of guerrilla operations is 'shamelessly attack the weak and shamelessly flee from the strong'.

We are convinced that this plan is capable of fulfilment. But only if the whole apparatus of the movement both here and abroad is mobilised for its implementation and if every member now prepares to make unlimited sacrifice for the achievement of our goal. The time for small thinking is over because history leaves us no choice.

PART 11
AREAS
1. Port Elizabeth-Mzimkulu.
2. Port Shepstone-Swaziland.
3. North Western Transvaal, bordering respectively Bechuanaland & Limpopo.
4. North Western Cape-South West.

PART 111
PLAN
1. Simultaneous landing of 4 groups of 30 based on our present resources whether by ship or air-armed and properly equipped in such a way as to be self sufficient in every respect for at least a month.
2. At the initial stages it is proposed that the 30 are split up into platoons of 10 each to operate more or less within a contiguous area and linking their activities with pre-arranged local groups.
3. Simultaneously with the landing of the groups of 30 and thereafter, there should be a supply of arms and other war material to arm the local populations which become integrated with the guerrilla units.
4. On landing, a detailed plan of attack on pre-selected targets with a view to taking the enemy by surprise, creating the maximum impact on the populace, creating as much chaos and confusion for the enemy as possible.
5. Choice of suitable areas will be based on the nature of the terrain, with a view to establishing base areas from which our units can attack and to which they can retreat.
6. Before these operations take place political authority will have been set up in secrecy in a friendly territory with a view to supervising the struggle both in its internal and external aspects. It is visualised that this authority will in due course of time develop into a Provisional Revolutionary Government.
7. This Political Authority should trim its machinery so that simultaneously with the commencement of operations it will throw out massive propaganda to win world support for our struggle, more particularly:
a) A complete enforcement of boycott,

b) Enlisting the support of the international trade union movement to refuse handling war materials and other goods for the South African Government.
c) Raising a storm at the United Nations which should be urged to intervene militarily in South West Africa.
d) Raising of large scale credits for the prosecution of the struggle,
e) Arranging for radio facilities for daily transmission to the world and to the people of South Africa.
f) If possible the Political Authority should arrange for the initial onslaught to bombard the country or certain areas with a flood of leaflets by plane announcing the commencement of our armed struggle as well as our aims, and calling upon the population to rise against the Government.
g) Stepping up transport plans, e.g. a weekly or bi weekly airlift of trainees outside the country in order to maintain a regular, if small flow of trained personnel.
h) In order to facilitate the implementation of the military aspect of the plan it is proposed the National High Command appoint personnel to be quartered at Dar under the auspices of the office there.

PART IV
INTERNAL ORGANISATION

In preparation for the commencement of operations when our external team lands, intensive as well as extensive work will have been done. For instance, guerrilla units will have been set up in the main areas mapped out in Part I above as well as in the other areas away from the immediate scene of operation.

Progressively, sabotage activity throughout the country will be stepped up before these operations. Political pressure, too, in the meanwhile will be stepped up in conjunction with the sabotage activity.

In furtherance of the general ideas set out above the plan for internal Organisation is along the following pattern:

1. Our target is that on arrival the external force should find at least 7 000 men in the four main areas ready to join the guerrilla army in the initial onslaught. Those will be allocated as follows:
   (a) Eastern Cape-Transkei   2 000
   (b) Natal-Zululand   2 000
   (c) North Western Transvaal   2 000
   (d) North Western Cape   1 000
2. To realise our target in each of the main areas it is proposed that each of the four areas should have an overall command whose task it will be to divide its area into regions, which in turn will be allocated a figure in proportion to their relative importance.
3. The preparation for equipping the initial force envisaged in I above will take place in three stages, thus:
   (a) By importation of Military Supply at two levels:
      (i) Build up of firearms, ammunition and explosives by maintaining a regular flow over a period of time.
      (ii) By landing additional supplies simultaneously with the arrival of our external force.
   (b) Acquisition and accumulation internally of firearms, ammunition and explosives at all levels of our Organisation.
   (c) Collection and accumulation of other military such as food, medicines, communication equipment etc.
4. It is proposed that auxiliary guerrilla/sabotage units in the four main areas be set up before and after the commencement of operations. They may engage in activities that may serve to disperse the enemy forces, assist to maintain the fighting ability of the guerrillas as well as draw in the masses in support of the guerrillas.
5. It is proposed that in areas falling outside the four main guerrilla areas M.K. units should be set up to act in support of the activities in the guerrilla areas, and to harass the enemy.
6. In order to draw in the masses of the population the political wing should arouse the people to participate in the struggles that are designed to create an upheaval throughout the country.

PART V
DETAILED PLAN OF IMPLEMENTATION

In order to implement the plans set out above in Parts I to III we establish Departments which are to be charged with duties to study and submit detailed reports and plans in respect of each of their Departments with the following terms of reference:

1. *Intelligence Department*

This Committee will be required to study and report on the following:
   (a) The exact extent of each area.
   (b) The portions of the country that are naturally suited for our operations and their location within each area.
   (c) Points along the coast which would be suitable for landing of men and supplies and how these are going to be transferred from the point of landing to the area of operations.
   (d) The situation of enemy forces in each area, thus:
      (i) the military and the police as well as their strength,
      (ii) military and police camps, and towns, and the distances between them,
      (iii) system of all forms of communication in the area,
      (iv) the location of trading stations and chiefs and headmen's kraals,
      (v) air fields and air strips in the areas.
   (e) Selection of targets to be tackled in initial phase of guerrilla operations with a view to causing maximum damage to the enemy as well as preventing the quick deployment of reinforcements.
   In its study the Committee should bear in mind the following main targets:
      (i) strategic roads, railways and other communications
      (ii) power stations
      (iii) police stations, camps and military forces
      (iv) irredeemable Government stooges
   (f) A study of climatic conditions in relation to seasons, as well as diseases common to the area.

(g) The population distribution in the areas as well as the main crops.
(h) Rivers and dams.
(i) And generally all other relevant matters.

2. *External Planning Committee* which shall be charged with the following tasks:
   (a) Obtaining of arms, ammunition and explosives and other equipment.
   (b) In co-operation with our internal machinery, making arrangements for the dispatch of items in I above into the country
   (c) Obtaining of transport by land, sea and air for the landing of our task force and for the continued supply of military equipment.

3. *Political Authority*
   We make a strong recommendation that the joint sponsoring organisations should immediately set about creating a political machinery for the direction of the revolutionary struggle as set out in Nos. 6, 7 and 8 of Part II and to set up a special committee to direct guerrilla political education.

4. *Transport Committee*
This Committee is assigned the following duties:
   (a) The Organisation of transport facilities for our trainees.
   (b) To organise transport for the re-entry of our trainees.
   (c) To undertake any transport duties assigned to them from time to time.

5. *Logistics Department – Technical and Supply Committee*
Its functions are:
   (a) To manufacture and build up a stock of arms, ammunition from internal sources.
   (b) To organise reception, distribution and storage of supplies from external sources.
   (c) To organise the training of personnel in the use of equipment referred to in (a) and (b) above.

(d) Obtaining of all other relevant supplies necessary to prosecute an armed struggle, to wit, inter alia, medical supplies, clothing, food, etc., and the storage of these at strategic points.
   (e) Acquiring equipment to facilitate communications.
   (f) To undertake all duties and functions that fall under the Department of Logistics.

PART V1
MISCELLANEOUS

1. *Immediate Duties of the National High Command in Relation to the Guerrilla Areas*
   (a) To map out regions in each area with a view to organising Regional and District Commands and N.K. [sic] units.
   (b) To achieve this we strongly recommend the employment of 10 full time organisers in each area.
   (c) The organisers shall be directly responsible to the National High Command.
   (d) The NHC is directed to recruit and arrange for the external training of at least 300 men in the next two months.

2. *Personal*
   (a) *Intelligence* Alex Secundus Otto
   (b) *External Planning Committee* Johnson, Thabo and Joseph together with a senior ANC rep. as well as co-opted personnel, seconded to us by friendly Govts.
   (c) *Transport Committee* Percy secundus Nbata.
   (d) *Logistics Dept.* Bri-bri secundus Frank

3. *Special Directives to Heads of Departments*
   The Heads of Departments are required to submit not later than the 30th May, 1963, plans detailing:
   (a) The structural Organisation of their Department.
   (b) The type and number of personnel they require to be allocated to them and their duties and functions.
   (c) The funds required for their work both for immediate and long term purposes.
   (d) Schedule of time required to enable them to fulfil given targets and what these are.

(e) Other matters relating to the efficient execution of the Departments' Plans.

4. *Organisation of Areas. Organisers and Setting up of proper Machinery* Rethau and James for this task.

CHAPTER 7

'WHAT IS WRONG?' by Ben Turok
A DISCUSSION ON THE PRESENT SITUATION IN THE SOUTH AFRICAN LIBERATION MOVEMENT

1. The present discussion will be based largely on experiences in Dar es Salaam and on information obtained from other comrades from time to time. I cannot pretend to know the situation further than that, although there is good reason to believe that the errors and omissions in Dar es Salaam are some reflection of the general position in our movement as a whole. In taking Dar es Salaam as basis I am of course also influenced by events in Morogoro which inevitably filter through to this city.

2. This paper will follow the following plan: First the faults of our work are itemised briefly, then the causes are analysed in a general way, then come proposals and conclusions. It is my intention to be constructive throughout and avoid personalities unless absolutely necessary.

3. WHAT IS WRONG? This question has been in the offing for a long time. Many comrades who have become dispirited and cynical have seized upon this or that explanation arising from their own experiences and attempted to blame certain individuals. Undoubtedly these accusations often reflected a true situation and were justified but the malaise has become so general that a partial approach is useless. No one in the movement can be content with the present situation; all must be aware of a deep-going malaise such as we have never known before. It is most convenient to list the problems under various heads:

4. **Theoretical:** Our movement, it is generally admitted, is facing an extremely difficult task. The difficulty arises not merely from the vicious character of the regime we are fighting but also from the isolation of our country from friendly borders. This affects not only military questions, it also affects our political work, and it will be remembered that for a very long period we had very little political contact with the outside world. It was only in the 60s that personnel were sent out for this purpose, before that we lived in political and theoretical isolation. As a result, our analysis at home tended to be insular in character, giving too little weight to world opinion and events in Africa. However, now that so many leaders have come to live abroad, the pendulum has gone the other way, and we find ourselves preoccupied with world problems to the detriment of our own.

5. **Links with Home:** This tendency is so marked that it requires little elaboration, but one must point to the absence of discussion documents of any kind for a long period, and to the utter failure of our leadership to introduce a political line in the movement which could orientate it to our main task: the struggle at home. Since there are so many comrades now outside the country it is necessary for us to develop a perspective among them to link their lives with those of our people at home, and reliance on our guerrilla units is far from sufficient in this respect. We require a total picture setting out the complexities of our struggle, the relative importance of the various segments, and how they fit together towards the common goal. The absence of such a picture is leading to the acceptance of exile – for life by many of our good comrades, and the consequent falling away of their interest.

6. **Political:** The absence of a political line has led to the absence of political work. In Dar es Salaam practically no efforts have been made over a very long time to keep the membership informed of the work of the leadership. There have been no report-backs from conferences, no formal reports on the fighting in Zimbabwe, no discussion of the difficulties around us. Instead, we seem to have been faced by bureaucracy, heavily entrenched in office, hostile to questions and tight-lipped in extreme. Without internal meet-

ings, without documentation and with the self-isolation of the officials there has been the predictable decline in morale and lack of involvement by comrades who, in other circumstances, would be wholly involved in the struggle.

7. Style of Work: The previous point leads naturally to this one. Where there is no political machinery there can be no proper style of work. Our officials have come to adopt authoritarian attitudes towards comrades in lower positions. Bossmanship is the rule of the day and commandism, a feature that is always a danger in an army, has come to stay in our political relations as well. A driver is treated as impersonally as his vehicle, a junior office worker is given orders like a lackey and the office which is supposed to be the political centre of gravity for all comrades in Dar es Salaam resembles some gone to seed commercial enterprise. The boss sits in some dark internal recess and one has to pass through a number of 'minor' officials before coming into his 'Presence'. That the relations between our comrades is poor is easily evident. There have been instances of open quarrelling over petty matters, over questions of prestige, over representation, over time off and numerous trifles. Unfortunately the disputes are more often than not settled by the heavy hand of authority and not by comradely discussion. The air is thick with grievance and suspicion.

None of these comments are made without an awareness of the requirements of security. Obviously this is a primary consideration these days. The leading member of an office is the natural custodian of many secrets, documents etc., and he must be sure of privacy in many discussions. But this should not become a cover for authoritarianism, for abuse of privileges and for the necessary mobilisation of other staff and members in the work of the Organisation.

Evidence of maladministration is massive. Letters are lost, appointments broken, numerous motorcycles have been wantonly destroyed and the wastage of petrol is immense. Considering the price of petrol in Dar es Salaam it would seem that motor transport would be treated with the greatest reserve; instead, the official cars are constantly in use, using petrol without restriction. The checking of accounts appears to be at fault. There have been a number of cases of cash embezzlement, which are known to many of us.

Officials are constantly invited to diplomatic parties to represent our organisations. While serious missions in Dar es Salaam regard these occasions as opportunities to make contacts, too many of our personnel have used them for their private craving for liquor. Drunkenness was a major feature of our office in Dar es Salaam – day and night. Some comrades were drunk for days on end, and those who should have set an example were sometimes no better. There has been an improvement recently, but the intention here is not to point a finger, it is to comment on a style of work wholly out of keeping with a serious movement. It has become apparent too often that some leading comrades, particularly those with full-time official duties, which take them into diplomatic contacts, have surrendered to the temptations offered them, thereby losing both self-respect and pride in their organisation. In this connection, it must be noted that leading personnel who visit Dar es Salaam for short periods often stay in a hotel. The reason for this is not clear. Firstly there are numerous comrades in this city with spare accommodation and whose duty it would seem to make it available for leaders passing through. Secondly, it would seem that the most obvious way out is to add some rooms to our camp, or to obtain some accommodation which could be the permanent quarters for visiting personnel. Hotel costs for the Organisation must be astronomical and the sight of leaders spending evening after evening in a bar is not one which can bring credit to our movement.

8. Diplomatic: Our movement has much need for diplomatic contacts. There is the question of aid, the problem of explaining our policies, and many other related matters. However, we must not make diplomacy a way of life, nor should we become a burden on other diplomatic personnel. In Dar es Salaam these tendencies are ever present in relation to various foreign missions, particularly the Socialist countries. Our people make demands on them, which are sometimes unreasonable, and on occasion for purely personal assistance thereby bringing our movement into disrepute. However, what is more important is the failure of our move-

ment to maintain good diplomatic relations with our hosts in Tanzania. Undoubtedly this is a difficult question, with a long history with which I am not familiar. I can only judge the situation as it exists and that leaves a great deal to be desired. It is common knowledge that the relations between our movement and that of Tanu and the government are unsatisfactory. Whatever the background to this development it is a situation which cannot be allowed to continue without constant effort to improve it. Unfortunately this is not the case at present and if anything we are drifting along accepting an unhealthy state of affairs. It should be said that the PAC is not so passive. Even taking into consideration that there are forces which are favourably disposed towards them, it is nevertheless true that they adopt an active attitude, using every opportunity to build bridges with Tanzanians, building contacts and putting over their line. By contrast our officials are reticent, on the retreat, apparently content to accept the situation. This position on our part is fraught with danger since suspicion thrives in such a vacuum and the distance between us and the Tanzanian authorities may increase to an intolerable extent.

9. Propaganda: Here again much of what has been said above is applicable. It is well realised that the possibilities for the ANC to propagate its views are extremely limited and that liberation movements are not permitted to use their offices for the purpose of conducting active political work among the Tanzanian people; in fact there is a distinct embargo on such activities. Yet some opportunities do come up from time to time. In Dar es Salaam there have been occasions when the students have offered a platform to the ANC, which were not used. Other liberation movements have not been so reluctant with the result that they made friends and influenced students and other youth to the benefit of their movements. There is considerable apathy in the ANC office and among our personnel generally in the propagation of our views and news about our struggle. As a result there is abysmal ignorance in Tanzania about South Africa and about our movement.

10. Solidarity Work: The principal weakness here is the failure to build contacts with leaders and activists of other liberation move-

ments. Whilst Dar es Salaam is the base for a great deal of activity for many movements, there is little contact among the personnel. Security considerations partly account for this gap, but it is insufficient in itself. There is also some unwillingness to break out of our self-imposed isolationism and make friendships and contacts, which can have great importance to the whole struggle in Southern Africa. Perhaps it is the South African liberation movement that has the most to gain by the unification of the struggle in this sub-continent, but certainly no one can be the loser thereby.

11. Mobilisation of Rank and File: Officials who regard their positions as privileged cannot be expected to bring into activity ordinary members who are felt to be external to the organisational machinery. Remembering that most ordinary members have their own problems of adjustment to a foreign country since they are regarded as refugees, these people cannot be expected to maintain their interest in the movement unless their presence is constantly sought and their participation invited. Officiousness by office personnel can only drive our members away from the Organisation. In Dar es Salaam such people are not ordinarily given any tasks and they are not made to feel that the movement expects anything from them.

Factors which contribute to the alienation of members from the Organisation are the absence of current newspapers from South Africa, the absence of news about the movement's activities and the lack of political discussion. Too many of our officials regard their work to be purely administrative, devoting themselves to detail routine work, neglecting the political issues of the day. Evidence of the non-involvement of our members of Dar es Salaam is to be found in their reluctance to contribute regular donations to the organisation and their slackness in fund raising. Non-South Africans have done far more for ANC fund raising than our own people in Dar es Salaam. And these friends of our movement have been sorely neglected by our officials. Rank and file members could well be appointed to keep in touch with our donors making them first and permanent friends of our movement. In this way further assistance could be obtained from them in the contacts with overseas Organisation, with South Africa and so on.

12. Our Army Men: Perhaps the most deplorable aspect of the work of the movement in Dar es Salaam is the treatment meted out to our military comrades. A number of officials working at political posts have openly shown the most appalling contempt for the army men, failing to exercise common courtesy let alone according them the honour they deserve. Our men in Mandela camp live in squalor. They sleep on the floor on thin mats, their building is in disrepair and there is every evidence of gross neglect. No one would suggest that our army personnel wishes to be coddled, nor would it be sound policy, but they deserve decent conditions and above all, they deserve respect. This is wanting at present and must at all costs be remedied. Furthermore, any person who shows a lack of respect for these men ought to be brought before authority and reprimanded. Our men are volunteers, they live a dull, monotonous existence of waiting. Anyone who adopts an arrogant, superior attitude towards them is not only insensitive but also lacking in political understanding. Furthermore, there is a marked absence of contact between leading personnel passing through Dar es Salaam and the men at Mandela. It is extraordinary that leaders should spend several days here without paying a visit to the men at the camp, particularly as it is largely for the sick who would appreciate a kindly word from persons in leading positions. The camp itself badly needs a face-lift. It needs some decoration, some facilities for amusement, a flag or two, a proper library with up to date magazines, in short, it must be turned into a home for the sick and the homeless. At present it is a slum.

WHY THINGS ARE GOING WRONG

13. In the first section of this report I have attempted to set out some of the major weaknesses in our movement in the limited area with which I have some acquaintance. The more difficult task of finding the reasons for these failures follows. If one is to be objective one is obliged to recognise that most of the problems arising in our movement are due to the extremely difficult objective situation in which we find ourselves today. There is no need to explain these difficulties – we are all painfully aware of them every day. And it should be recognised that no matter what has

been said in the first section on the privileges enjoyed by some leading comrades in exile, there can be no doubt but that everyone in the movement is deeply concerned with our frustrations in going home. No one can be happy in exile.

14. Objective difficulties have increased rather than decreased in the past few years and it cannot be said with confidence that the trend will change for the better. We have to come to terms with this possibility and work accordingly. But objective difficulties can explain but not excuse the weaknesses in our work. They certainly cannot excuse the decline in the overall political level of our work. Ultimately the devotion of our cadres, the tenacity of our military men and the constancy of our officials will depend on their political clarity, and it is here that so little has been done in the last few years. I refer not only to the concrete work that is the production of reports etc but the absence of actual analysis. The very foundation of political work has not been done.

15. Every revolution must go through a period of gestation, of churning out by means of intense internal discussion, of the fundamental strategy of that revolution. Practice is of course the testing ground of that theoretical work and the father of the ideas, but there can be no evading the task of original thought. In the stagnation that has set in, this process has come to a halt. As stated earlier, routine has taken the place of creativity, not least in the field of strategy.

16. Evidence of this poverty is to be found in the attention that is given to the task of infiltrating back home. Not only is the work skimpy and amateurish but it is obvious that the bulk of our leadership and of our membership are not oriented to this problem. THERE IS NO GOING-BACK OUTLOOK. While we must pay the highest tribute to the action of our immortal heroes of Zimbabwe battles, it is obvious that those actions could only be regarded as one of the steps necessary. If the great majority of our personnel spent most of their time on concentrated activity oriented around the question of going home, little of the weaknesses mentioned in Part I above would have emerged. What is required is a total approach to this problem, with exploration at every level, with

constant practical training in all related fields, for the numerous problems that the act of going home will bring out. How many of our leaders can read a compass proficiently? How many can move comfortably at night? How many are physically fit? How many know elementary first aid? Once we ask these questions it becomes immediately apparent that there are many who do not have the appearance of suitability for going home. This is obvious at a glance in some cases and in others, a little gentle probing will reveal the inadequacies of many of our personnel for a life of either guerrilla existence or even for that of a man in hiding underground. And while there will always be men whose task it will be to act externally, there should be no doubt about the willingness and ability of the majority of our leading personnel to return to a tough existence in South Africa itself. And what exists at the top has in some way filtered down to the lower levels, so that too many of our people are no longer concerned with the problems of the struggle but rather with those of adjustment to life in exile. And the temptations are often great for a life of comparative security and ease.

17. It is often said that for an Organisation to be healthy, the discrepancies between the leaders and the rank and file ought not to be too great. Obviously leaders need peace of mind, some comfort, and facilities for quiet work. However, it ought to be constantly borne in mind that these requirements ought not to be an excuse for the emergence of an elite. It has been suggested on a number of occasions that the leaders of the movement in exile have not had to face elections for very many years. Indeed one has to go further back than just the exile years to realise that there has been little elective democracy in our movement for well over a decade. Our leaders ought to ask themselves – are they not a little too secure? Have they not become complacent of criticism from below? Has this not led to some of the stagnation in our movement? It is not suggested here that the present leadership is not able or that there are better men around; what is meant is that democracy must be seen to operate – the power of recall is basic to discipline and mutual respect between leaders and led. And where this falls into disrepute, distortions are bound to arise. Even leaders are human!

18. It has been evident to many of us that there has been a growing breach between our military personnel and others. This was mentioned in the first section and it is repeated here as a cause of the general malaise. Army people speak as though they belong to a different world. It is for them to act and for others to think. This is a non-political attitude containing the seeds of militarism. We dare not allow such a psychology to grow in our army men, every one of whom must be a politically advanced person fully equipped for political leadership.

19. A further case of the disarray is to be found in the breakdown in the Congress Alliance. There is no secret that the ANC has as a matter of policy downgraded non-African Congressites in the many spheres of our activity. The reason for this development seems to be a desire to maintain an image of Africanness on the part of the ANC. There is undoubtedly considerable justification for this view and it must not be ignored, but equally important is the maintenance of faith with the racial minorities of South Africa and their revolutionary representatives in the liberation movement. There is little justification or political sense in counting heads in the present situation and the arguing that since there are only so many persons of a certain racial group active in the struggle therefore this negligible group can be left out. Not only is this wrong in that it is wasteful to exclude good revolutionaries, but it is political shortsightedness that those few are seen to be standard bearers for others of their group. And South Africa, as we all know, includes a complex of a number of minorities which cannot be left out of account.

20. However, more important than these practical questions on the Congress structure is the question of political principle. The history of Africa has shown again and again that narrow nationalism is a futile empty policy which defeats itself. Where nationalism has been advanced as a narrow vehicle for the self-assertion of a particular race to the exclusion of all others it has generally degenerated into racialism, tribalism and chauvinism. As such it feeds on its own narrowness and hatred, destroying its positive content from the historical point of view. If such policies have

failed elsewhere they are even more certain of utter failure in South Africa – a land of many peoples.

The final political point I have to make therefore is that narrow African nationalism will break the African revolution in South Africa and even if in some unforeseen way the revolution itself should succeed, it will be broken by a combined opposition of national minorities afterwards.

PROPOSALS AND CONCLUSIONS

21. Immediate Tasks

Since an atmosphere of crisis prevails in our ranks at present it is necessary to take such concrete immediate remedial action as will ease off the tension. The most helpful way this could be done is by a large-scale planning operation centred around the problems of 'going home'. Once it is felt that the years of stagnation in exile may be drawing to a close and that serious attention is being given to the main tasks of the day, our healthy cadres will fall back into a positive frame of mind and set the positive organisational processes into motion once again. Discipline will be restored on a voluntary basis.

The strategic problems involved in this exercise are immense. The most dynamic, imaginative and experienced personnel in the movement must be drawn into a special planning council to examine every aspect and every possibility. They will have to study all possible routes: land, sea and even perhaps air, in order that no possibility is missed. It is the height of folly to think in terms of one or other route into the country as being the only possible one; the more avenues that are explored and eventually used the better, for we must take advantage of the major strategic weakness of South Africa's defence – its vast borders, on land and sea.

Planning must be conducted, taking account not only of our own personnel immediately available but also of sympathisers who might be of some use. There are security problems involved here, but what is wanted is a vast network bearing vital information to the centre of operational planning and carrying instructions and suggestions for investigation. We must be cautious in using people, but we must also not leave a stone unturned in our constant processing and assessing the usability of friends of our movement, for we have many everywhere.

Part of the work of this planning council should be the setting up of highly specialised training schools where our personnel are put through carefully prepared courses in the kind of activities they will be engaged in on return. Not a single comrade should be idle at this time – everyone ought to be learning and developing his capabilities in a number of directions. The more highly skilled a man is the more his chances of survival in a police hunt. Hence an immediate requirement is maximum study and full-scale practice of what is learnt.

22. The Theoretical Aspects

While these practical activities are set in motion, we require of the leadership to carry through a full-scale analysis of our political prospects. A thoroughgoing analysis is required of our revolutionary strategy and our tactical line, and this task should be carried out with the utmost honesty, with as wide participation as possible, and the conclusions arrived at must be conveyed in clear terms to all our members. We desperately require to introduce some perspective into our political thinking, the present day-to-day drift must cease. As part of this analysis a special small-circulation theoretical bulletin should be established to provide scope for articles of an analytical nature to be circularised among our senior cadres wherever they must be stationed. This will assist in bringing into being a greater unity of thought and purpose into the movement.

23. Organisational

There can be little doubt that the present vacillation of the ANC on the question of the Congress Alliance has been injurious to our work. Many comrades are demanding to know what has happened to our former unity and what contribution some of our tried and trusted non-African comrades are making to the struggle. My proposal to overcome this problem is the unification of all Congress personnel within the ANC, at least as far as militants outside South African are concerned. The proposal has been made many times before and it has been rejected. Perhaps it will prove more acceptable in the light of the following argument. This is not the place to attempt a deep analysis of South African society, nor for a discussion of the political basis and origins of the Alliance, but it is assumed that there is general agreement that the principal feature of the struggle in South Africa today is the solution of the contradiction between a white ruling minority and a large non-white majority. At the same time, it is also understood that the most critical focus of this contradiction is the exploitation of the African masses who constitute a large segment element. Hence the most vital task of the liberation movement is to find forms for stimulating this revolutionary potential for organising its energy and giving it the means to move into action. This has traditionally been the task of the ANC. It is proposed that this position should remain fundamentally unchanged except that comrades of other races ought to be enrolled into the Organisation on the understanding that the African leadership of the Organisation must at all times and at all levels be maintained, that Africans must predominate in its work and be seen to so predominate, and that the rules of the structure of all committees etc be designed for this purpose. Some may be alarmed at this proposal on the grounds that this is a new form of race discrimination in reverse. The answer is that such procedures are not new in the organisations of the exploited and if one were to draw the obvious parallel in the experiences of the working class in other countries, it will be seen that there are very specific rules on the election and promotion of personnel to leading bodies on the basis of their class origin and of their professions. (The latter is explicitly laid down, the former is implicitly taken into account.) What is here proposed therefore is that the practice of working class organisations which are extremely vigilant to maintain the correct balance and predominance of worker leadership in relation to other sectors, intellectuals etc. ought to be emulated in our liberation movement. In sum, it is suggested that comrades of all races be admitted to full membership of the ANC outside South Africa on the condition that African comrades predominate and are seen to predominate on all committees and in the general work of the Organisation. It is my view that this will go a long way to consolidate the movement, to introduce a new spirit of comradeship and at the same time bringing new forces to bear on our gigantic tasks. It ought to be stressed however that the ANC must remain a largely African Organisation by virtue of its historical mission and in virtue of its standing. This must be clearly accepted by all its adherents to the extent of explicit rules of structure and method of operations.

24. Diplomatic

It is known to everyone that the world and Africa in particular is tiring of the plethora of anti-apartheid diplomats touring the world. It is apparent to the world that the proportion of activity outside the country directed at our people at home is tiny in comparison to our efforts in the rest of the world. This is bringing us into disrepute. Far too many leading people are spread around the capitals of the world and too many of those centred in E. Africa spend too much time away from base. It is proposed therefore that there be a drastic reduction in the number of our personnel engaged in external missions and that they may be brought back to participate in the preparations discussed in para 21. We repeat, we need the best brains in the principal area of operations, not in missions overseas.

25. Radio & Propaganda Generally

Many of these persons who return can be pressed into assisting the work on the radio broadcasts and on propaganda generally. It is common knowledge that far too little use is being made of the facilities offered to us by Radio Tanzania and that it is often regarded as a burden instead of a positive weapon in our struggle. There are many other possibilities for propaganda directed at South Africa from East Africa, none of which are being effectively explored.

26. The Other Liberation Movements

The discrepancy between the publicity given to the South African Alliance of liberation movements and the reality is remarkable. It is proposed that efforts be made to establish a permanent Standing Committee among the Big Four liberation organisations in order to bring us closer together. It is fairly common knowledge that co-operation in Dar es Salaam, at any rate, is still far from satisfactory, often for purely technical reasons. Co-operation ought to be consolidated on a political level and with the aim of political cohesiveness in view.

27. Dar es Salaam Office
In view of the above requirement and in the light of the need to strengthen constantly our relations with the Tanzanian authorities, it becomes urgently necessary to upgrade the Dar es Salaam office and the strengthening of our personnel there. The situation is extremely delicate in Dar es Salaam and the most able, flexible and efficient comrades are required to fill the posts there.

28. Style of Work
It is proposed that rules for conduct and a guide on style of work be issued to all offices, missions, camps etc and that a supervisory commission be set to check on implementation.

29. Education
Political and other education must be improved radically. All personnel ought to be studying something at all times in a formal way and under supervision.

30. Report Back
Regular report-back conferences to check up on work planned ought to be held every few months. Leaders should give an account of their work and subject themselves to scrutiny. The replacement of tired leaders or those who have failed in their duties ought to be given attention regularly. Machinery for the election of replacements must be developed.

CONCLUSION

There is a great deal more to be said if our struggle is to rise to the heights of former days. We have a proud history of political struggle, and the heroes of Zimbabwe have blazed a new path of military action. It is up to those of us who are now lying relatively immobilised in exile to take up with new resolve the fight to free South Africa. There is no more noble task before mankind today.

Within two weeks I received the following response:

REPLY TO DOCUMENT ENTITLED 'WHAT IS WRONG' BY COMRADE BEN TUROK

1) The Preparatory Committee has had an opportunity to study the document submitted by Comrade Turok which was found very interesting and illuminating. As with all documents submitted by units of the Organisation or individual comrades, it was considered necessary to respond to the document in order to clear up some matters and advance the discussion further. The aim is to ensure that by the time we get to conference there is general agreement on all major questions.

2) We note that the document begins by admitting a lack of information except such as has been gained in Dar es Salaam or from hearsay. It should be remarked that in the circumstances a great deal of caution would be required in drawing any general conclusions from such a limited experience.

3) Everyone in the movement is aware of the fact that the movement is in many ways going through a very difficult period. It is certainly not the most difficult we have ever faced. Most people would say that the period following the Rivonia arrests was undoubtedly the worst blow we suffered and in many ways our problems stem from the smashing of our leadership at home in one fell swoop, thus precipitating the most difficult situation. The shadow of Rivonia is never very far as far as our organisational machinery is concerned and we must never forget it. Before then we had a functioning machinery manned by some of our most significant leaders. Those outside were carrying out the directives of the people inside the country and were merely representatives of the movement abroad, as it should be. Suddenly those outside found themselves pitch-forked into a different situation for which there had been no preparation except in one sense. In anticipation that some such situation could arise a number of leading figures had shortly before Rivonia been sent out of the country so that when the event occurred, there was a cadre of leadership that

could endeavour to organise the recovery. Otherwise it must not be forgotten that the responsibilities thrust on the people outside were not the result of some theoretical mistake or faulty political analysis. It was a response to an emergency situation which was not of their making and which none of them desired then or now.

4) In the result the 'external mission' as it is perhaps erroneously called was formed, whose primary job became the building and training of an army – a job last done by Africans ninety years ago. It should be said that this task although it was being done outside the country is not what might be called 'external' work. It is vital work for our eventual recovery inside the country. Much of the running around or 'globe trotting' was devoted to arranging for training in various countries; collecting weapons; obtaining funds; persuading governments to allow camps in their countries which took years to achieve; to getting governments to agree to arms being brought into their countries and to allow them to be used for training; to go through the excruciatingly painful job of begging all kinds of governments and organisations for what appear to any revolutionary to be obvious and simple requests.

So that whilst it is true that more and more the work of the movement must be oriented towards 'home' and must as much as possible derive from an analysis of the situation inside the country, it is also true that we owe our substantial recovery from the blow at Rivonia to the external work that has been done in the last few years.

5) The point that the movement in S. Africa was previously isolated from the outside world is not clearly understood. The liberation movement in South Africa for various reasons had closer relations with international trends than most liberation movements and in fact the vast international solidarity movement against apartheid owes it successes precisely to work done long before there was an external mission of the movement. The real issue now and the danger is that the leadership, unlike the position in the past, is physically situated outside the borders of S. Africa and as long as this is the case all manner of problems will arise. This is an objective that is due to conditions. It is not some

sort of political deviation, which has gained currency in the movement. A solution of this issue is closely bound up with the fortunes of our revolutionary struggle and how quickly we can get the guerrilla war to spread to our own country. It is highly doubtful if this is an issue which presents us with the need to make a new theoretical analysis of the South African revolution and to raise the level of our ideological thinking. We are faced with actual, organisational and practical problems. How do you get well-armed men to designated bases in South Africa safely, so that they can carry out their tasks? How do you get trained underground workers into the country to do work and survive under those conditions? How do you set up efficient propaganda machinery inside the country? How do you get arms into the hands of the people in South Africa?

These are some of the very complicated problems the struggle is confronted with. In other words, whilst in no way minimising the importance of theory and discussion documents we must stress the overcoming of our organisational problems. Some people say the South African liberation movement has too much ideology, too much theory and too much discussion! All our guerrilla comrades have been training in the Soviet Union. Questions of theory have been stressed. The political education and literature has been pretty thorough and in fact we believe our army is highly politically conscious.

The point made in paragraph 6 regarding accountability and the making of reports to inform the membership and so on is well made. There has definitely been insufficient of this. Though it should be borne in mind that the matters on which most people seek information and which have important political meaning are precisely those which are sensitive militarily and politically dangerous in countries that are not ours.

Being away from our mass base and without democracy in the form of meetings, conferences, elections and so on quite clearly the danger of bureaucracy becomes sharp. On the other hand every illegal organisation is faced by this problem. To what extent is democracy to be allowed to function without disrupting the movement? An examination of the experiences of the PAC and other movements will soon show that the utmost vigilance is required in any revolutionary movement against possibility of infiltration and disruption by enemy agents – this is especially so where the internal mass movement is not there to sift and vouch for people who come outside claiming to be members of the movement. But even bearing these risks in mind it is true that some methods must be found to account to those who can be reached in ways that will minimise the dangers of bureaucratic complacency.

It should be remembered that many comrades came out for training when there was a leadership at home. It was then expected that they would return home immediately after completing their training. When Rivonia occurred and the plans then made fell into the hands of the enemy all this unexpectedly changed. The months men had expected to be away from home lengthened into years. All this is fundamental to a lot of frustration we all feel.

Paragraph 7 dealing with style of work seems to the Preparatory Committee to be too lurid, melodramatic and unjust. The statements are too general and sweeping and therefore cannot even be checked. There are so many allegations that it is not easy to know where to start.

(i) 'Our officials have come to adopt authoritarian attitudes towards comrades in lower positions.'

Is this a general attitude or is it confined to some individuals with whom you have come in contact? There are literally dozens of people in our movement in positions of responsibility either in the political movement or in the army. Are they all supposed to be 'authoritarian'?

(ii) 'Bossmanship is the rule of the day.' Is this a general problem in the ANC requiring a conference to put right? Is this really the issue we are faced with?

The office of the ANC in Dar at one time was the office of headquarters. It was a hive of activity with dozens of people in it. At that time the complaint was that the office had been turned into a virtual place where everybody could have a chat or spend the day. Reporters and all sorts of doubtful characters used to come roaming in. It was then that it was decided to divide the inner office off and put a reception counter etc. The aim was primarily 'security', not to give the impression of some 'gone to seed' commercial enterprise. This was long before there was the type of position we have today where a few comrades man the Dar office and there is a single chief representative.

The rest of the allegations clearly call for some massive enquiry to establish the facts.

'Evidence of maladminstration is massive' – 'Letters are lost' – 'appointments broken', 'Numerous motor cycles have been wantonly destroyed' and so on and so forth.

Is all this based on fact? What is meant by wanton destruction of motor cycles? Were they destroyed in accidents by careless drivers? 'There have been a number of cases of embezzlement.' This is a very serious charge. Our movement has severely punished some comrades found guilty of misusing funds. Fortunately this has not been a problem in our movement in contrast to some others. In fact we have had the opposite accusation that our Treasury is too tight-fisted with money. Therefore we would certainly be interested to crack down on any proven case of embezzlement. The fact that this is known 'to many of us' and has never been reported is an indictment in itself.

It is regrettable that a few comrades in our movement are given to excessive drinking. But is the whole of our machinery to be castigated for this fault? If it is confined to some individuals, however prominent, should we not in fact say so and to use your words 'point a finger'. Why condemn a whole host of innocent officials with the faults of a few.

What is meant by the expression 'Drunkenness was at one time a major feature of our office in Dar es Salaam – day and night.'

As regards the problem of accommodation of 'leading personnel who visit Dar es Salaam for short periods' they should stay at a hotel because they must be accommodated. The hotel they often go to is the worst in Dar es Salaam precisely to save on costs. There is no other available accommodation that is convenient. There was a time when our headquarters were in Dar es Salaam and there were many comrades accommodated there. Then it was possible for comrades to stay at the residences of other comrades. There definitely are not 'numerous comrades in Dar es Salaam' with rooms or beds to spare for visiting comrades. And those few who may have such accommodation may not find it convenient. Certainly leaders of the ANC are not desirous of begging their way round for accommodation as this could lead to other problems. There was a time when the Organisation had a place in an area called 'Mtonill'. This had to be abandoned when the government ordered organisations to leave Dar es Salaam. We do not know of leaders who spend 'evening after evening in a bar'.

Again in regard to paragraph 8 we must have some data and evidence. We would be very interested to discover comrades who make unreasonable demands or even 'reasonable' ones to our friends from the Socialist countries. The embassies never brought it to our attention and no individuals were allowed to approach Socialist or any embassies for personal demands. We know of no member of our Organisation who has sought personal assistance from any of the Socialist embassies and indeed they would not be likely to meet a response should they do so.

As regards our relations with Tanzania we reject utterly the suggestion that our movement has not done its utmost to develop and maintain good relations with Tanzania. On the contrary from long before independence came to Tanganyika, as it then was, we had good relations with TANU and its leaders. Since then we pioneered good relations between liberation movements and this country. We were the first to be granted facilities of any kind including camps etc.

The development of relations with a state is a very complex matter influenced by numerous factors, some of which are beyond our control.

It is not merely a matter of good public relations. And often the less said the better. The more the special policies of our Organisation are articulated in other countries, the more we may be setting off more problems than we can solve. A lot depends on what one intends to say at a students' meeting. All the Preparatory Committee wishes to stress is that such tertiary relations as being nice to everybody and being easily available for expressions of one's own opinion may not be the best means of fostering good relations. Our leadership is under fire for concentrating too much on foreign relations work and this could at least suggest that we have learnt something about the subtleties and imponderables of this question of foreign relations. The solidarity between various organisations fighting for liberation in Southern Africa is one in which the ANC has always, and everywhere taken the lead. In fact there have been suggestions that we are pursuing this policy with such persistence that there must be some ulterior motive behind it. It is surprising to hear that we have not been doing our job here.

One of the problems is that with the exception of Frelimo and Swapo the headquarters of the organisations have not been in Dar. Naturally relations would be pressed particularly at national level. There is an alliance with ZAPU, which is unique in history. This could hardly be the result of ignoring relations with organisations in Southern Africa. An examination of our literature will show that we do far more than most to publicise the Southern African alliance and to project the organisations such as MPLA, PAIGC, SWAPO, ZAPU, FRELIMO.

All these organisations have rendered a lot of assistance to us and we have rendered much assistance to them. Does this mean there are no individuals in these organisations who have attitudes against the interests of our Organisation for personal and other reasons? Perhaps. But then we do not base policies on gossip. We can only go by the official relations and contacts which we have established and in respect of which the position is sound. Are there no ways in which our relations could be even further developed? This is an absolute must.

Now that guerrilla operations are becoming more widespread, the need for co-ordination of operation in different countries has grown. It is in this direction our efforts are now mainly concentrated.

The paragraphs dealing with the need to involve our members more and those relating to the need to improve the conditions of MK men and also to intensify political work are high on the agenda of the conference. All proposals to this end are welcome. But here again, are some statements not too sweeping and generalised?

The suggestion that there has been an emergence of an 'elite' is amazing. The conditions in which leading personnel are forced to work, certainly in Tanzania, can hardly be described as inducing the emergence of an elite. It is true that Africans in South Africa generally live under such degrading conditions that for them to have anything better looks luxury. We totally reject the approach. It is tantamount to saying that because Europeans in our country live in very luxurious conditions compared with Africans, genuine revolutionaries cannot be expected from that quarter.

The ANC leadership can hardly be described as living the life of an 'elite' as compared with other members including the MK despite the remarks on Mandela camp. Naturally care has to be taken that a gap is not created between leaders and led. But in this and other matters we must not exaggerate. The conditions under which our top leadership such as Tambo, Kotane, Marks and other leaders are living ought to fill members of the Congress Movement with absolute shame if they had any conscience.

There ought to be a general review of the living conditions of all our personnel at all levels with a view to securing all-round improvements. But to talk of an 'elite' emerging is quite honestly nonsense.

The Congress Alliance is an issue of great importance, which has been discussed many times before, and in particular at a consultative conference held in December 1966. It is a very serious political problem with many aspects. It is just not helpful to try and shift the blame on the ANC for the problems in this connection. The policy that has been followed in the external mission on this issue was laid down by the entire Congress Movement back at home in 1962. All the factors were then gone into and decisions taken by many of the people who today complain about consequences. The decision that the ANC should be responsible for the external mission for the whole Congress Movement and that an 'African Image' (to use the cliche then current) was not taken by the leaders outside or by the ANC alone. The start of a solution is therefore definitely to get out of one's head the idea that somehow the ANC is at fault in carrying out some unilaterally conceived policy. This just makes a solution difficult.

Furthermore what does one now mean when talking about the 'Congress Alliance'? The ANC is the only Organisation in the former Congress Alliance officially committed to the armed struggle. The SAIC, CPC and SACTU are semi-legal in South Africa and the last we know is that they were not officially committed to armed struggle. The Communist Party was so committed. But it was never part of the Congress Alliance at home. Therefore what is needed is obviously not the old alliance except perhaps its spirit and its common programme – the Freedom Charter. What is required is a new united front machinery capable of mobilising 11 nationally oppressed groups, working class movements and Progressives behind armed struggle. This is a task that requires creative thinking. Any attempt to preach to the Africans and use such terms as 'narrow nationalism', 'racialism' or 'tribalism' to describe present ANC policies or to suggest such a trend is wholly rejected.

It is the Africans who are the victims of racialism and who are having 'tribalism' shoved down their throats by government policies. It is other movements in which Africans take a leading role and not the other way round. We therefore feel that there is need for caution before accusations, as distinct from analysis, are thrown around carelessly. The bringing together of all revolutionary forces is a matter of principle and a way must be found to accomplish this aim. It is not easy in any situation least of all that of South Africa. Warnings of doom uttered against the ANC are hardly the best way of going about this.

As far as the ANC is concerned part of the problem is the hesitation of comrades in accepting the necessity for ANC leadership of the revolution in a very real and honest manner. The one thing that will defeat our objectives is to try and evade, or to construct devices to dodge this issue of conducting our struggle under the banner of the ANC. It is this which Africans will construe as 'racialism' and the cause to delay in consummating revolutionary unity. It is hard for people in South Africa to conceive of Africans being the leadership of the country because of centuries of looking down on them by all groups in this country. But it is absolutely vital that this should be enshrined in any machinery we set up, otherwise, instead of losing the support of non-Africans the revolution will lose the support of Africans. Either of these eventualities would be a disaster for the revolution.

The proposals in your document are all very welcome indeed and in particular the one for integration of all personnel in the

ANC, we believe could be a tremendous step forward which could galvanise the whole movement. There is no doubt that something along these lines will emerge from our conference.

The other proposals also are interesting and will form the basis of much of the preparations. Many comrades have commented in greater detail on specific proposals on the same issues.

We must stress that the aforegoing represents the view of the Preparatory Committee which is responding to all contributions and will welcome further comments so as to ensure that we arrive at the conference completely united in our approach.

Some matters of an ideological and theoretical nature we have not dealt with because they will be with us for years during the revolution and are more long-term. The same applies to problems of strategy and tactics.

Joe Matthews
Secretary
Conference Committee

CHAPTER 8

Extract from *Inner-Party Bulletin – Number 1* (July 1970)

THE PARTY AS A LEADING FORCE AND RELATIONS WITH THE ANC

1. The post-Rivonia period in the South African struggle has revealed serious deficiencies in the assertion by our Party of its independence and its leading role.

The Central Committee, at its 1968 plenary session, resolved: 'This meeting declares that the central aim of our Party at this time is to promote the further unity of the national democratic movement for the liberation of our country as a step toward socialism. It recognises that this aim can only be achieved on the basis of close co-operation between our Party and the ANC and its allies, not by way of rivalry or competition.

'It believes that the strengthening of the socialist outlook in the movement can be a source of strength for the whole movement and for the future of our country in combating racialist, tribal and other divisive and reactionary influences.

'It believes, therefore, that the fullest development of our Party as an independent organisation playing a special role within the national united front is an essential part of this development.'

This meeting recognises that in the years from 1963 onwards the Party failed to play its leading role within the national movement, and its independent role as the vanguard Party for the following reasons, among others:

(a) The failure of the Party to re-establish a working Central Committee collective in which the members in leading positions in the national movement were an integrated and functioning part.
(b) The inability of the CC to resolve the issue of the reconstitution of the Party in the most crucial area of operation, namely in Mkhonto and among our members in Africa.

This meant that at both a leadership level and at the rank-and-file level the Party was immobilised. Our theory and our recent experience has shown that leading members of the Party, however strategically placed in the national movement or Mkhonto or in any other sector of our struggle, do not function as Party cadres unless they take part in continuous collective Party life and policy-making. This is why the political role of the Party in vital spheres has diminished in crucial years. This is why some of our members in Africa were rendered ineffective and suffered demoralisation. It is above all the reason why the Party failed in its role in the formulation of policy in the national movement and in our military organisation. And this led directly to the division in leadership between the political and military.

This meeting directs that steps be taken to ensure that all Party members function in units, subject to collective decisions; that individual members who are working in isolation from collectives be kept in regular contact with Party bodies; and that all leading members be answerable to a functioning Party collective.

This is essentially the way in which the Party will play its special vanguard role in the national movement to assert it ideology and the leadership of the working class. At the same time the Party will maintain and build its separate and independent political existence.

The ideology of Marxism and its specific class outlook distinguishes our Party and determines its separate existence as a vanguard force within the national liberatory movement. But the position of vanguard is not achieved automatically. It has to be won by the dedication of our members and by our conscious effort to gain for the Party its proper place within the liberation movement. Experience has shown that the Party can fulfil its vanguard role without 'being at the head' of the movement in the physical or public sense. Our leadership must rather depend on the correctness of our political line, on our ability to win non-Party comrades to supporting our line, and on our cohesiveness as an organisation.

The ability of the Party to play its proper role within the liberation movement will be advanced by the creation of clear institutional links between the Party and the ANC. We must follow up the steps already taken to create a closer working alliance between the Party and the ANC.

For this purpose regular consultations should be organised between the leaderships of the two organisations on the general conduct of our revolutionary strategy and on the most effective use of our joint resources for the prosecution of our common struggle.

2. The meeting expresses its firm support for the main resolutions and tendency of the Morogoro Conference of the ANC. It calls upon every member loyally to observe the letter and spirit of the Morogoro decisions, to fight for Congress unity and against all factional activities and intrigues.

The meeting feels that there is a danger that the decisions of the Morogoro Conference which condemned factionalism and incorrect styles of leadership and personal behaviour, will be undermined. Since the Morogoro Conference, factional activities of various kinds have appeared and attempts have been made to minimise and distort decisions of the Conference.

We call on the ANC to drive home the lessons of the Conference in an organised campaign against those styles of work and the activities of some in the leadership driven by personal and factional ambitions.

We call upon the Central Committee to exercise the utmost vigilance and maintain strict discipline so as to ensure that every member plays a full part in the implementation of this resolution.

Index

Abedian, Iraj 273
ACCDESS 258
Adedeji, Adebayo 258, 259
Adesola, OO 212
Africa Club 30
African Communist 50, 139, 213, 223, 224
African Metal Workers Union 43
African National Congress (ANC) (*see also* National Minded Block) 7-9, 11, 12, 29, 31-33, 38-40, 46-49, 51, 52, 57, 63, 65, 67, 68, 74-76, 80, 82, 83, 86, 88, 89, 92, 93, 96, 97-99, 101-104, 108, 109, 115-117, 119-123, 127, 134, 137-140, 146, 157, 158, 168, 178, 186, 187, 195, 197-200, 202, 203, 205, 210-214, 216-232, 236, 242-246, 248, 250, 251, 253-265, 268-275
African Railway Workers Union 21, 43, 71
African Union 66
African Women Against Passes 100
Afro-Asian Solidarity Movement 189
Alexander, Ray 14, 39, 40, 44, 64
Alexandra Township 76, 83, 92, 93, 100
Amato Textile Mills 83
Amra, Cassim 24
ANC *see* African National Congress
ANC Women's League 93
ANC Youth League 88
Andrews, Bill 28, 48, 110
Anti-Apartheid Movement 222, 223, 232
Anti-pass Campaign 102, 103
Anti-Semitism 13, 15, 17, 18, 37, 42, 233
Armed Resistance Movement 167, 171
Arrighi, Giovanni 201
Arthur *see* Hlapane, Bartholomew
Arusha Declaration of 1967 201, 202, 210
Aucamp, Colonel 163, 166, 172, 175
Aziz, Salim *see* Salim Aziz

Baker, Lewis 169
Bantu Education 52
Barenbladt, Yetta 80
Barnett, Don 232
Battersea Polytechnic 35
Begin, Menachim 138
Benjamin, John 111, 173
Benjamin, Pixie 111
Bennun, Tollie 113
Bernadt, Hymie 56
Bernstein, Hilda 69, 222, 226, 227
Bernstein, Rusty 47, 52, 69, 95, 119, 123, 127, 128, 130, 164, 165, 222, 223, 226, 227, 236, 240, 247
Berrange, Vernon 70
Bevan, Aneurin 38
Beyleveld, Piet 81, 82
Bill of Rights 271
Birobidzhan 18
Black Power 204
Blatchford, Robin 24
Bolshevik Revolution of 1917 13
Bond, Patrick 260
Boonzaaier, Gregoire 40
Boshielo, Flag 214
Boston Bag Workers Union 64
Botswana 180, 181, 183-186, 199
Brooks, Alan 168
Brown, Mannie 239
Brown, Rene 201
Bucharest Festival 36
Budlender, Geoff 271
Bulawayo 25-27
Bunge School 197
Bunting, Brian 29, 39-41, 44, 47, 49, 50, 59, 71, 222-224, 232
Bunting, Peter 236
Bunting, Sonia 58, 222, 223
Butcher, Jane 252
Butcher, Mary see Turok, Mary
Buthelezi, Mangosuthu 261
Byelorussia 13

Cachalia, Maulvi 123
Cachalia, Yusuf 31, 82, 123
Camps Bay 37
Cape Argus 252
Cape Provincial Council 70-73, 80
Cape Town 16, 17
Caprivi Strip 185
Carmichael, Stokely 204
Carneson, Fred 29, 39, 40, 47, 50
Carolus, Cheryl 260
Castro, Fidel 62
COD *see* Congress of Democrats
CODESA 257
Coetzee, Brigadier 175
Coetzee, Stef 258, 259
Colonial Youth Day 41
Cominform 230
Communist Party of Great Britain 35, 111, 238
Communist Party, South African *see* South African Communist Party

315

Comoros Liberation Movement 203
Congress Alliance 45, 51-54, 67, 82, 83, 87, 89, 90, 95, 117, 118, 126, 216, 225
Congress Movement 34, 39, 45, 59, 80-83, 95, 116, 216
Congress of Democrats (COD) 33, 34, 80-82, 86, 87, 89, 103, 111, 120, 125, 134, 137, 139, 146, 147, 154, 168, 169
Congress of the People (COP) 21, 22, 51, 53, 54, 58, 59, 63, 64, 67, 98, 99, 138, 257
Congress Youth League 31
Constitution Act 155
COP *see* Congress of the People
Cope, Jack 24, 40
Cope, Leslie 24
Cornforth, Maurice 92
Cosatu 261, 273
Cossacks 13
Counter Attack 86
Cox, Idris 35
Criminal Laws Amendment Act 33, 39
Cronin, Jeremy 256, 260, 274
Crossman, Dick 34
Curran, Bunny 72

Dadoo, Yusuf 7, 29, 31, 32, 47, 48, 82, 87, 104, 105, 107, 149, 190, 191, 220, 223, 224, 237
Daily Nation 188, 191, 203
Daniels, Professor John 266
Dar es Salaam 192, 196-202, 205-207, 210, 212, 218
Davies, Rob 258
De Klerk, President FW 250, 251, 253, 257, 258, 261, 266
Defiance Campaign 31, 32, 38, 51, 137, 138
Defiance of Unjust Laws Campaign *see* Defiance Campaign
Democratic Party 274
Die Burger 72
Dos Santos, Marcelino 206
Dos Santos, Pam 206
Duarte, Jesse 263

Eisenstein, Raymond 169
Engels, Friedrich 23
Erwin, Alec 260, 261, 272
Evans, Dave 169, 172

Fanon, Frantz 136
Federation of South African Women (Fedsaw) 93

Fedsaw *see* Federation of South African Women
Feinberg, Barry 235, 236, 240, 246
Fighting Talk 67
Finance Week 266
First, Ruth 7, 47, 79, 93-95, 105, 191, 231
Fischer, Bram 7, 73, 75, 113-115, 165, 177-179, 190, 191, 199, 227, 254
Food and Canning Workers Union 53
Forman, Lionel 24
Fort Hare University 189
Fort, The 77, 93, 141, 147
Freedom Charter 48, 51, 53, 54, 57-59, 61, 67, 68, 72, 74, 75, 81, 96, 98, 99, 225, 262
Frelimo 202, 203, 206, 223, 229
Friends of the Soviet Union 18

Gandhi, Mahatma 89
Gazides, Costa 169
GEAR *see* Growth, Employment and Redistribution
Githi, George 188, 191
Goldberg, Dennis 30, 165, 167, 172
Government of Provincial Unity 265
Greys, The 134
Grootboom Judgement 271
Group of Eight 80, 225, 229
Growth, Employment and Redistribution (GEAR) 273
Guardian (UK) 50
Guevara, Che 8, 62, 138
Guidelines 240

Hall, Eve 188
Hall, Tony 188
Hani, Chris 214, 254, 258
Harmel, Michael 7, 28, 29, 47, 58, 67, 95, 104-106, 108-110, 112, 113, 115-117, 139, 220
Hassani 197
Hay, Gordon 251, 252
Hayman, Ruth 116
Haysom, Fink 271
Hepple, Bob 117
Hill Committee 120-122
Hirson, Baruch 168, 175
Hlapane, Bartholomew (Arthur) 115, 116
Hodgson, Jack 7, 103, 105, 125, 126, 128, 129
Hungary and the Hungarian Uprising 50
Hutchinson, Alfred 35

IFAA *see* Institute For African Alternatives

INDEX

IMF *see* International Monetary Fund
Indian Congress *see* South African Indian Congress
Industrial Conciliation Act 52, 65, 90
Inkatha Freedom Party 257
Institute For African Alternatives (IFAA) 195, 242, 245, 253-256, 263
International Monetary Fund (IMF) 255, 258, 272
Isaacson, Rabbi Ben 111

Jasset, Harlene 269
Jele, Josiah 198, 246
Jewish Labour Movement 13
Jewishness *see* Judaism and Jewishness *and* Anti-Semitism *and* Zionism
Joffe, Joel 165
Jordan, Pallo 271, 274
Joseph, Helen 49, 74, 81, 118
Joseph, Paul 35
Judaism and Jewishness (*see also* Anti-Semitism *and* Zionism) 13, 14, 16-19, 41, 42, 156, 161, 234

Kahn, Sam 22, 39, 40, 46, 66, 68
Karume, Vice President 229
Kasrils, Ronnie 111, 248, 249
Kathrada, Ahmed (Kathy) 74, 134
Kaunda, Kenneth, President 30
Kawawa, Rashidi 207
Kazungula 185, 186
Kenyatta, Jomo 193
Ketley, Richard 273
Kitson, Dave 167, 168
Kodesh, Wolfie 105, 111, 125, 222
Kotane, Moses 7, 11, 12, 22, 29, 47-49, 76, 77, 78, 88, 95, 104-109, 112, 113, 115-117, 119, 123, 137, 199, 200, 211, 212, 220
Krige, Uys 68
Krugman, Paul 272
Krushchev, Nikita 50
Kuper, Justice 146, 158

La Guma, Alex 29, 234
Labour and Democratic Movement 36
Labour Movement 35
Labour Party (South Africa) 81
Labour Party (UK) 34
Langa location 46, 47
Laredo, John 168
Latvia 13-15
Leballo, Potlako 102
Lee-Warden, Len 44
Leipzig option 257
Lenin, Krupskaya 41

Lenin, Vladimir 19, 20, 23, 62, 97, 110, 139
Leninism *see* Marxism/Leninism
Levy, Leon 82
Levy, Norman 169, 175
Lewin, Hugh 168, 235, 246
Libau 13, 14
Liberal Party 34, 58, 70, 72, 81, 85, 96, 168
Liberation 67
Liberation Committee *see* OAU Liberation Committee
Liberation Support Movement 232
Liebenberg, Sandy 271
Life is More Joyous 50
Lilliesleaf Farm 124, 164, 166
London 16, 218, 219, 221-223, 225, 230, 234, 245, 253
Long Walk to Freedom 7
LSM *see* Liberation Support Movement
Luthuli, Chief Albert 11, 12, 49, 51, 52, 67-70, 76, 77, 82, 91, 95, 98, 103, 108, 118, 123, 135
Lystra Zip Factory 65

Mabhida, Moses 218
MacKay, Peter 185
Macro-economic Research Group (MERG) 260
Maisels, Issy 73, 75
Makiwane, Tennyson 118, 186, 187, 217, 231, 254
Malan, Prime Minister Dr Daniel 29, 32
Mandela, Nelson 7, 9, 12, 31-33, 39, 48, 69, 74, 75, 78, 98, 111, 116, 124-126, 152, 156, 164, 177, 250, 253, 257, 261, 262, 266, 267, 271, 272, 275
Mandela, Winnie 111, 253
Manuel, Trevor 258, 259, 261, 272, 273
Mao Tse-Tung 62, 139
Marks, JB 31, 32, 47, 90, 199, 212, 213
Martin, Kingsley 34
Marx, Karl (*see also* Marxism/Leninism) 23, 34
Marxism/Leninism 23-25, 30, 49, 62, 67, 75, 91, 92, 97, 110, 114, 118, 139, 201, 202, 211, 212, 224, 229, 238, 240, 266
Mashatile, Paul 262, 264
Masina, Leslie 82
Masondo, Andrew 246
Mathews, John 167
Matlou, Joe 224
Matsowane, Ruth 115
Matthews, Joe 116, 215
Matthews, ZK 67, 77, 91

Mau Mau 190
Mbeki, Govan 39, 113, 137, 164
Mbeki, Thabo 98, 195, 262
Mboweni, Tito 258, 261, 272
Mboya, Tom 187, 189
Mdingi, Leonard 120, 121
Mdladlana, Shepherd 270
MERG *see* Macro-economic Research Group
Metal Workers Union 41
Metcalfe, Mary 263, 264, 268
Mhlaba, Raymond 39, 113
Mhlambiso, Thambi 224
Mixed Economy in Focus: Zambia 245
MK *see* Umkhonto we Sizwe
Mkwayi, Wilton 167
Modern Youth Society (MYS) 29, 30, 32, 40, 41
Modise, Joe 126, 130, 247, 248
Moi, Daniel Arap 189
Moleketi, Jabu 268, 269
Molotov, VM 38
Mondlane, Eduardo 206
Mondlane, Janet 206
Morogoro Conference 215, 218, 223, 225, 228, 229
Moroka, James 31
Morris 234
Moscow 233
Mosunkutu, Elias 270
Motlante, Kgalema 274
Motsegha, Mathole 264
Mphahlele, Ezekiel 188
MPLA 202, 203, 223
Mposho, Florence 92
Mqota, Temba 79
Mquikana, Sobizana 232
Msimang, Mendi 253
Mungai, Njoroge 189
Murray, Andrew 75
Murumbi, Joseph, Vice-President 187, 188
Museveni, Yoweri, President 203, 205
MYS *see* Modern Youth Society

Naicker, MP 223
Naidoo, Jay 260, 268
Naidoo, MD 35, 235, 239, 247
Naidoo, Shanti 81
Nair, Billy 59, 60
Nairobi 187-191
National Action Council 55, 57-59, 67
National Consultative Committee 67
National Democratic Movement 48
National Democratic Revolution 59
National Minded Block (ANC) 31

National Union of Mineworkers 255
Nationalist Party 56, 63, 71, 72, 113, 132, 141, 168, 265
Native Affairs Department 71
Nazism 63, 64
New Age 169
New Agenda – South African Journal of Social and Economic Policy 275
New Statesman 34
Ngakane, Lionel 224
Ngotyana, Greenwood 21, 22, 42, 46, 47, 53
Ngwevela, Johnson 46
Nkobi, Tom 92, 121, 122
Nkosi Sikelel' iAfrika 127
Nkrumah, Kwame 8, 142, 193, 199
Nokwe, Duma 35, 36, 74, 82, 86, 120, 213
Northern Rhodesia *see* Rhodesia
Nyerere, President Julius 192, 200-202, 205, 207, 209, 266
Nzo, Alfred 92, 246, 245

OAU Liberation Committee 203, 211, 212
Ollie, Councillor 28
Open University 231, 232, 235, 241, 246
Operation Mayibuye 165, 166, 169, 190
Ossewabrandwag 142

Paarl 17
PAC *see* Pan-Africanist Congress
Pahad, Amina 87
Pahad, Aziz 87, 248
Pahad, Essop 7, 257
Pahad, Goolam 87
PAIGC 223
Palestine 18
Pan-Africanist Congress (PAC) 95, 96, 101, 103, 104, 199, 202-204, 211
Peake, George 54, 58, 82
People's Republic of South Vietnam 205
Philips, Mark 265
Piliso, Mzwai 198
Pillay, Vella 35
Pirow, Oswald 74
Plato 24
Plekhanov, GV 97
Pogrund, Benjamin 130
Pondoland rebellion 120, 122
Potato Boycott 93
Pound a Day Campaign 83, 90, 138
Pretoria Central Prison 147-148
Pretoria Local Prison 158

Rademeyer, Major General 102
Ramaphosa, Cyril 255

INDEX

Rand Daily Mail 130, 131, 176
Randeree, Doc 245
RDP *see* Reconstruction and Development Programme
Ready to Govern 261
Reconstruction and Development Programme (RDP) 259-261, 264, 266-269, 272, 273
Red Youth Movement 14
Reeves, Bishop Ambrose 69
Resha, Robert 69, 80, 94, 224
Revolutionary Council 223, 224, 229
Revolutionary Thought in the Twentieth Century 270
Rhodesia (*incl* Southern and Northern Rhodesia) 24-26, 28
Rissik Street Post Office 128, 130, 134, 140, 143, 146
Rivonia farm, The *see* Lilliesleaf Farm
Rivonia Trial 113, 114, 165, 166, 227, 228
Road Transportation Act 56
Robben Island 191, 262, 270
Rochman, Hymie 111
Roderik, Dani 272
Rodney, Walter 204
Rufiji 207, 209, 216
Rumpff, Justice Franz 73
Russia 13, 19, 22

SABC *see* South African Broadcasting Corporation
Sabotage Act 165
Sachs, Albie, Justice 30, 32, 271
Sachs, Jeffrey 272
Sachs, Solly 34
SACOD 51
SACP *see* South African Communist Party
SACPO *see* South African Coloured People's Organisation
SACS *see* South African College High School
SACTU *see* South African Congress of Trade Unions
SAIC *see* South African Indian Congress
Salim Aziz 267
Saul, John 201
Schermbrucker, Ivan 120, 169, 239, 254
Schoon, Marius 87, 170
Sechaba 223, 226, 230, 231
Second World War 18, 22, 138, 166
September, Reg 223
Sexwale, Tokyo 262-266, 268, 269
Sharpeville 100, 102, 103, 132
Sibeko, Archie 42, 43, 66, 71, 117
Sibeko, David 204
Simons, Jack 24, 30, 39, 40, 191, 199, 230, 244
Simons, Ray 191, 199, 230, 245
Sisulu, Walter 22, 31, 35, 36, 39, 48, 52, 69, 74, 75, 82, 84, 86-88, 95, 101, 102, 120, 122, 127, 131, 134, 137, 164, 249, 252, 261
Sisulu, Zwelakhe 255
Sizokunyatela ma Africa 164
Slovo, Joe 14, 47, 69, 78, 79, 95, 105, 119, 133, 143, 146, 212, 219, 222-224, 226, 227, 230-232, 235, 248, 255, 256
Smith, Ian 27
Snitcher, Harry 24
Sobukwe, Robert 102
Socialist Revolution 48
Songambele, Commissioner 209, 215
Sophiatown 52, 80, 93
South African Broadcasting Corporation (SABC) 30
South African College High School (SACS) 23
South African Coloured People's Organisation (SACPO) 34, 51, 54, 58, 82
South African Communist Party (SACP) 7, 8, 11, 21, 22, 24, 25, 28, 31, 40, 42, 44, 45, 48, 54, 58, 62, 76, 81, 82, 91, 108, 111, 114-116, 135, 139, 140, 169, 211, 222, 225, 237, 239, 240, 246, 250, 255, 269, 273
South African Congress of Trade Unions (SACTU) 34, 52, 82, 83, 89, 90, 222, 236, 240
South African Indian Congress (SAIC) 24, 31, 33, 39, 51, 82, 89, 118, 235
South African Trade Union Council 52
South Vietnam *see* People's Republic of South Vietnam
South West African People's Organisation (SWAPO) 30, 185, 186, 202
Southern Rhodesia *see* Rhodesia
Soviet Union 18, 24
Soweto 20, 104, 115, 126, 174, 257, 268
Special Branch 29, 30, 41, 43, 53, 55, 60, 65, 68, 88, 103, 104, 113, 134, 140, 154, 155, 165, 168, 170, 173, 178, 184, 185, 188, 192, 227, 251
Spotlight 210, 223
SSP *see* Students Socialist Party
Stalin, Josef (*see also* Stalinism) 50
Stalinism 50, 110, 238
Steenkamp, Officer 150-152, 155-157

Stiglitz, Joseph 272
Stormjaers 146
Strachan, Harold (Jock) 127, 147, 153, 154, 159-162, 164, 165, 171, 176, 181, 234, 235, 239, 246, 247, 254
Strachan, Maggie 165, 234, 235
Strategic Problems in South Africa's Liberation Struggle: a critical analysis by Ben Turok 232, 244
Strategy and Tactics 98
Strijdom, Prime Minister JG 57
Students Socialist Party (SSP) 24, 187
Students' Revolutionary Association 203
Sunday Times 186
Suppression of Communism Act 32, 48, 52, 80, 179
SWAPO *see* South West African People's Organisation
Swart, State President CR 154

Tamana, Dora 46
Tambo, Oliver 9, 31, 39, 48, 49, 52, 70, 78, 98, 105, 108, 177, 190, 199, 200, 210, 217, 219, 220, 223, 225, 242-245, 257
Tanu 203, 210
Tanzania 192, 196
Tanzanian Youth League 202
Tarshish, Jack 163, 164
Tembo, Nephas 30
The Africa Groups of Sweden 232
The Enemy Hidden Under The Same Colour 225
The Guardian 22, 29, 32, 39, 40, 45, 49, 50, 59, 64, 93, 186, 232
The Socialist Register 232
Third World Youth Festival 35
Thoms, Raymond 170
Thorn, Athol 44
Timber Workers Union 66
Togliatti, Palmiro 50
Toivo, Herman Andimba Toivo Ya 29, 30
Trades and Labour Council 52
Transvaal Congress 123
Treason Trial of 1957 22, 63, 69, 70, 72, 74-76, 83, 85, 88, 92, 97-100, 107, 113, 114, 127, 137, 142, 187
Trew, Tony 169
Trewhela, Paul 169
Trotsky, Leon 19
Tshunungwa, TE 47, 55-57
Tsomo 22

Turok, Fred 42, 85, 157, 175, 207, 222
Turok, Hillel 14, 42, 73, 251, 252
Turok, Ivan 42, 157, 175, 206, 222
Turok, Mary (Mary Butcher) 32, 40-42, 79, 84, 86, 89, 104, 111, 120, 130, 133, 134, 141, 143, 146, 147, 153, 154, 157, 171-175, 178-181, 184, 185, 189, 192, 196, 197, 203, 212, 215, 216, 222, 232, 235, 245, 249-253, 256, 257, 264, 266, 270
Turok, Neil 42, 111, 157, 175, 206, 222
Turok, Sol 42

Ujamaa 201, 202, 206-210
Umkhonto we Sizwe (MK) 87, 125-127, 130-133, 136, 139, 164, 165, 166, 168, 169, 174, 198, 199, 213, 218, 228, 239, 240, 247, 248, 249, 253, 254
United Party 72
University of Cape Town 23, 32, 187
University of London 34, 231
University of Zambia 242
Unzima Lomtwalo 61

Van der Ross, Dick 53
Van Zyl, Olaas 265, 266
Verwoerd, Prime Minister Dr Hendrik 52, 92, 93, 113
Vorster, Prime Minister JB 142, 166

Washington Consensus 272
Weinberg, Eli 169
Western Areas Removal Campaign 52, 138
Western Cape Action Council 55
White Terror 13
Williamson, Craig 235, 247
Woddis, Jack 238
Wolpe, Harold 151
Wood, Professor Chris 197
World Bank 255, 258, 273
World Communist Movement 49, 51, 110, 139
World Marxist Review 111, 230

Youth League *see* ANC Youth League

Zambia 214, 246
Zanu 185, 203, 244
Zapu 185, 202, 203, 244
Zionism 18, 146
Zukas, Simon 24, 187